How Drugs,
Thugs, and
Crime are
reshaping the
Afghan War

SEEDS OF TERROR

Gretchen Peters

ONEWORLD

A Oneworld Book

First published in the USA by St. Martin's Press 2009
First published in Great Britain by Oneworld Publications 2009
This paperback edition first published by Oneworld Publications 2012

A CIP record for this title is available
from the British Library
Not for exclusive sale outside of the UK and Commonwealth

ISBN 978–1–85168–751–0

Printed and bound in Great Britain by Page Bros, Norwich

Front cover images:
Soldier © AFP/Stringer/Getty Images;
Poppy field and mountains © Paula Bronstein/Getty Images

Oneworld Publications
185 Banbury Road
Oxford
OX2 7AR
England

This book is for Isabella and Sophia.
Never believe it isn't possible.

And in memory of Abdul Samad Rohani (1982–2008).

CONTENTS

ACKNOWLEDGMENTS

This book would not exist today were it not for the brave and tireless efforts of six individuals who have chosen, for their own protection, to get no public credit for their work. Blandly cited throughout the pages that follow as research assistants 1, 2, 3, 4, 5, and 6, they took extraordinary risks to collect a detailed catalogue of information. Any insights provided in this book are theirs and the mistakes all mine.

The danger they faced became painfully real when Abdul Samad Rohani, the BBC's reporter in Helmand, was abducted and killed by unidentified gunmen in June 2008. Rohani, who also wrote poetry in his native Pashtun, had reported extensively on the drug trade. Friends who investigated Rohani's murder believe he was killed by corrupt provincial police officials whom he had implicated in the heroin trade.

Some may interpret this book as anti-Pakistan or anti-Afghanistan. That's not the case at all, and I hope my friends in both countries—both those who serve in government and those who do not—understand that I wrote this book because I think the great people of both nations deserve better. The international community talks about the importance of building a stable South Asia but seems to look the other way when it comes to the deeply corrosive issues of corruption and criminality. This must stop if we are to truly help this region.

As the *ABC News* reporter in Pakistan and Afghanistan, I had the great pleasure of working with Habibullah Khan, Nasir Mehmood, Islam Mujahid, and Aleem Agha. A woman could not ask for better travel companions along the border, and I thank them for patiently explaining their culture to me and for putting up with my frequent faux pas. I am also indebted to David Westin, Chuck Lustig, Chris Isham, and Rhonda Schwartz, who from early on supported my efforts to pursue this complex story.

My indefatigable agent, Helen Rees, devoted the same energy and zeal to my book as she does to life in general. Marcia Markland, my editor at St. Martin's/Thomas Dunne, has expertly steered the project through the publishing process. I'd also like to thank Sally Richardson, Tom Dunne, Steve Cohen, Joseph Rinaldi, Dori Weintraub, Kerry Nordling, Julie Gutin, Diana Szu, and everyone else at St. Martin's who made this book possible. I am indebted to Frederick Hitz for his kind foreword and to Niko Price, Warrick Page, and Michele Jaffe for their thoughtful edits.

An earlier version of this book was written as a report for the U.S. Institute of Peace, which generously awarded me a research grant. There, I'd like to thank Carola Weil, Kathleen Kuehnast, April Hall, and Mauna Dosso for their help in administering the project. Robert Templer, Blair Murray, and Ulrike Hellmann at the International Crisis Group provided the project a nonprofit umbrella and were instrumental in helping me fulfil technical requirements. I am grateful to Samina Ahmed, William Olson, Barnett Rubin, Andrew Wilder, and Lisa Pinsley for providing commentary on early versions of the USIP report and for pointing out flaws. I'd also like to thank the staff at the National Security Archives at George Washington University.

Many sources for this book can't be thanked by name; hopefully you all know how grateful I am. In no particular order I would also like to acknowledge friends, journalists, diplomats, scholars, and other officials who have helped guide or support my research, shaped my thoughts, engaged me in lively argument, or listened to my tirades about the Afghan heroin trade: Ahmed Rashid, Ghulam Hasnain, Rahimullah Yusufzai, Zahid Hussein, Pir Zubair Shah, Rehmat Meshud, Arian Sharifi, Bilal Sarwary, Daoud Yaqub, Ryan Crocker, Elizabeth Colton, Beverly Eighmy, Ken Thomas, Doug Wankal, Bobby Charles, John Cassara, Steve Coll, William Maley, Ali Jalali, David Smith, Raymond Baker, Hannah Bloch, Peter Tomsen, Jack Lawn, Richard Fiano, Seth Jones, Christine Fair, Chris Alexander, Samina Ahmed, Joanna Nathan, Vikram Parekh, Michael Shaikh, Ali Dayan Hasan, Aamir Mansoor, Talat Massood, Adan Adar, Whit Mason, Rodolfo Martin and Susana Saravia, José María Robles Fraga, Anna Fumarola, Sophie Barry, Tim McGirk, Graeme Smith, Carlotta Gall, Kim Barker, Tamur Mueenuddin, Romano Yusuf, Fayesa Amin, Lulu Tabbarah-Nana, Mimo Khan, Phil Goodwin, Liz Cotton, and the great Afghan reporters at IWPR. Thank you to my hiking buddies Zulfiqar, Lauren, and Bronwyn, because climbing up the Margallas kept me sane. And I'd like to mention Tariq Amin, because he is the only person who, when he found out I was writing a book about drugs, said, "Ooh, I hope there is a part about me in it."

My wonderful parents, who probably hoped I'd do something more respectable with my life, have been nonetheless supportive and loving. Thanks also to my sister, Jenny, whom I adore and admire, and to my extended family: Leslie, Jan, Bud, and Casey. I am lucky to have you.

My fabulous husband, John, and my near-perfect daughters, Isabella and Sophia, have put up with a wife and mother who has been exhausted and mostly foul-tempered for about two years straight. I love you more than anything and thank you for your understanding. Hopefully, I will be less busy now.

Este libro nunca habría sido completado sin Socorro Espinosa Jiménez. Ella ha sido una segunda madre para mis hijas, y es una persona que hace todo en su vida con mucho amor y cariño. Este libro también es tuyo, Coco.

FOREWORD

On page 167 of this detailed and readable study of the poppy trade in Afghanistan, Gretchen Peters observes: "Eight years after 9/11, the single greatest failure in the war on terror is not that Osama bin Laden continues to elude capture, or that the Taliban has staged a comeback, or even that al Qaeda is regrouping in Pakistan's tribal areas and probably planning fresh attacks on the West. Rather, it's the spectacular incapacity of western law enforcement to disrupt the flow of money that is keeping their networks afloat."

By tracing masterfully the enormous success of the illegal heroin trade in the region, Ms. Peters means it, and she proves her case. It is a case that becomes more compelling as a reinvigorated Taliban challenges NATO and Afghan government troops more boldly each week.

Ms. Peters brings a wealth of area knowledge and experience to her report. She has worked as a journalist in Pakistan and Afghanistan for more than a decade. Her reporting shows a firm knowledge of Afghan history as well as the mountainous countryside. Her contacts appear to be with a broad range of U.S. and local officials, including those from the spy services.

Ms. Peters's well-written odyssey takes us through the economics of the poppy trade and points out the distinction and conflict between the Taliban's prohibition of personal consumption of heroin by Muslims and their need to grow and sell the poppy in order to finance their war against the government in Kabul. What is so compelling about Ms. Peters's story line is the simple and obvious equation she draws. Some regions of the world possess petroleum, uranium, or land that is ideal for the production of rubber or cocoa—Afghanistan has the poppy and has grown it for centuries. It is what pays the bills and cements the loyalties, individually and for ethnic groups.

To have imagined that the creation of an unproven, western-supported regime in Kabul would have the power to eliminate the traditional cash crop of hundreds of tribal chieftains without an enormous and lengthy struggle is once again the height of western hubris and ignorance.

Ms. Peters makes that point colourfully and clearly in this highly readable account.

—Frederick P. Hitz,
Inspector General of the CIA (1990–1998)

INTRODUCTION

It was early 1998 when an official I used to meet regularly from the U.S. embassy begged me to do more reporting on the terrorist camps inside Afghanistan. "We can't get anyone in Washington to focus on this issue," he told me.

We were speaking at an Islamabad diplomatic reception. It was, like most of them, a fairly stiff affair, where diplomats, politicians, and pundits dissected Pakistan's latest intrigue over cocktails and bland-tasting snacks served by uniformed waiters.

Amid the mild-mannered parlour room chatter, my contact was visibly agitated, and he gripped my arm tightly. "I am worried sick about what they are up to," he said. "Please don't ignore this story."

But in fact, that was exactly what I did do, along with most of the other journalists covering Pakistan and Afghanistan.

At the time, I was the junior reporter at the tiny Associated Press bureau in Islamabad. We worked hard there, and the stories we filed were important. We sent daily reports on the sectarian violence wracking Pakistan. We travelled extensively in Afghanistan, reporting on the Taliban's reprehensible policies toward women. We covered grisly public executions and their bizarre edicts banning music, kite flying, and white socks. We wrote about food shortages, earthquakes, teeming refugee camps, and the tragedy of a nation devastated by war.

From time to time, we reported on Osama bin Laden and the various terror groups training in Afghanistan, but it never received much play. What got published were stories about the plight of Afghan women, so that's what we wrote.

I was young then—still in my twenties—but that's no excuse for missing one of the biggest stories of our time. I failed as a journalist to report on a key event happening all around me. It wasn't that I didn't know about the training camps, and my contact at the diplomatic party wasn't the only one who suggested I focus on them. But there always seemed to be other, more pressing stories to write first.

The following year, I moved to London and left the story, until days after the 9/11 attacks when I returned to Afghanistan, this time working for *ABC News.*

By 2003, a time when many U.S. officials considered the Taliban virtually extinct, there was an explosion of poppy farming across southern Afghanistan. I began to hear that the insurgents were profiting.

At first, I faced considerable resistance researching the link between the two. U.S. officials scoffed at the notion the Taliban were reaping extensive profits off drugs. Leading experts dismissed my analysis as a misrepresentation of the facts. My editors at *ABC* listened with vague interest whenever I pitched stories, but they always got knocked off the air when something blew up in Iraq.

I often got discouraged, but this time around I stuck with the story, trusting my instincts and continuing to collect information, which I squirrelled away, even at moments when I doubted it would ever see the light of day. The more I learned, the more convinced I became that the nexus of smugglers and extremists presented a critical security threat, to both Afghanistan and the West.

Journalists today are slaves to the twenty-four-hour news cycle, forever feeding the beast, as we say, filing the latest sound bite, bullet point, or factoid. But *Seeds of Terror* is not just another up-to-the-minute item banged out on my battered laptop. I bring the determination of a journalist who didn't get it right the first time, and the concern of a mother fearful for the future my children will inherit. This subject, as anyone who knows me well can attest, has become my passion. This time I will continue to report on it, and I will not stop. I hope someone is listening.

Opium Poppy Cultivation in Afghanistan, 2008 (at province level)

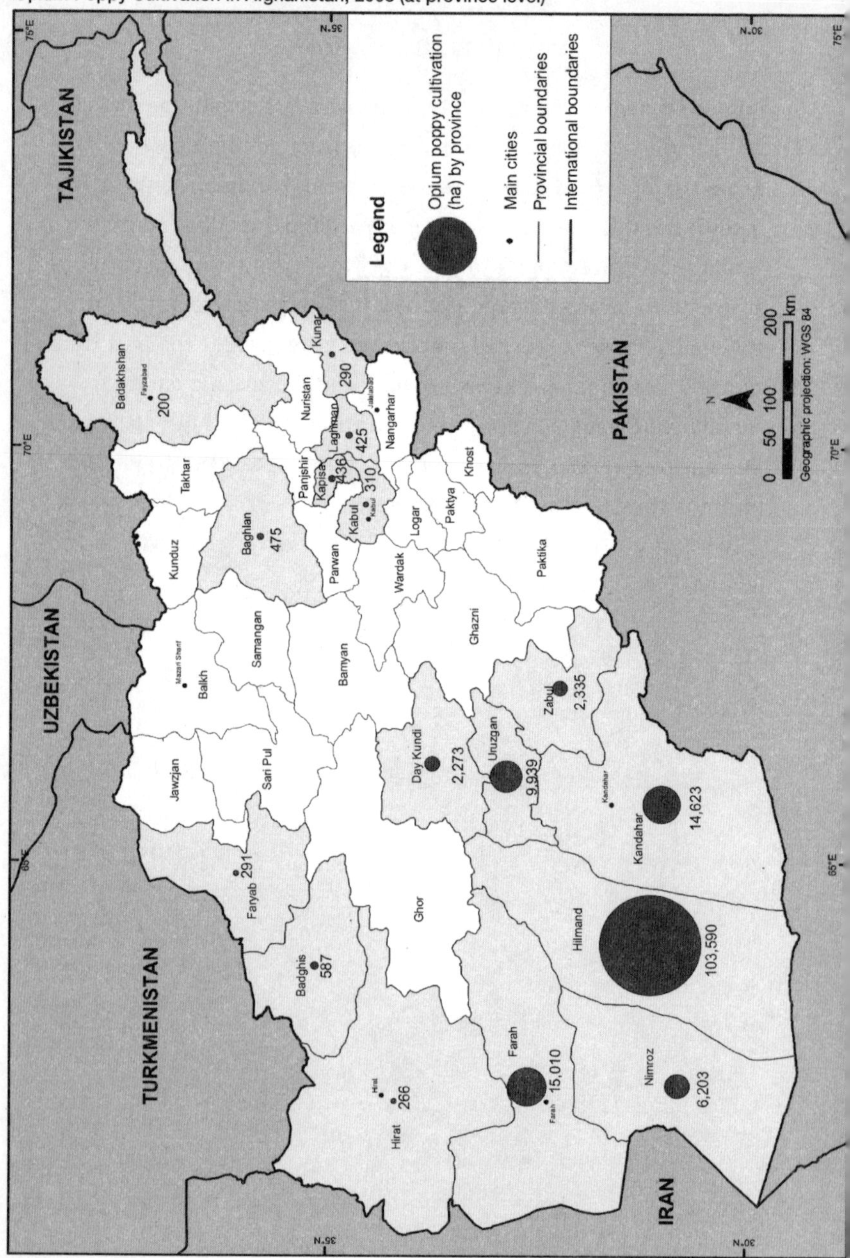

Source: Government of Afghanistan - National monitoring system implemented by UNODC

Note: The boundaries and names shown and the designations used on this map do not imply official endorsement or acceptance by the United Nations.

SEEDS OF TERROR

1. THE NEW AXIS OF EVIL

OUR BATTLE GROUP WAS A RAGTAG CREW OF SCRUFFY AFghan cops and stony-faced American mercenaries. Our target was opium fields profiting the Taliban.

As the first light of day cast a pink glow across the desert, the Afghans rewound their turbans to cover noses and mouths, clicked ammunition clips into Kalashnikovs, and piled onto tractors and Bedford trucks. Wearing flak jackets, baseball caps, and dark sunglasses, the men from DynCorp silently checked their M4 rifles, and peered out across the bleak horizon.

I scribbled into my notebook as my colleague Nasir filmed the scene. John, my husband, was busy taking photos. Journalists rarely had access to ERAD, the poppy eradication force, especially in remote, lawless Helmand. Armed to the teeth and already covered in dust, our convoy looked like something out of *Mad Max.* We wanted to capture it all.

That morning before dawn, an advance team patrolling the roads had come upon a group of insurgents planting an IED in our path. Once the Afghan police colonel and the DynCorp team leader identified where the would-be bombers came from, they decided to pay their village a visit. As punishment, the ERAD team would destroy their opium crops.

Around the cloud of dust that rose as we bumped along the

Zamindavar Plains, poppy fields stretched as far as the eye could see: intense fuchsia blossoms floating in brilliant seas of green. Simple mud huts hugged the banks of irrigation canals. Veiled women hoisted buckets of water out of wells. Turbaned farmers tended their crops, staining their fingers black with the opium gum as they scraped it off the buds. The scenery actually looked lovely, not that I was able to sit back and enjoy it. We were deep in Taliban country and would be lucky to make it through the day without an attack.

Inside our four-by-four, we rode in nervous silence. My mind replayed the array of nightmares that might befall us: ambush, IED, suicide bomb. Villagers along the road watched stonily as our convoy lumbered past. Each time a man approached on a motorcycle, or we slowed down to cross over a stream, my teeth clenched and my heart rose in my chest. It took about an hour to reach the target village. It felt like forever.

The Afghan police and the DynCorp soldiers quickly fanned out in a perimeter around the lush fields, their weapons ready. Tractors went to work churning up the poppy buds. Overhead, a Huey-2 helicopter buzzed the pastures, patrolling for ambushes. We were hundreds of miles from any place that could justifiably be called civilization, with about a hundred boots on the ground and one bird in the sky to protect against a ferocious, battle-hardened enemy.

In the end, the only confrontation came when a skinny farmer, tears streaming down his face, emerged from his mud hut with two filthy children to hurl insults at the eradicators. "Why don't you just shoot us now?" he shouted. "If you cut down my fields, we'll all die anyway."

Next to him on her knees was his wife, toothless, in dust-covered robes. She reached her arms toward the sky and wailed loudly, beseeching Allah to inflict his wrath upon us. In this neighbourhood, we all knew, her prayers had a decent chance of being answered.

That trip to Helmand, in April 2006, put a face to the fragmentary information I had been hearing for more than two years. I had already interviewed truck drivers, farmers, police, and several governors from the southern provinces. The insurgents, they said, had teamed up with criminals. Kandahar's top counternarcotics cop, Ahmadullah Alizai, put it this way: "The smugglers forged a direct link to the Taliban and al Qaeda. They get the terrorists to move their drugs."[1]

U.S. authorities started seeing the trend, too. In late 2003, American sailors boarded two rickety-looking dhows in the Persian Gulf. On board, they found a couple of wanted al Qaeda terrorists sitting on bales of heroin worth $3 million.[2] A few months later, U.S. counternarcotics agents raided a drug smugglers' lair in Kabul, confiscating a satellite telephone. When CIA agents ran numbers stored in its memory, they discovered the telephone had been used repeatedly to call suspected terrorist cells in western Europe, Turkey, and the Balkans.[3]

Suddenly, links between terror groups and narco-traffickers began popping up all over Afghanistan and Pakistan. It was the start of things to come. The Taliban insurgency launched a comeback in the spring of 2003, just as opium cultivation exploded across southern Afghanistan.[4] U.S. troops searching a terrorist hideout in Uruzgan Province found a drug stash worth millions of dollars.[5] U.S. spy satellites tracked cargo ships leaving Pakistani shores laden with Afghan heroin, and returning with weapons and ammunition for the insurgency.[6] DEA agents brought smugglers with ties to Mullah Mohammed Omar and Osama bin Laden to the United States to face justice.

If the accumulating incidents were troubling, it wasn't until I saw the vast scope of Helmand's poppy crop that I felt real alarm. Sloshing about the muddy fields, I realized these lovely flowers could one day fund whatever deadly ambitions terrorist groups based in this region had. "Drugs are going to change everything," I thought.

In 2006, Afghanistan produced the largest illegal narcotics crop a modern nation ever cultivated in a single harvest. Two-thirds of it was grown in areas where the Taliban held sway, if not outright control.[7] It's no coincidence that it was also the bloodiest fighting season since Mullah Omar's regime was toppled five years earlier, with about four thousand deaths. These two circumstances are codependent: the insurgency is exploding precisely because the opium trade is booming. In 2007, Afghanistan's poppy crop expanded a further 17 percent, with 70 percent grown and processed in the Taliban-dominated south. In 2008, drought reduced Afghanistan's poppy output by 19 percent. But more than 98 percent of it was cultivated in insurgent-held areas, where more than three thousand tons of opium were stockpiled, according to the United Nations Office on Drugs and Crime (UNODC). Senior U.S. commanders now predict Afghanistan will turn out to be America's "bad" war and Iraq the "good" one.[8] An American soldier was more than twice as likely to die in Afghanistan as in Iraq by the end of 2007, reversing earlier trends, while Jane's Information Group rated Afghanistan the third most unstable territory after Somalia and the Gaza Strip.[9]

In video statements, the insurgents no longer speak of their ambition to take Kabul; their battlefield tactics have shifted to protecting poppy fields and drug convoys. Campaigns for territorial gain, such as a 2007 Taliban push into Deh Rawood district in Uruzgan, now support smuggling activities.[10] Deh Rawood is perched along the most important drugs- and arms-trafficking route in Uruzgan, connecting to Iran in the west and Pakistan in the south. Poor security in general is vital to the opium trade, preventing aid programmes and other development that might offer poor villagers alternatives to the narcotics trade. "Drug smugglers do not want to see this country become stable," said Ashraf Ghani, the former finance minister.[11]

Helmand Province, where I travelled with the poppy eradication force, is about the size of West Virginia. If it were a separate country, it would be the world's leading opium producer, with the rest of Afghanistan in second place. It's also where links between the Taliban and the opium trade are strongest. "Most of the insurgency there is drug-related," says Ali Jalali, Afghanistan's former interior minister. "It's 100 percent intertwined."[12] The province's total population is less than 1 million—with tens of thousands of families displaced by the fighting. Taliban gunmen patrol the streets of towns they control, hanging alleged spies for the NATO coalition in public squares.[13]

In 2007, UNODC valued Helmand's total poppy output at $528 million, a figure that prompted the conclusion among U.S. and UN officials that Helmand is a wealthy place.[14] Poppy can fetch as much as twelve times more than other staple crops, like wheat and melons. "Helmand's farmers are not poor," a senior UNODC official told me in 2006. "Actually there are a lot of rich ones among them."[15] It is true traffickers and a handful of large landowners earn tens of millions off Helmand's poppy crop, and we need to go after those individuals. However, the vast majority of farmers and sharecroppers are barely eking out a living. Household data collected by the Afghan government, and analyzed by two leading scholars on the Afghan drug trade, calculate a per capita daily income of $1, hardly reflecting Helmand as a land of plenty.[16] "We grow poppy, but the drug smugglers take it from us," said Haji Ramtullah, a farmer in Maarja district. "We sell it cheaply. Then they take it over the border into Pakistan. They make twice as much as we do."[17]

Another argument one hears from U.S. officials is that the poppy farmers have alternatives but do not take them. Helmand receives more U.S. aid than any other Afghan province, they often add. That's true; however, much of the money has been spent on large infrastructural projects that won't show concrete change for ordinary Afghans for years. Meanwhile, cash-for-work and alternative livelihood programmes funded by USAID have been costly failures. One $18 million, U.S.-funded programme shut down in 2005 after gunmen killed eleven of the local staff and guards.[18]

Everywhere you look, there are horrific reports filtering out about daily life in this violent and lawless province. Farmers there often say they must grow opium to survive, and they are not exaggerating. The Taliban threaten dire consequences for anyone who fails to meet opium quotas set by the traffickers. With too few foreign troops to launch a proper counterinsurgency campaign, NATO commanders are forced to rely on aerial bombardments, killing hundreds of civilians and hardening the Afghan villagers against the West. The provincial government and police are notoriously corrupt—with most profiting from the opium trade as well. "We are caught here between the Taliban and government," said Dastoor Khan, a Helmand farmer, expressing a commonly heard sentiment.[19]

Yet instead of intensifying efforts to go after the traffickers and money launderers behind the insurgency, the U.S. government has pushed for broadscale aerial spraying of poppy fields. Wide-scale spraying would play into the hands of traffickers and terrorists. If implemented, this policy would drive up opium prices, thus increasing profits for drug dealers and the Taliban, and make life even harder for already debt-ridden Afghan farmers—exactly the results the U.S. government and NATO don't want.

It's easy to see how we got into this mess. Finding a way out presents a greater challenge. One can blame the current predicament on a combination of geography, poverty, and the "light footprint" approach. Landlocked Afghanistan is one of the poorest and most backward countries in the world, with social indicators on par with places like Burundi and Ethiopia. Almost one in four Afghan children die before they reach age five and average life expectancy is just forty-three years. Per capita GDP was estimated by the World Bank in 2003 to be a mere $310.

The nation's infrastructure is pitiable, with one phone line for every five hundred people, few paved roads, not a single functioning sewage system, and a capital city that grinds along on just a few hours of city power per day. The economy is in shambles, inflation is skyrocketing, and along the rugged Pakistan frontier, many tribes have survived for centuries by smuggling goods through the forbidding mountain passes. Financial hardships weigh on ordinary Afghans as much as security concerns. In a 2006 survey by the Asia Foundation, Afghans named poverty and unemployment as more critical concerns than the Taliban.[20]

After 9/11, the international community paid lip service to the strategic importance of a stable Afghanistan, but never committed the resources to actually create one. Despite troop increases to the NATO-led mission, Afghanistan has the lowest troop-to-population ratio and one of the lowest international aid-to-population ratios of any major conflict zone in the past ten years.[21] The mandate for peacekeepers with the International Security Assistance Force (ISAF) did not go beyond Kabul for its first two years of existence, and there were fewer than ten thousand U.S. troops deployed to Operation Enduring Freedom—which covered the rest of the country—through 2002. As former national security advisor Richard Clarke put it, "There were more cops in New York City than soldiers on the ground in Afghanistan."[22] It was the perfect soil for an insurgency and a criminal economy to take root and flourish.

As poppy output mushroomed, donor nations started bickering over how to deal with it. The Pentagon, with the largest number of people and greatest amount of resources to throw at the problem, refused to take command, saying it blurred the central mission of hunting down terrorists. Top U.S. commanders, including former defence secretary Donald Rumsfeld, often quipped: "We don't do drugs."[23]

But many recognized what was coming. "Nobody in the military who's been out here questions that drugs are the problem," says a U.S. official who used to be based in Kabul. "They just don't want to deal with it." Before long, the problem became impossible to ignore. "The commanders all know how bad it is," continues the official. "I have been to landing zones where there's poppy growing right up to their freaking wire."[24] The Pentagon's reluctance to take on the problem backfired badly for the Bush administration, which had to deploy more American soldiers rather than bring them home. Although public attention in the United States focused on the high numbers of U.S. troops in Iraq, there are now more American troops dedicated to the Afghan conflict than ever. And it's still not enough.

The NATO-led force in Afghanistan now numbers more than 50,000 soldiers, but only some 10,000 are for combat, owing to large administration and logistical support ratios. Estimates of how many insurgents are fighting range from 5,000 to 20,000, with the total swelling or contracting depending on the season. Even with 3,200 U.S. Marines deployed to Helmand in 2008, NATO was only able to slow the insurgency's expansion.[25]

The international aid community has also shortchanged Afghanistan. Since 2001, the international community pledged $25 billion in aid but delivered only $15 billion, according to the Agency Coordinating Body for Afghan Relief, an alliance of ninety-four international aid agencies. An astounding 40 percent of that sum—$6 billion—goes back to donor nations in the form of corporate profits and the exorbitant salaries paid to foreign aid workers.[26] Meanwhile opium income in 2003—estimated at $4.8 billion—was more than 70 percent greater than the $2.8 billion dispersed in foreign aid.[27] "The poppy economy has filled the vacuum we created by not engaging in nation building," says Marvin Weinbaum, a former State Department intelligence analyst. "The danger that we reach a point where drug armies are controlling large areas of territory is real now."[28]

It's hardly unusual, however. In hot spots around the globe, terrorist and other anti-state groups have forged symbiotic relationships with dope runners and the criminal underworld. Of the State Department's forty-two designated terrorist groups, eighteen have ties to drug trafficking, according to the Drug Enforcement Administration. And thirteen of the smuggling organizations the DEA believes are primarily responsible for the United States' illegal drug supply have links to terrorist groups.[29] "In the new era of globalization, both terror and crime organizations have expanded and diversified their activities," said Michael A. Braun, the DEA's chief of operations. "As a result, the traditional boundaries between terrorist groups and other criminal groups have begun to blur."[30]

They flourish around the globe in places where good governance does not. The players may change by region, but the script remains largely the same. Whether it's the Irish Republican Army moving ecstasy into Northern Ireland, Maoist insurgent groups in Nepal running hash into East Asia, or Sri Lanka's Tamil Tigers moving Burmese heroin to the West, anti-state groups the world over have engaged in criminal enterprise, from drug smuggling to kidnap for ransom, credit card fraud, and extortion. Some, like Turkey's Kurdistan Workers Party, or PKK, get their start by taxing traffickers who pass through their control zones. Their role deepens over time. French law enforcement estimates the PKK now smuggles 80 percent of the heroin sold in Paris.

For other groups, drugs provide an opportunity to break free from state sponsors whose support may be dwindling or politically conditional. Hezbollah, for example, got into drug production in Lebanon's Bekaa Valley to fill the void when funding from Iran declined.[31] Terror groups have every incentive to seek financial independence. According to a Stanford University study that examined why some conflicts last so much longer than others, crime was a crucial factor. Out of 128 conflicts, the 17 in which insurgents relied heavily on "contraband finances" lasted five times longer than the rest.[32]

Around Kabul, one often hears concerns that Afghanistan is turning into another Iraq.[33] The parallels are actually closer to Colombia. The Taliban and the Revolutionary Armed Forces of Colombia, known by their Spanish acronym, FARC, both got their start like modern-day Robin Hoods, protecting rural peasants from the excesses of a corrupt government. Strapped for cash and needing the support of local farmers, both groups began levying a tax on drug crops. Over time in Colombia, the FARC was slowly sucked into the coca trade. They began using their soldiers to protect drugs shipments, and then took control of the factories refining coca into cocaine. FARC commanders started forcing farmers in the zones they control to grow coca. Eventually, the FARC became financially self-sufficient, and set up a parallel government.

The pattern sounds eerily familiar to police and military officials in Afghanistan, where the Taliban is undergoing a similar metamorphosis—only much faster. As one senior U.S. official who moved from Colombia to South Asia put it, "It's like watching a bad movie all over again."[34] As Afghanistan's poppy crop explodes past $4 billion a year, "there is no question, no question at all, that the Taliban has been increasingly involved both directly and indirectly in narcotics," says Seth Jones, a Rand Corporation analyst and author of books on Afghanistan.[35] "Nowhere, except perhaps in Colombia, has the linkage between the drugs trade and terrorism been stronger," writes Robert Charles, a former director of the State Department's Bureau of International Narcotics and Law Enforcement Affairs (INL).[36]

The Taliban still mainly confine their role in the drug trade to taxing farmers and protecting drug shipments, but that is changing, just as it did with the FARC, as opportunities for income grow. More important, the definition of Taliban member and drug smuggler is blurring. Taliban help organize farm output in the regions they control, and some commanders even run their own heroin labs.

Today's battles are more often diversionary attacks to protect big drug shipments, rather than campaigns for strategic territorial gain. In many areas, drug smugglers have their own armies whose fighters are widely referred to as "Taliban." Unravelling the details is complicated by the fact that the Taliban itself is less of a unified movement today than it was at its start. In many parts of the Afghanistan-Pakistan border, it's more a gangland-style grouping of tribal leaders, businessmen, regional warlords, and thugs. Media reports often describe the Taliban as profiting off the drug trade, but it's more accurate to say they service it, working for opium smugglers and the mammoth international organized crime rings behind them.

One thing is clear: as the insurgents get sucked deeper into drugs, commanders are losing ties to ideological roots of the Taliban movement. "There's a very small core of true believers still left in the Taliban," says a top U.S. military official. "But our intel is that most of the guys are just in it to make a buck."[37] My research came to a similar conclusion. Using local reporters, I surveyed 350 people who work in or alongside the drug trade in twelve areas along the Pakistan-Afghanistan border where the insurgency holds power or significant influence. Eighty-one percent of respondents said Taliban commanders' first priority was to make money, rather than to recapture territory and impose the strict brand of Islam they had espoused while in power.

Again, the Taliban is following a pattern demonstrated by the FARC. They are no less violent—and in fact are far more ruthless—but their terrorist acts now serve to further their drug ambitions as often as their political ones. Individual commanders may be corrupted by the race for the almighty dollar, but I don't mean to suggest the Taliban and their al Qaeda allies have put aside their ambitions to wreak havoc in the West. Far from it. As earnings soar, criminalized insurgents could make significant gains against the Kabul government—and beyond. Consider this: the FARC now controls 35 percent of Colombia, and earns more than $500 million from the cocaine trade every year. "People should be concerned about the FARCification of the Taliban," says Doug Wankal, who headed the counternarcotics task force at the U.S. embassy in Kabul until mid-2007. "It does not take a lot of drugs money to fund their terrorist operations."

But how much are they making? Where does al Qaeda come into the picture? And what do they plan to do with all that money?

A senior Afghan security official says Taliban soldiers captured in battle have confessed that the bulk of their operational funding—including their salaries and cash for fuel, food, weapons, and bombs—comes from drugs. "It's reached the point where about half of the opium we seize in the provinces has some link to the Taliban,"

General Ali Shah Paktiawal, director of the anti-criminal branch of the Kabul police, told me in 2006.

The DEA in 2007 estimated opium provided the Taliban with as much as 70 percent of its financing.[38] UNODC estimates that approximately 80 percent of Afghanistan's 8,200-metric-ton opium yield in 2007 came from Taliban regions and sold at an average of US$86 per kilogram. This would have netted the Taliban more than $56 million in 2007 from the 10 percent tax known as *ushr* (from the Arabic *ashr*, which means "ten") that is collected at the farm level. Additionally, more than fifty refineries reportedly operate in Taliban-held areas, where insurgents collect about $250 for every kilogram refined.[39] UNODC estimates that those refineries produced 666 metric tons of heroin and morphine base in 2007, which yields another $133 million and change per year.[40] The Taliban also earn as much as $250 million annually providing armed protection for drug shipments moving through their region, as well as receiving tens of millions of dollars' worth of material supplies from smugglers, including vehicles, food, and satellite phones.[41]

Added together, their drug revenue may even outpace that of the FARC. When putting numbers on criminal activity—especially in such a fluid atmosphere—even the best estimates are just that. But one thing is clear: the Taliban's profits from the drug trade are now astonishingly high.

Nailing down how Osama bin Laden comes into the drug trade is far tougher, especially since the issue became embroiled in Washington politics. Today, senior U.S. officials often say evidence of al Qaeda's ties to opium is fragmentary. The argument goes like this: bin Laden's two public statements on drugs indicate that he, like

Mullah Omar, is deeply opposed to the *use* of narcotics. (Neither man has gone public with his opinion on *trafficking* drugs.)[42] As well, officials claim captured al Qaeda operatives have told U.S. interrogators that bin Laden warned his people to stay away from the trade, fearing it would expose them to greater risk.

There are indications al Qaeda has struggled for money, including a six-thousand-word letter allegedly intercepted in 2005 where the number two figure in al Qaeda, Ayman al-Zawahiri, asked the late Iraqi insurgent Abu Musab Zarqawi to send money, saying many of its "lines have been cut off" and "we'll be very grateful" for financial help.[43] American officials say donations from the Persian Gulf are what keep the movement flush, and argue that even though al Qaeda operates in a region where the opium business is booming, it doesn't necessarily prove the terrorists are into it.[44] "Our reporting was they were very worried drugs would corrupt their movement," a senior U.S. counternarcotics official told me. "I have seen nothing to indicate that has changed."[45]

This wasn't always Washington's official line, however. Back in 2000, CIA director George Tenet testified to the Senate Select Committee on Intelligence that "there is ample evidence that Islamic extremists such as Osama Bin Ladin use profits from the drug trade to support their terror campaign."[46] In March 2002, former INL chief Rand Beers told the Senate's Judiciary Committee: "Afghanistan's opiate trafficking . . . was reportedly advocated by Osama bin Ladin as a way to weaken the West."[47] A month later, Asa Hutchinson, the DEA administrator at the time, said his agency "has received multi-source information that Osama bin Laden himself has been involved in the financing and facilitation of heroin-trafficking activities."[48]

Then suddenly, as the Bush administration ramped up for war in Iraq, the official language on this issue took a 180-degree turn, to the immense frustration of U.S. officials who track it closely. "Suddenly I was only permitted to say that we had a 'high probability' of drug money going to the Taliban and 'the possibility' of it going to al Qaeda," says Charles, the former INL chief.[49] It wasn't clear whether top aides to Bush didn't know how to deal with the narcoterror threat or if they simply worried the issue would distract the general public from their wider ambition to invade Iraq. Either way, the administration tried to stir up confusion over whether it was really happening. "It's kind of like déjà vu all over again," complains a senior Republican aide, recalling years of debate in Washington over whether the FARC in Colombia was involved in cocaine smuggling. "We lost precious years there not fighting drugs and terrorists simultaneously, and we are doing the same thing in Afghanistan."[50]

Jack Lawn, a former DEA administrator and FBI agent, became so concerned about the nexus between terrorists and heroin in Afghanistan that he sat down and wrote letters to all relevant officials in the Bush administration, and to the chairs of all relevant committees of Congress. No one even bothered to answer him. "Why we are not speaking out on this—much less doing something about it—confounds me," Lawn says, adding, "Ultimately, we are all going to have to care."[51] Other U.S. officials point to two July 2007 intelligence reports describing al Qaeda as better organized and better funded than any time since 9/11.[52] "If you can't figure out what opium is doing in that mix, you don't deserve to be in this game," says one.[53]

Based on my research, Islamic extremists connected to al Qaeda don't move large quantities of drugs themselves, and there's scant evidence of an organized network involving their leaders in the drug trade. However, low-level al Qaeda operatives appear to get involved at the Pakistan-Afghanistan border, once the opium has been refined into heroin and is ready to get smuggled to the West. This is exactly the point where the profit margin is the highest. Respondents to our survey along the Pakistan-Afghanistan border had no evidence top leaders like bin Laden or his deputy al Zawahiri personally took a role, but 41 percent said low-level al Qaeda fighters regularly helped to protect heroin shipments for money.

The data makes sense when you consider that western intelligence officials believe top-tier al Qaeda leaders are largely cut off from the day-to-day running of their organization, leaving lower-level operatives to fend for themselves. "It's wrong to think you'll find Osama bin Laden with a bag of opium in one hand and a dirty bomb in the other," says a western official. "But the link is there. Increasingly, there are signs that al Qaeda fighters have learned to live off of drug money."[54]

That's certainly true among terror cells in Europe. "Crime is now the main source of cash for Islamic radicals [here]," says attorney Lorenzo Vidino, author of *Al Qaeda in Europe*. "They do not need to get money wired from abroad like ten years ago. They're generating their own as criminal gangs."[55] Take the terrorists behind the March 2004 train blasts in Madrid, which killed 191 people and left 1,500 wounded. They got their hands on explosives by trading hashish to a former miner, and learned to construct bombs—all connected to Mitsubishi Trium T110 mobile phones—from Internet sites linked to radical Islamic groups. When police raided the home of one plotter, they found 125,800 ecstasy tablets, one of the largest drug hauls in Spanish history. Eventually, investigators recovered almost $2 million in drugs and cash—far more than they needed to pull off the operation. Although a man who identified himself as Abu Dujan al-Afghani, and who said he was al Qaeda's "European military spokesman," claimed responsibility in a video released two days later, authorities never found any evidence that al Qaeda's top leaders ever provided the Madrid bombers with financing or direct guidance.[56]

European authorities have linked drug money to the 2003 attacks in Casablanca, which killed forty-five people, and the attempted bombings of U.S. and British ships off Gibraltar in 2002. European police knew for years that Islamic fundamentalists—some through links to Afghanistan dating back to the anti-Soviet resistance—were peddling drugs around the continent.[57] "What is new is the scale of this toxic mix of jihad and dope," writes journalist David Kaplan.[58] Investigators believe extremist groups have broken into as much as a third of the $12.5 billion Moroccan hashish trade, Kaplan reports, meaning they can not only reap enormous profits but also take advantage of extensive smuggling routes through Europe.

The message here is not that Osama bin Laden has morphed into Pablo Escobar, the notorious Colombian cocaine kingpin. Nor has Mullah Omar become the world's new Khun Sa, the infamous Burmese heroin warlord. Rather, there is a blurring of distinction between terrorist and criminal. They may not share the same values, and sometimes even come into conflict, but they are fellow travellers in the underworld, locked in an increasingly symbiotic relationship. One crucial distinction remains: The classic drug smuggler is driven by greed. The terrorist raises money as a means to an end.

So what are they saving up for? By mid-2004, U.S. Treasury

Department agents monitoring drug and terrorist finance flows started watching large sums of illicit money moving *out* of Afghanistan and Pakistan—a region that had traditionally attracted large *inflows* of cash, mostly in the form of donations to jihadi groups.[59] Where that money ended up—and just what it might eventually pay for—no one quite knows. One thing everyone agrees on: the world should be worried. September 11 cost al Qaeda only $500,000, according to the 9/11 Commission. Terrorist groups can now earn that from the dope trade every week.

Just days before the 2004 U.S. presidential election, my office in Pakistan received a mysterious delivery. It was the taped statement of a man claiming to be a new spokesman for al Qaeda. His face was wrapped in a kaffiyeh and he spoke English with an American accent. He turned out to be Adam Yahiye Gadahn, the Orange County native turned al Qaeda front man who has since been indicted for treason. One thing Gadahn said in that statement always stuck with me as I researched this project. When the next 9/11 comes, he warned, "the casualties will be too high to count." For years, western intelligence has documented al Qaeda's efforts to get its hands on weapons of mass destruction. Former CIA director George Tenet repeatedly called it the thing that kept him up at night.[60] Extremists have widely disseminated assembly instructions for an improvised chemical weapon on the Internet and experimented with rudimentary biological-chemical attacks in their former camps in Afghanistan. Experts say it will be technically difficult for a terrorist group to successfully pull off an attack using weapons of mass destruction. But one thing will make their goal a lot easier to reach: lots and lots of money.

I hope it won't take a massive terrorist attack to focus the international community's attention on this problem. Debate finally seems to be ending among senior policymakers over whether the Taliban is making money from Afghan opium. But so far the world's governments have not responded coherently to the tempest brewing along the Afghanistan-Pakistan border. Militarily, the NATO coalition in Afghanistan has failed to adapt to the changing nature of its enemy. Even after UNODC released 2007 crop figures showing the clearest link yet between the poppy trade and the Taliban, senior NATO officials reiterated their disinterest in getting involved. "The fight against narcotics is first and foremost an Afghan responsibility, but they need help," declared Jim Pardew, NATO deputy assistant secretary-general for operations, adding blandly: "We are doing the best we can. We would ask others to do more."[61]

It's unclear who NATO's commanders hope will step up to the plate. No one has much hope for the corrupt and inept administration of Hamid Karzai. The president of Afghanistan, an ethnic Pashtun, derives much of his political support from the country's Pashtun-dominated south, where he has resisted efforts to curtail poppy cultivation. Karzai has refused to dismiss, much less prosecute, high-level officials in his administration widely believed to be tied to drugs, prompting some former officials to conclude that he's protecting relatives and cronies suspected of earning enormous profits. "Karzai was playing us like a fiddle," wrote Thomas Schweich, the State Department's former point man on counternarcotics in Afghanistan, in an unusually frank 2008 editorial. "The U.S. would spend billions on infrastructure improvement; the U.S. and its allies would fight the Taliban; Karzai's friends could get rich off the drug trade; he could blame the West for his problems; and in 2009 he would be elected to a new term."[62]

Washington hasn't done a very good job of choosing allies in Afghanistan. Since 9/11, the U.S. government—the Pentagon and the CIA in particular—has worked with unsavoury individuals in Afghanistan, regional warlords and thugs with known ties to drug smuggling, saying they were helpful in the effort to capture al Qaeda fugitives. In fact, few high-value terror targets have been snared, thanks to such dubious allies, and Washington possesses a wealth of evidence that some of these individuals are enriching themselves through the opium trade. Fighting corruption and official involvement in drug trafficking in Afghanistan is as critical a challenge to rebuilding the country as defeating the Taliban. A central reason the Taliban insurgency is now flourishing is the failure of the Kabul regime and the international community to establish good governance in Afghanistan.

On top of that, it's not possible to handle the insurgency and the opium trade as separate issues. Whether NATO's commanders like it or not, they are already fighting a drug war in Afghanistan. In 2006, Antonio Maria Costa, the executive director of UNODC, made a dramatic call for a shift in NATO operations across Afghanistan "to stop the vicious circle of drugs funding terrorists and terrorists protecting drug traffickers." He publicly asked the NATO-led coalition to destroy heroin labs, disband opium bazaars, attack opium convoys, and bring to justice the major narco-traffickers. "In Afghanistan," Costa declared, "drugs are now a clear and present danger."[63] Costa is right. It's time the international community stops bickering over who has responsibility for counternarcotics, and starts putting resources toward programmes that will cut the profits reaching traffickers and insurgents.

The purpose of trafficking narcotics is to make money: lots of money. It's crucial to keep that simple fact in mind. The United Nations calculates the global illegal drug trade to be worth $400 billion a year—more than the entire U.S. Department of Defense budget. Illegal drugs make up 8 percent of global trade, while textiles make up 7.5 percent and motor vehicles just 5.3 percent.[64] The harder we make it for the traffickers and terrorists to access these vast profits, the closer we will come to defeating them.

The union of narco-traffickers, terrorist groups, and the international criminal underworld is the new axis of evil. It doesn't stop at Afghanistan's porous borders. This is a transnational problem and so, too, must be the response. As insurgent and criminal networks become more deeply intertwined, they will swell in economic and military might, and then what began as a regional headache will become a global security nightmare: the perfect storm. Chasing down heroin smugglers along the Pakistan-Afghanistan border is not only crucial to beating back the Taliban and stabilizing Afghanistan. It's essential to winning the global war on terror.

My message here is simple: if you want to go after terrorists, you have to go after drugs and the smugglers' ability to profit from them. Just as this shift in strategy presents a fresh challenge to the intelligence community, which has been stymied in its efforts to kill or capture top terrorist leaders, it also presents an opportunity. Because traffickers and terrorists are working closely together, the way to find terrorists is to track smugglers. As one U.S. official observed, "When you run with the dogs, you're going to find fleas."

In Chapters 2 and 3, I will map out how the heroin trade has shaped the conflict in Afghanistan since the 1980s. Recent history set the stage for today's mess and shows how the international community, and Washington in particular, is repeating the mistakes of the past. In Chapter 4, I'll examine how heroin money saved the Taliban from the brink of extinction and show how this reincarnated, reloaded Taliban is a very different and far more ruthless animal from the one that governed Afghanistan in the 1990s. Chapter 5 profiles a sheepherder-turned-kingpin whose heroin network moves quantities of dope that put him in a league with world-renowned drug smugglers like Pablo Escobar or Mexico's Arellano-Felix brothers. Yet he remains unknown to the general public and even to many U.S. policymakers focused on Afghanistan and Pakistan. It is critical to grasp the power wielded by such businessmen, who bankroll the insurgency and who could fund wider violence.

I'll follow the money trail in Chapter 6, tracing the shadowy South Asian crime boss Dawood Ibrahim, who is linked to Pakistan's spy agency and powerful Arab sheiks. This is not fanciful conspiracy theory: individuals profiled in this book are listed in government indictments and most-wanted lists. In Chapter 7, I'll follow muddled U.S. counternarcotics policy in Afghanistan and the botched case against Haji Bashir Noorzai, an opium smuggler with links to the Taliban and al Qaeda who is behind bars in a high-security Manhattan jail, awaiting sentence. The long journey bringing him there reveals the challenges and complexities international law enforcement faces.

I'll examine why our policy has failed in Afghanistan, and put forward ideas for a way out in Chapter 8. One thing is clear: counter-narcotics experts, longtime Afghanistan observers, and our own

2. OPERATION JIHAD

UNDER THE SHADOW OF THE LARGEST COVERT U.S. OPERAtion in history, two American federal agents crept over the Afghan border in January 1988 on a top-secret mission.

Across the devastated countryside, the final chapter of the cold war was drawing to a bloody close. For nine years Muslim guerrillas, secretly funded by the CIA, had waged jihad against their Soviet invaders. The conflict had united thousands of Islamic radicals (among them a young Osama bin Laden) who flocked to Afghanistan from around the globe to join what they considered a holy cause. Poppy fields and heroin labs had sprung up across the territory controlled by the rebels, who were known as mujahideen, Arabic for "strugglers." By the time the two U.S. agents snuck across the border, the American spies who ran the clandestine programme to train and equip the Afghan rebels knew the mujahideen were winning.

A month later, Soviet leader Mikhail Gorbachev would stun the world by announcing plans to withdraw the hundred thousand Red Army troops from Afghanistan. It would be an astounding victory for the mujahideen, and a CIA triumph. But even before Soviet tanks began their long retreat over the Hindu Kush, there was growing unease in some U.S. government circles that a deadly mix of heroin smugglers and Islamic extremists would one day emerge as a by-product of the conflict. With that concern in mind, Charles Carter and Richard Fiano, two DEA agents posted to the U.S. embassy in Islamabad, grew out their beards and wrapped themselves in the flowing robes of the mujahideen.[1] Riding in the back of a dusty truck, they rumbled up a smugglers' trail into Helmand Province, with a handful of Afghans as their guards and guides.

Alongside the CIA's multibillion-dollar campaign to bring down the Soviet army, the DEA had concocted a relatively modest effort using mujahideen informants to identify and destroy labs where raw opium was processed into heroin. Most labs were nestled in the hilly Chaghi district of Helmand Province along the Pakistan border. "We trained the mujahideen with cameras, and if they found a place that looked like a lab, they would photograph it," said Carter, then agent in charge of the Islamabad station. The camps weren't much—just a couple of rudimentary mud huts, often strewn with grimy plastic barrels for mixing precursor chemicals like hydrochloric acid and acetic anhydride. "This wasn't Bristol-Myers Squib," Fiano said. Together, DEA and CIA agents in Islamabad analyzed photos their informants brought back. When the agents concluded a site was producing crystal heroin, "then we would go in with the mujahideen and take out the lab," Carter said. They dubbed the programme "Operation Jihad."

Both the DEA and CIA pitched in funds to destroy the labs, paying the mujahideen as much as $25,000 per site. It was a small outlay given the millions of dollars' worth of heroin each lab produced in a thirty-day cycle. "Some of those labs were doing five, even six hundred Ks a month," Fiano said. They destroyed drugs on site, keeping small samples for the DEA's global tracking registry known as the System to Retrieve Information from Drug Evidence, or STRIDE. "As far as we were concerned, whatever else they seized was theirs," Carter said. There was often buried treasure hidden in the ground around the labs—British pounds, German marks, Iranian dinars, and Pakistani rupees valued at tens of thousands of dollars. "The mujahideen would take the money and turn it back around into their war effort," Carter said.

Fiano and Carter's three-week journey into Afghanistan, travelling with a half-dozen mujahideen, was aimed at verifying that Operation Jihad was working as intended. At a time when Americans were officially forbidden from crossing the border, it would end up being the longest and most extensive journey inside Afghanistan by any U.S. agents during the war.[2] Seeing the labs firsthand brought home the scale of the problem for the two DEA agents. "Especially when you caught them off guard and the lab was flush—with like three hundred kilos just sitting there," Fiano recalled. "And you think, 'Holy smokes, this is a bathtub operation, and they are putting out this much?' That surprised the hell out of me." The group travelled on foot along smugglers' trails through southern Helmand, taking along a goat, which their Afghan companions killed and ate along the way. "The nights were freezing, and it was a hundred degrees by day," recalled Fiano. "And after two weeks, that goat didn't smell very appetizing." Those were the days before satellite phones and GPS. If they came under attack, Fiano and Carter knew there would be no air support. If they got sick or injured, there would be no rescue. "Out there," Fiano said, "we had no one to count on but those mujahideen."

Operating as it did on a wing and a prayer, Operation Jihad eventually ran into trouble, mainly since the holy warriors the DEA hired to roll over heroin labs got into the habit of tying up the lab workers and executing them. "I got a call one day, and they said, 'We have a problem,'" recalled Jack Lawn, the DEA administrator in those days. "I listened, and then I said, 'How about we come up with a Plan B?'" Before long, Lawn and his agents were brought before the Senate Intelligence Committee for a grilling. The lawmakers were incensed that the programme had turned lethal. They asked why the DEA never got permission from the host nation, something Lawn pointed out was impossible given that Afghanistan was run by the Soviets. The DEA chief defended Operation Jihad, saying that labs along the border produced more than half the heroin sold on U.S. streets. His agents were just trying to do something about it, Lawn said. If you had to do it all over again, the senators wanted to know, would you do anything differently? "Not one bit," Lawn replied, to the delight of his men. Years later, Carter still recalled the moment fondly: "I think Jack has a gigantic set of *huevos*."

After all, it was one of the few times in those days that a senior U.S. official took the stand to say stopping Afghanistan's drug output mattered enough to take a risk or two. For much of the 1980s, the U.S. government acted like the problem didn't exist at all.

The United States' clandestine adventure in Afghanistan bears remarkable parallels to today's state of affairs. It began in 1979, when Pakistan was ruled by Zia ul-Haq, a mustachioed general who took power in a bloodless coup in 1977, ousting a democratically elected leader. The international community at first isolated the ruling junta, and then abruptly reversed its policy when the Soviets invaded Afghanistan. Overnight, Pakistan became a frontline state in the cold war, and the conduit for billions of dollars in military and other aid flowing to the Afghan resistance.

Washington embraced the mujahideen as valiant freedom fighters, and their jihad in the forbidding Hindu Kush became a cause célèbre bursting with drama and intrigue.

Strategically, the goal was to give the Soviets "a black eye," as one former U.S. official put it, and get revenge for the United States' humiliation in Vietnam. But no one wanted to start World War III or get sucked into Afghanistan's complex political quagmire. A "light footprint" approach was better, the CIA reasoned. Using Pakistan's spy agency, the Inter-Services Intelligence (ISI), as a proxy coordinator gave the United States deniability and freed the agency from muddying its hands in local politics. The downside to this approach was that it gave Pakistan free rein—and unprecedented funding—to pursue its own Islamist agenda in the region. Zia hoped that by waving the flag of Islam he could stamp out ethno-nationalist aspirations among Pashtun tribes living along the 1,500-mile Pakistan-Afghanistan border.

Opium was hardly new to the region. Poppy has flourished along the Golden Crescent—Afghanistan, Pakistan, Iran—throughout recorded history. By some accounts, Alexander the Great first introduced opium to Persia and India in 330 B.C. Moghul leader Zahiruddin Mohammad Babar wrote about smoking it (and then vomiting) when he conquered Kabul in 1504. It was consumed socially across Central Asia by the mid-sixteenth century. Through much of the twentieth century, Afghanistan's opium trade was controlled by the ruling family, headed by Zahir Shah, and largely exported to Iran. Afghanistan became a popular stop on the "hippie trail" in the 1960s because of its cheap hashish and striking scenery. When King Zahir Shah was ousted in a 1973 coup, Washington considered Afghanistan's drug trade worrisome, but Pakistan's tribal areas, a lawless border region slightly larger than Rhode Island, was a far bigger concern.[3]

The opium poppy flourishes in warm, dry climates, like the one along the Pakistan-Afghanistan frontier. Its vivid flowers bloom three months after its tiny black seeds are planted. When the petals drop off, they expose a green pod containing a thick, milky sap—opium in its purest form. Farmers harvest the sap as they have for centuries, by scoring the buds with a curved scraping knife and collecting the sticky brown resin that dries on the buds. In rudimentary "laboratories," often nothing more than a mud hut with metal mixing drums and a brick stove, raw opium is mixed with lime and boiled in water to make morphine base. Once poured into moulds and sun-dried into hard bricks, it is reduced in weight and volume by a factor of 10, making it easier to smuggle.

More elaborate refineries cook the morphine bricks with acetic anhydride and hydrochloric acid to create heroin base, a coarse granular substance. Referred to locally as "brown sugar" for its colour and coarse consistency, this low-grade heroin is what gets sold on the streets of Pakistan and Iran. Injectable crystal heroin—highly potent and white in colour—is what gets exported to the West. More complex to produce, it requires elaborate charcoal filtration and further cooking stages using chloroform and sodium carbonate. At the time, most labs along the frontier could only produce the so-called brown sugar, and normally exported partially refined heroin to more elaborate facilities along the Turkish border for the final stage of refinement, according to counternarcotics officials.

When the Afghan resistance began, Pashtun tribes in Pakistan's tribal areas grew more poppy than all of Afghanistan put together, and had been smuggling all sorts of commodities for centuries. A 1965 bilateral agreement allowing goods to be transported duty-free from Pakistan's coast to landlocked Afghanistan worked to the benefit of the tribes, giving birth to an elaborate network briskly ferrying commodities in and drugs out. This was known as the "U-turn scheme": Pashtun trucking companies carried goods ranging from refrigerators to foodstuffs from the port city of Karachi up to the tribal areas across the border, whereupon they would be smuggled back into Pakistan to avoid Islamabad's protectionist customs fees. The trucks would return to the coast laden with hashish, heroin, and other contraband. From time to time, Karachi authorities launched raids into the coastal smuggling dens at Sohrab Goth, a teeming Pashtun slum hugging the seaboard, where they uncovered massive underground narcotics bunkers.[4] After Jimmy Carter's administration signed off on the first secret aid for the anti-Soviet resistance in 1979, members of his own administration worried in a *New York Times* editorial that the United States was making a mistake by supporting Pashtun guerrillas who also moved dope. They wrote: "Are we erring in befriending these tribes as we did in Laos?"[5]

Their concerns were well founded. Reports filtering out of the war zone in the early years of the resistance asserted that rebel-held areas had begun growing poppy on an unprecedented scale.[6] Opium production more than doubled in Afghanistan between 1984 and 1985, from 140 metric tons to 400, according to U.S. government estimates at the time, doubling again in 1986.[7] Ali Ahmad, a young rebel commander from Sangin, in Helmand Province, said it was a matter of simple economics. He could sell a pound of opium for as much as $50—roughly one hundred times what other crops would bring in. "Everyone is taking it up," he said.[8]

The devastation the war inflicted on the countryside was largely to blame. Millions of refugees had fled over the border to Pakistan, leaving fewer people to work the land. Meanwhile, the Soviets' scorched-earth policy left far less land to work. Opium is a sturdy, drought-resistant crop that has few pests or ailments and doesn't rot. Afghan farmers found that there was an endless demand for it. "A farmer does not worry about selling his opium," said Daud Khan, another commander. "Dealers come from Iran with money in their hands. If a farmer thinks he can get a better price at the border, he can hire a camel for the trip."[9]

From early on, a system developed where farmers would hire rebel soldiers to protect their drug shipments, and the guerrillas would use the money to support the resistance. "If one of our soldiers is sick or wounded we must send money to his family," said Ali Ahmad. "We must also feed them and give them money for shoes and clothes."[10] When a *New York Times* reporter asked how strict Muslims could condone trafficking in narcotics, another mujahideen commander offered up a dubious rationalization that is still heard today across Afghanistan's poppy belt: Islamic law forbids *taking* drugs, but not *growing* them. (Leading Islamic scholars dispute this interpretation, saying Islam bans any and all involvement in narcotics production, use, or trade.) "How else can we get money?" said Mohammed Rasul, whose brother, Mullah Nasim Akhundzada, was then regarded as the most powerful warlord in Helmand Province. "We must grow and sell opium to fight our holy war against the Russian nonbelievers."[11]

This trend would dominate the final years of the resistance, and become exacerbated by the inconsistencies in the way that foreign military assistance was distributed among the mujahideen parties, which created intense competition for funds and fierce infighting. The United States and Saudi Arabia were the central donors to the Afghan resistance, providing matching annual funds worth hundreds of millions of dollars. Britain, China, and various European nations also contributed. All the money was funnelled through the ISI, giving the Pakistani spy agency tremendous control over which commanders and parties would benefit.

When the resistance began, there were more than eighty Afghan political groups clamouring for foreign money, each claiming to represent the Afghan people. "We told the ISI to bring this down to a manageable number," says a former U.S. official. "We said, 'You know the language and the culture, not us. You deal with this.' "[12] Pakistan's spy agency reorganized the eighty groups into seven parties, which became known as the Peshawar Seven, since their leaders had to travel to the Pakistani frontier city to collect their funds and marching orders. Some of the parties were more loose amalgamations of regional warlords than functioning syndicates. "The loyalty of the commanders was often pretty fleeting," says Milton Bearden, the CIA's chief of station from 1986 to 1989.

Hundreds of millions in private donations also flowed in from wealthy Arabs, and tended to benefit mainly fundamentalist Islamic factions. The ISI also favoured the fundamentalists, claiming they were more disciplined. In fact, Pakistan feared the rise of ethnic Pashtun nationalism—espoused by some of the moderate parties—along its border. The fundamentalists received more money, weapons, food, and medical supplies, while others struggled for money. The ISI would routinely withhold food and medical aid when they needed errant commanders to fall in line.[13]

Some commanders like Mullah Akhundzada sought early on to establish independence through the opium trade or other illicit activities, such as smuggling timber and gemstones.[14] "Akhundzada had his own power base," said Peter Tomsen, the State Department's special envoy to the Afghan resistance from 1989 to 1992. "A guy like that wasn't controlled by Peshawar."[15] Mujahideen commanders were generally satisfied to collect a 10 percent tax on the crops grown in their region. Akhundzada went further, setting production quotas and offering loans to farmers who planted poppy. Under the "salaam system," farmers would presell their crops at planting time at a price that was lower than its market value at harvest.

The system still functions today, and has trapped thousands of poor farm families into a crippling debt cycle.[16] Akhundzada also tapped into trafficking, opening an office in the Iranian town of Zaidan to manage his shipments west. By the time the Soviets withdrew, he ran Helmand like his personal fiefdom. In 1989, he demanded half the Helmand Valley farmland be planted with poppy.[17] He threatened farmers who did not comply with castration or death.[18] That year, the valley produced more than 250 metric tons of opium, earning Akhundzada the nickname "King of Heroin."[19]

Such abundances caught the attention of Gulbuddin Hekmatyar, a notoriously ruthless commander of the fundamentalist Hizb-i-Islami Party.[20] Hekmatyar was effectively a creation of the ISI and operated mainly along the Pakistan border. The power-hungry commander launched a two-year internal war against Mullah Akhundzada for control of Helmand's rich poppy fields.[21] By the end of the Soviet resistance, he reportedly invested in heroin labs along the border, working in partnership with Pakistani smuggling networks.[22] "All the big traffickers in those days tended to be from Hizb-i-Islami and that was principally because Hekmatyar was a border person," said Edmund McWilliams, another special envoy to the resistance who served from 1988 to 1989. "He was very much operating along the border because he was so dependent on Pakistani support."[23] Heroin money and ISI assistance helped Hekmatyar transform his network from a fledgling militia into a centralized military organization.

American officials assisting the war effort grudgingly acknowledged Hekmatyar's managerial prowess, but feared his rabid brand of Islam and vicious thirst for power. "He supported Saddam Hussein publicly. He was the deepest into drugs. He was killing modern Afghans and intellectuals. He had ordered his forces inside Afghanistan to kill westerners," said Tomsen. Yet repeated efforts by the Americans to cut Hekmatyar off failed because of his ISI connections. Years later, Bearden, the former CIA station chief, growled: "I always complain I should have shot that guy when I had the chance."

Yunis Khalis, who headed a breakaway Hizb-i-Islami faction, was the third fundamentalist commander deep in the heroin trade, according to ex-officials, historians, and mujahideen commanders. "Khalis was a drug dealer and a thief," says a former U.S. official. "He was also an effective fighter."[24] As with Hekmatyar, Khalis's rise to power was fully dependent on his manipulation of the heroin trade and his ties to Pakistan. Unique among the Peshawar Seven leaders, he came from a humble background, growing into a powerful businessman as his military strength swelled. According to one news report, Khalis ran a simple bicycle repair shop before the war; by 1989 he was operating a bus service with a fleet of fifty vehicles, and a huge auto parts store in Peshawar.[25]

Khalis worked systematically to gain power in Nangarhar, a province which had grown poppy for centuries. He reportedly skirmished with other mujahideen for control over poppy fields and roads leading to three heroin labs and hashish shops he ran on the border.[26] His party included the powerful eastern commander Jalaluddin Haqqani, who operated along the border and had close ties to both smuggling networks and the Arab fighters who would one day form al Qaeda. Another key associate was Haji Abdul Qadir, a Nangarhar commander nicknamed "Mr. Powder" who ran a rickety fleet of Antonovs that flew out of Jalalabad Airport under the flag of Khyber Airlines. The airline was widely believed to carry heroin on flights to the Gulf and return to Afghanistan loaded with electronic goods that would be smuggled over the Khyber Pass into Pakistan.[27]

The fundamentalist commanders weren't the only ones moving dope. Most Afghan resistance fighters got in on the exploding poppy market to some extent—mainly just taking a cut out of whatever passed through their region. "Drugs were behind everything," said a prominent former commander, who didn't want his name used, even years later. The extremist Islamic factions were more organized in their approach, however, integrating their operations horizontally across the narcotics trade, and investing in transport businesses and import-export schemes to conceal their shipments and launder money. Mujahideen leaders like Khalis and Hekmatyar never directly ran drug operations; a better comparison, say western officials, is the mafia overlord with his fingers in many pots of a diversified illegal empire. Lower-level commanders would actually do the dirty work, but the boss took a cut of everything. "Think of Tony Soprano and how he controls his guys," says a former CIA agent.

The next generation of Afghanistan's leaders would spring from the ranks of these fundamentalist commanders, and there are clear signs they were informed by this practice of fundraising. A young Mullah Omar fought under Yunis Khalis, and many senior Taliban officials served with Akhundzada. It was Khalis who gave Osama bin Laden refuge when the Saudi national fled Sudan in 1994. Meanwhile, Jalaluddin Haqqani and Hekmatyar still operate along the border with Pakistan, today fighting the NATO-led coalition. U.S. military intelligence believes both Hekmatyar and Haqqani remain deeply dependent on smuggling heroin.[28]

If the emerging mujahideen links to the drug trade were troubling, more worrisome still were reports Pakistan's military government was deeply involved, too. By 1984, 70 percent of the world's supply of high-grade heroin was produced in or smuggled through Pakistan, according to European police estimates. There were also widespread reports the covert pipeline run by the ISI, which brought weapons and materiel to Afghan guerrillas, was carrying vast amounts of heroin in the return direction.[29] The secret military aid for the mujahideen arrived at Pakistan's seaport, Karachi, and travelled to the North-West Frontier Province (NWFP) in trucks run by the National Logistics Cell (NLC), a trucking company wholly owned and staffed by the military. In 1985, a Pakistani news magazine, *The Herald*, reported the military trucks carried heroin back to the seaport. "The drug is carried in NLC trucks which come sealed from the NWFP and are never checked by police," the report said, quoting eyewitnesses. A senior Pakistani police official complained to another reporter, "If we want to investigate the NLC or military personnel who we may believe are involved we are told to 'keep out' by the army. If you push too hard, you are transferred. It's that simple."[30]

In a detailed memoir explaining how the pipeline worked, Brigadier Mohammed Yousaf, the ISI officer in charge of logistics, wrote that "the overall security of our methods" was helped by martial law. "The military was in complete control. They were both the makers and executors of the law."[31] Yousaf later insisted military trucks did not carry drugs, but even if that were so, it is hard to imagine Pakistani officers were not aware of and complicit in the huge amount of heroin crisscrossing the border region. The ISI controlled all traffic and inspected all cargo passing in and out of Afghanistan. Pakistan's spy agency also closely monitored vehicles plying roads into Iran.[32]

In fact, a number of incidents suggested the existence of a major heroin syndicate within the Pakistan military. In June 1986, an army major was arrested driving from Peshawar to Karachi carrying 220 kilograms of high-grade heroin. It was the largest heroin seizure ever made in Pakistan. Two months later, an air force officer was caught with an identical amount hidden in his car. He admitted to police it was his fifth mission. In both cases, military squads swiftly removed the men from police custody, shifting them to a high-security facility outside Karachi. Before any substantial investigation got underway—let alone a trial—the two officers made a highly suspicious "escape." In all, sixteen military officers were arrested in 1986 on drug charges. None were investigated.[33] A heavily redacted 1987 CIA analysis entitled "Narcotics Trafficking and the Military" concluded "corruption is widespread . . . and because of the generally low level of military salaries, it is likely to grow in the near term."[34] The late Baluch tribal leader Mohammad Akbar Khan Bugti put it more bluntly: "They deliver drugs under their own bayonets."[35]

Despite the growing evidence, U.S. officials working in support of the Afghan resistance largely ignored and even suppressed indications that America's allies were peddling heroin. *The Washington Post* reported in 1990 that U.S. diplomats had "received but declined to investigate" firsthand accounts that Afghan guerrillas and ISI agents "protect and participate" in heroin trafficking.[36] Lawrence Lifschultz, an American journalist who reported extensively on the issue, wrote that Afghan intellectuals who tried to alert the U.S. embassy to the problem were "politely noted but not acted upon."[37]

Years later, former senior officials at the U.S. embassy in Pakistan admitted they were aware of the rumours, but rarely followed them up, lest narcotics distract from the central focus. "We wanted to give the Soviets the biggest black eye and kick in the pants we possibly could," said Larry Crandall, who ran USAID operations from 1985 to 1990. McWilliams, the former special envoy, said: "You have to put yourself in the mind-set of the period. Raising issues like Hekmatyar and the ISI's involvement in the drug trade was on no one's agenda."[38] When President Ronald Reagan met visiting mujahideen leaders in the White House in 1987, he never mentioned heroin.[39] As the DEA's Rich Fiano put it, "Reagan did not want the mujahideen to be involved in drugs."

Although there were widespread indications that Afghan rebels were neck-deep in the dope trade, proving the allegations was another matter, even if anyone wanted to do so. Former CIA agents interviewed for this book said they vetted mujahideen commanders with the help of the DEA, but found it nearly impossible to collect concrete evidence of wrongdoing. Agents were frustrated by the lack of information in general filtering out of the war zone. "Part of the problem is this mythical American interpretation that if you put enough money into something you will know what is going on," said William Piekney, a former U.S. Navy officer who ran the CIA's Islamabad station from 1984 to 1986. "We could never get a reliable estimate of how many mujahideen were under arms. No one even knew who was fighting, let alone if they were dealing in drugs." Because the logistics and training had been outsourced to the ISI, getting direct, reliable information was all but impossible. "Once you put the weapons in the hands of a bunch of tough fighters who owe their allegiance to their tribe first and foremost, the best you can do is try and find out what happened later," said Piekney.[40]

Officially barred from crossing into Afghan territory and largely prevented by the ISI from meeting mujahideen commanders directly, CIA agents say they developed various methods to try to gather independent accounts of what was going on. Along the way, they collected scraps of information about the drug trade: who was active in financing farmers, moving drug loads, and running labs. "I do not remember seeing too many commanders who were really heavily into drugs," said Bearden. "And there was never any reliable proof." When Carter and Fiano toured southern Afghanistan, destroying about sixteen labs along the way, they were able to identify individuals running the labs they hit, but gleaned little information on how their operations fit into larger networks. The DEA had a clear sense of who the kingpins were in Pakistan, but Afghanistan was a black hole. "Quite honestly, we did not even look for the major players," Fiano said. The DEA's Kabul office had been closed since 1979 when the Soviets invaded. "We had extremely limited information on how the trade worked inside Afghanistan," he said. "There was no way for us to know who was making a cut."

For senior administration officials back in Washington, the vague level of understanding was useful. When U.S. lawmakers brought up media reports suggesting U.S. allies were peddling heroin, the lack of finished analysis provided plausible deniability. One could acknowledge that individual mujahideen commanders might be lining their pockets, but still deny evidence of a systemic smuggling effort. The haphazard nature of the drug trade in Afghanistan made it easy for everyone to describe the problem as circumstantial rather than a matter of mujahideen policy.

A May 1986 statement by Robert Peck from the State Department's Bureau of Near Eastern Affairs was typical. In a hearing before the House Foreign Affairs Committee, Peck testified that there "was no evidence of organized resistance involvement in narcotics production or trafficking."[41] In 1987, Ann Wrobleski, then assistant secretary of state for international narcotics matters, actually went so far as to defend the Afghan rebels for dealing in "the only currency they have."[42]

In dozens of declassified documents and interviews with former officials, the pattern of behaviour becomes clear: despite a wealth of evidence and intelligence reporting that showed mujahideen fighters were engaged in drug trafficking, there was never any systematic effort to map out the scale of the problem. At least one former CIA official is disparaging about former colleagues who claim there was no clear evidence. "We all knew what was going on," he said. "The people who could do something about it wouldn't hear about it, or they would listen and do nothing."[43]

Rather than trying to investigate the heroin trade inside Afghanistan, U.S. diplomats and counternarcotics officials in Islamabad busied themselves stamping out poppy cultivation in Pakistan's tribal belt. This was arguably an equally critical concern since more of the heroin produced there ended up on U.S. streets.[44] Between 1979 and 1986, a carrot-and-stick approach combining alternative livelihood projects and forced eradication succeeded in reducing the area planted with poppy by almost 80 percent. It was a Herculean effort that often erupted into violence. In 1985 alone, twelve poppy farmers and one law enforcement officer lost their lives when tribesmen attacked eradication teams arriving to destroy their crops.[45]

The Pakistan government repeatedly claimed stamping out poppy in the tribal areas demonstrated Islamabad's commitment to fighting narcotics. But actually, the programme did little more than kick the poppy fields over the Afghan border, which local Pashtun tribes didn't recognize anyway. "Moving it five hundred meters in either direction hardly made much of a difference up there," said Teresita Schaffer, a former deputy secretary of state for South Asia.[46] The fields being planted may have shifted slightly, but for the smugglers based in Pakistan, it was business as usual. And business was better than ever.

The new cross-border nature of the trade made it even harder to track. Pakistan rapidly became a net importer of opium, and annual heroin production rocketed from six tons in 1984 to thirty tons by 1988. By then, more than one hundred labs were operational, most of them located just inside the Afghan border, in the tribal areas.[47] Pakistani authorities proved to be much less enthusiastic about stamping out trafficking than stopping poppy cultivation. They routinely arrested truck drivers moving drugs and rounded up tens of thousands of drug addicts every year, but high-level traffickers and lab owners operated with almost total impunity.

In October 1990, for example, troops with the paramilitary Frontier Corps (FC) near the Afghan border in Baluchistan stumbled upon what was then the biggest heroin seizure in world history: a shipment of nearly two tons of crystal heroin and nine tons of hashish. According to a State Department cable on the seizure, quoting a "highly accurate" local investigative news report, the incident was buried after calls to "high-placed federal officials" by a cartel of Pakistani heroin dealers referred to as the "Quetta Alliance." So powerful was the tribal alliance, according to the report, that three men accused in the seizure were granted bail by a local court before they were even arrested; the eight top counternarcotics officers in Quetta simultaneously applied for four months' leave of absence and the inspector-general of the FC immediately transferred.

The news report described a massive flow of opium and cannabis from guerrilla-controlled parts of Afghanistan to Baluchistan, where Pakistani smugglers processed it and moved it west. "The problem is now out of official control," said an unnamed FC officer quoted in the U.S. cable.[48] A DEA report said U.S. counternarcotics agents had identified forty major smuggling groups operating in Pakistan. Agents estimated as little as 5 percent of the heroin produced in or shipped through the country ever got caught.[49] When Wrobleski complained about that issue during a September 1987 meeting with

General Zia, the military ruler refused to budge, replying blandly that "current problems" limited action unless a "massive force" could be raised.[50]

In fact, there were indications that Pakistani drug syndicates had penetrated the highest levels of Zia's administration. In 1983, a young Pakistani smuggler arrested in Norway carrying 3.5 kilos of crystal heroin identified Hamid Hasnain, President Zia's personal banker, as a key player in a major heroin syndicate moving drugs into Europe. Zia's pilot, Major Farooq Hamid, was arrested on separate drug charges in 1988 following the president's death. And the man widely believed to provide protection for the heroin trade along the Afghan border was Lieutenant General Fazle Haq, the powerful chief minister of the North-West Frontier Province and one of Zia's closest advisers. Efforts by the Pakistani police to investigate Haq's activities were repeatedly blocked by top officials, according to news reports at the time. Haq, often referred to as "Pakistan's Noriega," once described heroin as a valuable "mineral."[51]

Inside Afghanistan, the heroin explosion was taking its toll on the Russian troops, according to a Rand study commissioned by the U.S. Army. The report detailed a staggeringly low level of morale among the occupying force and reported that "a majority, perhaps even a substantial majority, of the Soviet soldiers in the DRA [Democratic Republic of Afghanistan] used drugs on a fairly regular basis." Almost all the soldiers interviewed in the project freely admitted having used narcotics—mainly hashish—saying getting high helped them escape the horrifying drudgery of their existence on the Afghan front. "Most people smoked," read a typical response, "but in 1986 many started shooting with the needles that we have in our first-aid kit." Soldiers described going into battle while stoned, trying to manoeuvre military convoys down Afghanistan's treacherous highways under the influence, and looting Soviet military stores to trade weapons for heroin.[52] A *New York Times* reporter who separately interviewed Russian defectors to the resistance wrote that "Russian troops in Afghanistan have turned to drugs for the same reasons that many Americans did in Vietnam: They are young, away from home constraints, bored, frightened and under fierce pressure to prove themselves."[53]

Perhaps it was no accident that Soviet soldiers got hooked on heroin. The former French spy chief Count Alexandre de Marenches wrote in his memoirs that during a 1981 Oval Office meeting he proposed undermining Soviet morale by flooding them with hard drugs, Russian-language Bibles, and fake copies of Soviet newspapers full of demoralizing stories. Reagan and CIA director William Casey loved the plan, according to Marenches, who dubbed it Operation Mosquito, "because one tiny mosquito can drive a bear crazy." In his memoirs and in later interviews, the Frenchman claimed he subsequently pulled out of the plan because he wanted the Americans to promise it would never end up on the front page of *The New York Times.* Sorry, Casey reportedly told him, Washington leaks like a sieve.[54]

Brigadier Yousaf, the ISI agent, claimed years later Casey floated the idea of "flooding the Russian troops with heroin" to the ISI chief, General Akhtar Abdul Rehman Khan, during a brainstorming session that Yousaf also attended. The meeting took place at ISI headquarters when Casey made his second visit to Pakistan in late 1984, Yousaf said.[55] Casey died of brain cancer in 1987 and Akhtar perished alongside President Zia in a 1988 plane crash, but

Piekney, who was the CIA station chief at the time, rejects Yousaf's story as absurd. "I remember the visit," he said, "I certainly don't remember that idea coming up in conversation."[56]

Author Steve Coll, also quoting Yousaf, writes in *The Ghost Wars* that another proposal was also mulled at the same meeting: covertly backing uprisings by the Muslim population in Central Asia, then part of Soviet territory.[57] Both proposals would have been highly illegal under U.S. rules of engagement, and Yousaf is hardly the most accurate of historians. In his book *The Bear Trap*, for example, Yousaf rejects allegations of corruption among ISI officers who ran the notoriously leaky arms pipeline, insisting "nothing much went astray."[58] But, as Coll writes of the covert attacks inside the Soviet Union, Casey's floating such proposals to the ISI would have given the American spy chief "the perfect cutout" and total deniability.[59] Both phenomena—heroin use among the Soviet troops and Muslim uprisings inside the USSR—later became reality.

A former Soviet foreign service officer posted to Kabul in the 1980s said his government pieced together clear evidence that the United States and Pakistan intentionally tried to make addicts of their soldiers. "It was well known that they had a plan to spread drugs among Soviet troops and we indeed had a problem," said Zamir Kabulov, today Russia's ambassador to Afghanistan.[60] The issue raises the question of how much the CIA knew about the ISI's ties to the narcotics trade and when. This has remained one of the most closely guarded secrets of the Soviet-Afghanistan war. Most U.S. government documents from the era have been meticulously excised whenever the twin subjects of ISI and heroin come up.

Years later, former U.S. agents say they believed some of their Pakistani counterparts were deeply involved in the heroin trade, but concluded it was more a case of individual officers trying to enrich themselves rather than a government-wide policy. "You have to understand it's a totally corrupt outfit," said one former CIA agent.[61] While American spies did make efforts to figure out which mujahideen commanders were moving heroin, there was never any official investigation on how Pakistani officials tied in to the trade. "We heard things," said another American spy. "And it certainly looked like the ISI was involved in drug smuggling. But proving it was another matter."[62]

Since Langley never asked them to probe the issue further, no one took it up, agents said. "There were no requirements to collect on what the ISI was doing," said a former Islamabad station chief. "My sense is that no administration really wanted to know."[63] Other former officials at the U.S. embassy felt the agency blocked investigations into the issue, lest it discredit a crucial, though admittedly faulty, ally in the region. "One of my great frustrations at the time was that the CIA would not give us information on narcotics," said the former ambassador to Pakistan, Robert Oakley. "My belief was then and still is that they wanted to protect their contacts in Pakistani intelligence. We were convinced the ISI was involved but we could not get any hard evidence on it."[64]

From Laos to Nicaragua, the CIA's tendency to get into bed with rebel groups prone to illegal drug smuggling repeatedly landed the agency in hot water and spawned no end of fanciful conspiracy theories. Following news reports that the CIA-supported Contras were subsidizing their activities by smuggling crack cocaine into the United States, the agency launched an extensive investigation into the role its agents played in the matter. A subsequent analysis written by Frederick P. Hitz, the CIA inspector general who led the

Iran-Contra investigation, concluded that the problem—at least with regard to the Contras—came down to a lack of concrete guidance rather than the grand conspiracy so often imagined to exist. Until 1986, no relevant statutes within the agency governed the conduct of CIA agents who received information that people they worked with or funded were also smuggling drugs. Nor did individual agents act in a consistent manner when they received such allegations, Hitz wrote.[65] It's not clear if this glaring policy omission was left out by design or by mistake, but it did give CIA agents working with the Contras the ability to dismiss the drug issue if they did not want to deal with it, Hitz wrote. Similarly, at the Islamabad station, a "see no evil" approach defined the CIA's response to the swelling narcotics problem. It wasn't that the agents didn't know it was happening, but probing it too closely would have interfered with their central mission.

Overall, the policy of the U.S. embassy was to itemize and prioritize the various issues considered critical to American interests, rather than to try to create a holistic approach to the region's many overlapping problems. DEA agent Rich Fiano recalled his first meeting with then U.S. ambassador Deane Hinton when he arrived at the post in June 1986. The U.S. envoy asked him, "Mr. Fiano, what do you think our biggest priority is out here?"

Fiano answered, "Drugs, sir?"

No, the ambassador replied curtly. It was fighting the Soviets. "Do you know what our second biggest priority is?"

Fiano took another shot, "Drugs, sir?"

Again, wrong. "It's stopping nuclear proliferation," the ambassador said. "Can you tell me what our third priority is here?"

By this point, Fiano was stumped.

"Guess what," said Hinton. "It's drugs."[66]

To the frustration of Fiano and the rest of the DEA team, the fight against narcotics would remain off centre stage for another two years, during which time two subsequent ambassadors would be posted to the region and more than $1 billion in military aid would be allocated to the Afghan resistance. "Until we were sure the Soviets would go in 1988," explained Crandall, who was USAID chief at the time, "we basically put drugs on the back burner."[67] By then a powerful and well-connected drug mafia had taken root on both sides of the Pakistan-Afghanistan border.

Mujahideen leaders competing for a stake in the new Kabul government turned their guns on each other as Russian forces began their pullout that spring. The vicious civil war that erupted would continue into the 1990s, dividing the country and the capital itself into warring fiefdoms. Afghan commanders would come to depend ever more heavily on opium profits. The lack of U.S. oversight into drug smuggling by the mujahideen had set up the preconditions for the complete integration of narcotics—and reliance on drug money—into the politics of the region.

Just as the war was shifting course in Afghanistan, a plane crash would set Pakistan in a new direction, too. On August 17, 1988, a C-130 transport plane carrying President Zia, U.S. Ambassador Arnold Raphel, and ISI Chief General Akhtar went down shortly after takeoff, killing everyone on board. Mirza Aslam Beg, the army chief who succeeded Zia, announced general elections and ordered the army to retreat from politics, ending eleven years of military rule. Benazir Bhutto, the Harvard- and Oxford-educated daughter of the ex–prime minister Zia had ousted and later hanged, was swept into power. She was just thirty-six years old, completely inexperienced in government, and deeply distrustful of the ISI. She pledged immediately to make the fight against narcotics one of the priorities of her administration.[68]

Robert Oakley, the U.S. ambassador posted to Islamabad to replace Raphel, also embraced the counternarcotics cause, addressing how crucial the issue had become in a prophetic December 1988 cable:

> Widespread Pakistani belief that Afghan war has caused major upswing in narcotics traffic is well founded. Not only has war resulted in a flow of large amounts of weaponry to Pakistan, it has also led to increase in heroin traffic into and through Pakistan, through the hands of Afghan refugees as well as Pakistanis. We and the Pakistan government believe the situation will become much worse in terms of both heroin and arms entering Pakistan from Afghanistan as the war winds down unless urgent, effective measures are taken right away. The fight against "heroin-Kalashnikov culture" is almost as critical to the future of Pakistan's security as the fight against Soviet domination of Afghanistan has been.[69]

The cable warned that opium output in Afghanistan—estimated at 750 metric tons in 1987—could surge another several hundred tons when millions of refugees living along the borders of Pakistan and Iran returned home in need of a cash crop. Afghans in camps along the border were already refining opium into heroin, storing it in the refugee camps, and then shipping it onward, Oakley wrote. There were increasing reports of massive heroin shipments travelling west to Iran in heavily armed convoys, "and observers in the area say both the Afghan resistance parties and ISI are directly involved."

That same year, USAID launched its first counternarcotics pilot programme for Afghanistan. "In 1988, I made the call," said Crandall, then chief of the USAID mission in Pakistan. "Since it now looked like we were going to win this thing, we couldn't countenance a situation where we were supporting a group of people who were freedom fighters but also drug traders." The embassy hired a U.S. contractor to develop a programme it hoped would mirror earlier successful programmes in Thailand, where the poppy crop had been reduced to almost zero, Crandall said. They hoped to blend forced eradication with support for alternative crops.

A CIA assessment circulated in September 1988 took up the narcotics problem on the Pakistani side of the border. Islamabad was "losing ground to an expanding drug industry," the report said, blaming "major increases in production in landlocked Afghanistan." Massive hundred-kilo heroin cargos were "moving routinely through Pakistan" and being smuggled west by boat from Karachi. The partially redacted document described a system that functions in much the same way today, according to police and counternarcotics officials: trucks coming from the NWFP deposit drug shipments at drop-off points along the main highways into the southern port city. Private vehicles then ferry smaller packages into the port.

"The size of such smuggling operations is, in fact, reflected in . . . a police investigation of a Pashtun-dominated section of the city—Sohrab Goth—that uncovered 11 underground storage facilities, each capable of holding up to one ton of heroin," it said.[70] At any given time three tons of heroin were "awaiting shipment to the United States or western Europe," the report said, adding that Pakistan's own addict population had tripled since the Afghan war began. Citing widespread corruption and a reluctance on the part of Pakistani authorities to tackle the problem, the CIA predicted "the narcotics situation in Pakistan will probably get worse before it gets better."[71]

Just as the drug issue leapt into the limelight, so did concern over the future aspirations of Afghanistan's holy warriors, many of them hostile toward the United States and now heavily armed and battle-hardened. The 1980s had witnessed a disturbing rise in terrorist attacks by Islamic radicals, from the 1983 bombing of the U.S. embassy in Lebanon to the 1985 hijacking of the *Achille Lauro.* In Washington and within the U.S. embassy in Islamabad, American officials were deeply divided over the best course of action for Afghanistan's post-Soviet future.

In October 1988, Special Envoy Edmund McWilliams clashed with Milton Bearden, the CIA chief of station, by suggesting in a classified cable that the United States needed to distance itself from the ISI and its ruthless protégé, Gulbuddin Hekmatyar. McWilliams's interviews with mujahideen leaders and Afghan intellectuals left him deeply alarmed about Afghanistan's future. As soon as the Soviet pullout had begun, Hekmatyar had launched a systematic campaign to wipe out his rivals in the resistance, butchering dozens of liberals, academics, and royalist politicians who might have stood against him in the political arena. Liberal Afghans worried what the fundamentalists would do if they ever got control of the country. "For God's sake," one warned McWilliams, "you're financing your own assassins."[72]

Bearden worked to maintain a balance of funding to the commanders by making unilateral payments outside the ISI's control to rival commanders like Ahmed Shah Massood and Abdul Haq.[73] But this effort was offset by the steady flow of Arab donations to the fundamentalist mujahideen and a shift in ISI policy from supporting the Peshawar Seven parties to supporting individual commanders, mainly Hekmatyar. It was a course of action that contradicted the international community's goal of strengthening a central council of leaders who would eventually share power. It also put the various resistance leaders under new pressure to raise funds any way they could.

With the Soviet army gone, agriculture and trade began to recover in the Afghan countryside. "Much of this renewed production took the form of opium growing, heroin refining, and smuggling; these enterprises were organized by combines of mujahideen parties, Pakistani military officers, and Pakistani drug syndicates," wrote historian Barnett Rubin.[74] Hekmatyar built up his forces into a conventional army and increased his involvement in the poppy trade, probably realizing that U.S. and Saudi funding was about to end. Other commanders shifted policy to shore up their military and financial positions, behaving more like feudal lords than allied members of a rebel army. Another new factor was the Arab radical Islamist fighters who arrived in eastern Afghanistan, bringing their own regional and global ambitions to the conflict.[75]

In the west, massive, heavily armed drug convoys were streaming out of Helmand, snaking their way across Pakistan's Baluchistan Province into Iran and on to Turkey. In March 1989, a confidential cable based on McWilliams's interviews with Afghan refugees reported: "The trafficking route entails cooperation of the mujahideen, Kabul regime, and GOP [government of Pakistan] officials and some elements inside the Iran government." It identified officials from the Pasdaran, Iran's Revolutionary Guard, as the main players in the illegal drug trade. "The convoys consist of approximately 30 specially equipped *Pajeros.* Each convoy is armed . . . and carries up to 10 armed Afghans." Stinger missiles, which had been provided to the mujahideen by the CIA to down Soviet helicopters, were now being used to protect heroin shipments, it said. "Convoy operators have been known to warn police checkpoints ahead of time," the cable said. "The police, who are thoroughly outgunned, arrange to be elsewhere."[76]

The partially excised document went on to describe the battle for control of Helmand's poppy fields between Nasim Akhundzada and Hekmatyar, accurately predicting that their internecine conflict was about to explode. In the course of the coming year, this war within the war would receive scant attention. The Soviet troops were completing their withdrawal from Afghanistan, and the ISI was busy cajoling the main rebel commanders into a shaky coalition that would set its sights on the vulnerable pro-Soviet regime still in power in Kabul. Without the Soviet troops there, the CIA predicted its imminent collapse. The moderate Sibghatullah Mojaddedi, one of the Peshawar Seven leaders routinely marginalized by the ISI, was selected to lead a new interim Afghan government in exile. Washington warned Mojaddedi to curb soaring opium production in mujahideen-held areas or face a cut in U.S. support. In meetings with Ambassador Oakley and President George H. W. Bush, Mojaddedi pledged to issue a religious fatwa banning opium. But he was powerless to move further on the issue and in any case would remain the titular head of government for just months.[77]

Beset by rivalries and infighting from the start, the rebel coalition mounted a spring 1989 attack on the western town of Jalalabad, hoping to instal Mojaddedi's government there and proceed swiftly to Kabul. It would not go as CIA and ISI planners predicted. Bloody fighting dragged on for months, with casualties numbering in the thousands. Meanwhile, a separate turf war raged between Hekmatyar and Ahmed Shah Massood, a powerful commander from the Panjshir Valley who relied on smuggling gemstones to fund his operations. Historian Alfred McCoy later blamed the battlefield chaos on a diffident attitude among mujahideen commanders too busy fighting over spoils of Nangarhar's brisk opium trade to bother with the march on Kabul.[78] In the 1989–1990 planting season, Nangarhar Province produced a whopping 355 tons of opium.[79]

The situation out west was similar. By mid-1989, the U.S. embassy was reporting "chronic fighting" in northern Helmand over control of the production areas and trafficking. Several thousand families had been displaced, U.S. diplomats cabled in June, and the brutal Akhundzada had ordered those who remained to grow poppy. With more than four thousand troops under his command, villagers had little choice but to obey. Akhundzada sent massive drug convoys out to Pakistan every four to six weeks, the cable reported.[80]

A senior official at the U.S. embassy decided it was time to try to do something about the problem. He flew to Quetta, the capital of Baluchistan, and put out word he wanted to see Mullah Akhundzada. "I told him he was a disgrace to his people, calling himself a mullah and dealing drugs," said the former official, who did not want to be identified. "The good mullah said he needed narcotics to support his fighters, so I offered to help set up new ways to pay the fighters and build health clinics."[81] Akhundzada wanted a personal guarantee from Ambassador Oakley. So they set up a meeting, and, to everyone's surprise, Afghanistan's biggest drug dealer turned up at the U.S. mission in Islamabad a week later. He proposed to cut opium production by half in Helmand if the United States would invest $2 million in alternative development programmes and help restart the Kajaki Dam, which provided hydroelectric power to the entire southwest region.

"I talked to him and he said, 'Look, we'd like to get the dam working again,'" Oakley recalled. "It was all rural development stuff—nothing outlandish."[82] Washington wanted a guarantee Akhundzada was going to deliver on his side of the deal before it handed out the cash. "The next year we had covert aerial reconnaissance, and we also sent ground teams with Nasim [Akhundzada]," Oakley said. "Both came back and reported the poppy was gone." But by then USAID in Washington had gotten cold feet, said former officials closely tied to the project. "Washington came back and said, 'You can't do deals with a known drug dealer,'" Oakley said.

Six months later, in March 1990, gunmen opened up their automatic rifles on Mullah Akhundzada as he and five subordinates walked out of a meeting in Peshawar. "They emptied a banana clip on him, literally cut him in half," said a former U.S. official. The bold assassination was widely blamed on Hekmatyar. With the cut in production in Helmand, raw opium prices had more than tripled, making it far more costly to supply Hekmatyar's refineries in Koh-i-Soltan. "Whoever did the killing, Nasim's death pretty much threw a wet blanket on anyone's willingness to cooperate on anti-narcotics for a while," said the U.S. official. "It showed everyone what a down and dirty business it had become." Akhundzada's brother, Ghulam Rasul, swiftly took over in Helmand. He ordered farmers in Helmand to return to "full production."[83]

The war in Afghanistan entered a new phase, as bloody and complex as ever. With the dawn of a new decade, Washington faced a new era of global geopolitics. Iraqi leader Saddam Hussein invaded Kuwait in August 1990, and the Soviet Union collapsed a year later. These two seminal events shifted the United States' focus away from Afghanistan, a cause that had fallen from grace anyway. Allegations of drug running and concerns about Islamic extremism suddenly made the mujahideen seem distasteful, if not downright worrisome. Indications that money had been funnelled to the rebels using the disgraced Bank of Commerce and Credit International (BCCI), and that up to 70 percent of the money never even reached them, added the stench of scandal.[84] When William Gray, then chairman of the House Budget Committee, asked the General Accounting Office to look for the missing cash, they were rebuffed by the CIA, saying there would be "phenomenal security implications" if the GAO probed too closely.[85]

Just at a time when reconstruction funding might have provided poor Afghan farmers with an alternative to poppy farming, U.S. funding for the mujahideen, and Afghanistan in general, dropped off sharply. "The minute an issue becomes unpopular in Washington, interest in it dries up totally," said a U.S. official who worked on Afghanistan in the early 1990s. "That's what happened here. Everyone turned on it." Amid predictions that the pro-Communist government of Najibullah was about to disintegrate, the U.S. Congress allocated just $280 million in fiscal year 1990 for the final push on Kabul. It was a 60 percent cut over the previous year's grant.[86] Arab nations continued to kick in money—mainly to Hekmatyar and other fundamentalist commanders—until the Kuwait invasion distracted them, too.

In June 1991, the administration of George H. W. Bush approved an "off-budget" transfer of just $30 million in captured Iraqi weapons to the mujahideen. Although private Arab donations—mainly profiting fundamentalist parties—would continue to the tune of hundreds of millions of dollars, the secret U.S. programme to aid the mujahideen was terminated in 1992.[87] "Overnight, that left 135,000 armed Afghans and their families with no way to support themselves," said a former CIA officer. "And what do you expect happened? The commanders turned to gun running to make money, and in no short time, most of them turned to drugs too." The agent realized then that what little influence the United States ever had on the rebel commanders had just evaporated. "I thought, hell, I am going to lose all my Afghan sources," he said.[88]

In April 1992, Najibullah's regime collapsed. Hekmatyar and his Panjshiri rival, Ahmed Shah Massood, entered Kabul and began to fight each other for control. Just a month earlier, Najibullah had begged the West to help cobble together a moderate new government. "If fundamentalism comes to Afghanistan, war will continue for many years," he told the *International Herald Tribune.* Otherwise, he warned, "Afghanistan will turn into a centre of world smuggling of narcotic drugs. Afghanistan will be turned into a centre for terrorism."[89]

But no one was listening. Shortly after shutting off military aid to the mujahideen, the Bush administration slashed relief and reconstruction aid to Afghanistan by more than 60 percent. The UN had just calculated that $1 billion would be needed to rebuild the devastated Afghan countryside.[90] The outgoing U.S. special envoy, Peter Tomsen, sent a confidential 1992 cable suggesting that the "drastic reduction" to the USAID budget would strip Washington of the "only political leverage we have with Afghanistan" and give the Afghans the impression the United States was abandoning them. It was in the interest of the United States, he warned, to stop Islamic radicals from using Afghanistan as "a training/staging base for terrorism."[91] It was the last serious effort a senior U.S. official would make to keep Washington sincerely engaged in Afghanistan.

When the new administration of President Bill Clinton took office in 1993, it zeroed the USAID budget for Afghanistan, according to former officials. As far as Washington was concerned, the country fell off the map entirely until 1998, when al Qaeda bombed the U.S. embassies in Kenya and Tanzania. "The Soviets left and America just lost interest," said Beverly Eighmy, who ran a counternarcotics pilot programme for USAID that got shut down with the budget cuts. "Personally, it broke our hearts," she said. "We left them all high and dry." Added Bearden, the former station chief, "We just walked away, walked away from it all."

In the coming years, mujahideen forces would reduce Kabul to a pitiable state of rubble and ravage the countryside as they fought for dominance. Smuggling routes, before mainly limited to Pakistan, Iran, and Afghanistan, now snaked up into Central Asia, where the Soviet Union's collapse left a law enforcement vacuum and a population desperate for hard currency.[92] Commodities ranging from Iranian oil to Firestone tires and Sony televisions wound their way over the Afghan border, taking advantage of Pakistan's transit trade agreement and loose regional tax enforcement. By 1997, the World Bank estimated the illegal trade in legal goods to be worth $2.5 billion.[93] Afghanistan was by now the world's leading opium producer, having outpaced Burma. As author Michael Griffin wrote in *Reaping the Whirlwind*:

> The concentricity of the drugs, arms and smuggling rings around a single imploded state created the conditions for the birth of a unique, post-modern phenomenon: an illegal trading empire that defied customs, frontiers and laws . . . controlled by scarcely literate warlords living hundreds of miles from the nearest bank or fax.[94]

Next door, the heroin trade was now worth an estimated $8 to $10 billion, more than the government's annual budget and as much as one-quarter of Pakistan's entire GDP.[95] It had created a class of billionaire tycoons with tremendous influence over the new civilian government.[96] The leading smuggler was Haji Ayub Afridi, a tribal chief who ran a massive heroin empire from a luxury fortress in the Khyber Pass. Afridi worked closely with Zia's government to help smuggle weapons to the mujahideen and was believed to coordinate shipments of heroin smuggled out in NLC trucks.[97] Following Zia's death, he allied himself with the Punjabi politician Nawaz Sharif, actually winning himself a seat in the National Assembly in the 1990 general elections.[98] The second most powerful Pakistani trafficker, also tied to moving Afghan heroin, was Mirza Iqbal Baig, a Punjabi cinema owner with close ties to Benazir Bhutto's People's Party and a tendency to ruthlessness.

When two BBC reporters showed up at his office to interview him for a 1986 documentary, they were soundly beaten by a gang of thugs.[99]

Despite the huge amount of narcotics crossing their country, Pakistani officials for years blithely rejected American warnings that heroin addiction would one day become a domestic crisis. "Their attitude was always, 'We are sorry you Americans have this problem, but it's your problem,'" said Teresita Schaffer, the former deputy secretary of state for South Asia. By the early 1990s, Pakistan had more than 1.2 million heroin addicts. Suddenly, Schaffer said, there was "this dawning awareness" that they, too, had a major social problem on their hands.

Declassified U.S. documents reveal a high level of frustration among American diplomats over Islamabad's refusal to go after big-league drug lords like Afridi and Baig. An undated DEA analysis had especially sharp words for Islamabad's "weak policy" toward heroin lab owners in the federally administered tribal areas (FATA):

> The GOP has now and then arranged for the surrender of some equipment (pots and pans) used at heroin manufacturing sites in the FATA and extracting formal promises from the operators that they will nevermore engage in heroin manufacturing. These surrenders and promises have been used by the GOP to fool itself and the international community into believing that at least something is being done against heroin manufacturing in Pakistan. Nothing could be farther from the truth. Never have these surrenders included seizures of heroin, morphine, opium

> or precursor chemicals in any significant quantity, and never have any important lab owners, profiteers or financiers been arrested, prosecuted and imprisoned in connection with these lab surrenders.[100]

But as it had done with the mujahideen, Washington began taking a tough line with Islamabad over drugs only once it became clear that the Soviets were withdrawing from neighbouring Afghanistan. Legislation passed by the U.S. Congress meant Washington "certified" countries where narcotics were produced to signal they were making efforts to fight drugs. A confidential list of "talking points" distributed in September 1988 instructed American diplomats to warn their Pakistani contacts to "cooperate fully" with the United States on counternarcotics "in order to avoid the threat of decertification and the loss of most [U.S.] assistance to Pakistan." A handwritten note on the incoming telegram calculated that Pakistan stood to lose $228 million in military aid, economic assistance, and loan forgiveness for fiscal year 1989 alone.[101]

The pressure appears to have worked. By the following year, the Bhutto administration launched an aerial spraying campaign in the tribal belt, created an elite counternarcotics police force, and raided a notorious Afghan refugee camp, capturing one hundred kilos of opium and a large cache of gold and weapons.[102] In March 1989, Ambassador Oakley cabled that Pakistan "appears finally to be getting its act together on narcotics." He asked for a $5 million increase in the counternarcotics aid budget for Islamabad, writing: "We have poured a great deal of money into Pakistan over the years to fight narcotics and we are just beginning to see some important results."[103]

But by the end of 1990, Pakistan would get left out in the cold, too. Just as the CIA was disentangling itself from its decade-long partnership with the ISI over Afghanistan, American agents monitoring Pakistan's nuclear ambitions discovered Islamabad had recently approached Tehran about technological cooperation.[104] By October 1990, the Pressler amendment kicked in, cutting off most U.S. assistance to Pakistan. Relations between Islamabad and Washington plunged. CIA agents in Islamabad suddenly found themselves in the position of trying to get weapons back from the ISI and the mujahideen. "We actually had to destroy seven hundred tons of ammunition at one point," said a former intelligence official. Fearful that fundamentalist commanders might use the shoulder-fired, heat-seeking Stinger missiles for terrorist attacks, Washington launched a programme to buy back the weapons. It provided U.S. agents the only cash leverage they had left to get information out of Afghanistan. The Stingers were now being put to use guarding two-hundred-vehicle convoys ferrying heroin west across the Iranian border. When U.S. agents found a way to put an informant on a convoy, the Department of Justice quashed the plan, ruling that it would mean the CIA was participating in the drug trade.[105] In just two years, the region had gone from being a central focus of U.S. foreign policy to falling off the radar screen almost entirely.

On its own, the region seemed dangerously adrift. A study commissioned by the CIA and leaked to the media in 1993 stopped just short of calling Pakistan a narco-state.[106] Since the cutoff of U.S. aid to Islamabad, the CIA report said heroin had become "the lifeblood" of the country's economic and social systems. Known drug lords held seats in the national and provincial assemblies, and had access to Prime Minister Nawaz Sharif's "inner circle." Drug mafias regularly paid off Pakistan's corps commanders and senior military officials, it said, citing an "underworld source." Many experts, the report declared, said Pakistan's military—and specifically the ISI—was "significantly involved in narcotics, and perhaps even using heroin money to finance covert operations and weapons purchases." The report also noted:

> Many believe the ISI allowed the Afghan resistance groups to trade in narcotics after the cut-off of U.S. assistance and that individual ISI officers participated in the trade, either as part of sanctioned operations or to enrich themselves. The ISI is also deeply involved with Sikh militants, who use Pakistan for sanctuary and who do use heroin for arms purchases. At the very least, the ISI tolerates Sikh involvement in heroin. The Kashmiri insurgency may also be partly funded by heroin. The strongest pro-Pakistan group, the Hezb-ul Mujahidin, is backed by the ISI . . . and the Hezb-i-Islami of Gulbuddin Hekmatyar.

The Pakistan government stoutly rejected the CIA report—a spokesman at their embassy in Washington called it "stupid . . . totally baseless."[107] But a year later, Nawaz Sharif himself, who by then had been kicked out of office after having been accused of corruption, would suggest it had been accurate. In September 1994, he told *The Washington Post* that in 1990, three months after his election as prime minister, General Aslam Beg, then army chief, and General Asad Durrani, then ISI chief, told him the Pakistan military needed money for covert foreign operations and wanted to raise it through large-scale drug deals. "I was totally flabbergasted," he claimed.[108] By the time the *Washington Post* story ran, Sharif had developed a reputation as a troublemaker, and the information was widely discredited (not least due to the former premier's alleged connections to heroin syndicates). Later, when he returned to power in 1997, Sharif denied the meeting ever took place. However shaky the information, it was another disquieting indication that a murky web of Pakistani intelligence agents, Islamic extremists, and international drug traffickers were cooperating, at least on some level.

Next door in Afghanistan, the situation was yet more disturbing. By the early 1990s, Jalalabad Airport, in eastern Nangarhar Province, had become a central clearing station for massive shipments of drugs, gemstones, electronic goods, and other contraband being smuggled to and from the Persian Gulf, according to former workers there. Mujahideen working for Yunis Khalis and Haji Qadir would arrive on the tarmac with truckloads of carpets laden with heroin powder. "We could always tell which carpets had heroin, since they were so much heavier than normal," said a cargo loader, still terrified to be identified two decades later. "They would shake out the carpets once they reached their destination, and the heroin would fall out."

Another trick, said a senior airport official, was to smuggle powder out in timber shipments—the logs would appear solid but have holes drilled inside, stuffed with heroin. Airport staff earned up to $2,000 a week—far more than they would normally take home—to pack and load drug shipments, both men said. Arab fighters often appeared alongside Khalis or his top deputies, boarding flights without clearing immigration and returning days later to hand out dates, a delicacy in the Gulf. Airport workers didn't see the "Arab

Afghans," as they came to be known, actively engaged in the heroin trade, but described them as "fellow travellers" on frequent heroin flights to the Gulf.[109] Along the border, smuggling mushroomed even more. "By this point, the entire jihad was funded by drugs," said a senior Pakistani police official then based in the border area.[110]

As Pakistan and Afghanistan sank further into chaos, a handful of former American officials continued to defend U.S. involvement there, saying the principal objective of bringing down the Soviet Empire outweighed continued instability in the remote mountains of Southwest Asia. "What was more important in the worldview of history?" asked Jimmy Carter's national security advisor, Zbigniew Brzezinski, in a 1998 interview. "A few stirred up Muslims or the liberation of Central Europe and the end of the cold war?"[111]

Far away in Kandahar, a few stirred-up Muslims who called themselves the Taliban were about to set their war-shattered nation on a collision course with the West. In the bloody new chapter of the Afghan saga, heroin would play a central role.

3. NARCO-TERROR STATE

THE TALIBAN DROPPED A BRUISED, SHIVERING WRETCH AT our feet, his legs in shackles. "This is what we do to addicts," declared Abdul Rashid, head of their anti-drug force in Kandahar.

It was spring of 1997. I had travelled to the southern Afghan city—then the Taliban's de facto capital—with the Pakistani journalist Ahmed Rashid. I was writing a story about the opium trade for the Associated Press. Ahmed was researching his book *The Taliban,* which would become an overnight bestseller after the 9/11 attacks.

We met the counternarcotics chief in his shoebox-sized office. I made a joke about how the two men might be related, since they shared the same last name. Neither man found it funny. Ahmed was meticulously turned out in an Italian sports coat. His namesake picked bits of food from his greasy beard while he explained the Taliban's unique approach to curing drug addiction. First, he said, addicts got beaten until they confessed the name of their supplier. After that, they were thrown in jail. "Then we dunk them in ice-cold water for two or three hours a day," Rashid explained, adding brightly, "It's a very good cure." To prove his point, he ordered his minions to drag out Bakht Mohammed, a local shopkeeper recently caught smoking a joint.

"When they put me in that cold water, I forget all about

hashish," said Mohammed, slumped on the floor before us.[1] Normally I discount interviews with prisoners when their jailers are present, especially when it's clear they have been tortured. However, I was pretty sure this guy was telling the truth. As they dragged him off, Ahmed and I exchanged looks of horror.

A day earlier, we had driven to Arghandab, a fertile suburb of Kandahar where poppy fields stretched as far as the eye could see. "We could not be more grateful to the Taliban," a toothless farmer named Wali Jan told us, crediting the bearded crusaders with bringing security that allowed him to tend his crops in peace. Even though the Taliban cracked down on hash smoking, they gave full support to the poppy trade, farmers and Taliban officials told us. The next day, when Ahmed and I asked Rashid, the anti-drug cop, about this apparent contradiction in drug policy, he just smiled. "Opium is allowed because it is consumed by infidels in the West and not by Muslim Afghans," he said.

Largely because of its one-year ban on poppy cultivation, there is a widespread misperception in the West that the Taliban regime opposed drugs. Nothing could be further from the truth. The Taliban meted out harsh penalties to anyone caught using intoxicants: they crushed bottles of whiskey under tanks and beat up pot smokers. However, Mullah Omar's movement—almost from its inception—was highly dependent on and intertwined with the opium network spanning the Pakistan-Afghanistan border. Drug traffickers and tribes growing poppy were critical to the Taliban's swift and astonishing rise to power. Later on, the opium trade provided vital tax revenue, which kept the pariah state afloat despite global economic sanctions. It also funded the military campaign against the Northern Alliance and supported the global ambitions of Osama bin Laden, who plotted the 9/11 attacks at terrorist training camps he ran in southern and eastern Afghanistan. Fuelled by drug money and joined at the hip with al Qaeda, the Taliban turned Afghanistan into the world's first fully fledged narco-terror state.

Three years of vicious fighting between various mujahideen warlords had put a chokehold on Afghanistan's multibillion-dollar transit trade. Rival commanders erected roadblocks—often just a few hundred yards from each other—where they extorted fees for safe passage along the highways. Roadblocks were especially numerous in southern Kandahar Province, where there was no clear strongman. The Pashtun trucking mafia controlling most shipping from Karachi, Pakistan, which passes through Quetta and into Kandahar Province at the Chaman border, was taking huge losses. Trucking firms wanted to end the intolerable situation.

When the Taliban first appeared on the scene, most assumed—not entirely incorrectly—that the new fighting force was a creation of Pakistan's security agencies. ISI officials had watched with dismay as their fundamentalist offspring Gulbuddin Hekmatyar got repeatedly trounced on the battlefield by his rival Ahmed Shah Massood. Benazir Bhutto, the newly reelected Pakistani prime minister, wanted to open up trade routes into the now independent Central Asian states. Islamabad was in the market for a new protégé across the border.

The origins of the Taliban are steeped in legend, aimed at elevating the group's barely literate, one-eyed leader to a semidivine status among Afghanistan's uneducated masses. The story begins in mid-1994 when rival warlords were ravaging the Afghan countryside and terrorizing the public. Neighbours came to Mullah Omar, then a teacher in a small religious school, or madrassa, outside Kandahar, to tell him that two young girls in their village of Maiwand had been abducted by a local warlord and repeatedly raped. Horrified, Omar raised a force of thirty madrassa students (or Talibs), armed with half as many rifles, and attacked the commander's base. They freed the girls and hanged the commander from his tank barrel.

A few months later, Omar's force intervened again when two rival commanders fought over a young boy both men wanted to take as a lover.[2] "Commanders were looting people, raping women and boys for days, and then killing them," said Mullah Roketi, a former mujahideen fighter who later joined the Taliban and now sits in the Afghan parliament. "Mullah Omar raised his voice against these people and said, 'I am going to fight them.'"[3] As Omar's reputation as a local Robin Hood grew, Afghanistan's war-weary public embraced the Taliban, which swept across the country, capturing many towns without a shot being fired.

Although Omar was inarticulate, reclusive, and barely able to write his own name, his supporters believed he was possessed with a profound, God-given wisdom. They spread the perception that his campaign to stabilize the nation was backed by divine forces. Later, in 1996, to legitimize the notion that he had been chosen by Allah to lead Afghans, Omar gathered supporters in front of the Shrine of the Cloak of the Prophet, one of Afghanistan's holiest sites. He took out the ancient relic and wrapped himself in it, whereupon the tumultuous crowd ordained him Amir-ul-Momineen, the Leader of the Faithful. It was a ranking in Islam nearly second to the prophet Mohammed himself.[4]

Like all good myths, aspects of the tale were true. Many who encountered the Taliban at their outset say the group was well-intentioned, even if their behaviour was medieval. In their initial meetings with foreigners, the Taliban appeared to be village simpletons—unkempt, naïve, and utterly devout. On my first visit to Kandahar, senior Taliban officials I met had piled furniture in the corners of their offices and received guests sitting cross-legged on the carpet, their seating area inevitably adorned with a vase of dusty plastic flowers. "My God, these people don't even know how to sit on chairs," I thought. The Taliban publicly stoned women accused of committing adultery and whipped men caught trimming their beards. They were ignorant of the outside world and had little understanding of international diplomacy, modern technology, or how to run a government.

According to people who witnessed the early movement, the Taliban initially made commitments to stamp out the poppy trade—but only acted on them a handful of times. These commitments were swiftly dropped as political realities and need for funds overcame their original objectives.[5] Despite their good intentions and efforts at myth making, the Taliban's rise to power in Afghanistan had little to do with the grace of Allah, as they claimed. In fact, from its inception, the movement relied on the financial backing of a distinctly unholy alliance with drug smugglers and trucking companies. During their first year in power in Kandahar, the Taliban issued a book outlining what was permissible under their strict brand of sharia law. Most forms of simple entertainment, like music and television, were banned; alcohol and cannabis were "absolutely forbidden." But on one issue Kandahar's new leaders were conspicuously ambiguous: "The consumption of opiates is forbidden, as is the manufacture of heroin," the book said. "But the production and trading in opium is not forbidden."[6]

By the end of 1994, diplomats at the U.S. embassy in Pakistan were scrambling to determine who exactly was backing the Taliban, according to declassified documents. The Islamabad mission sent a rash of cables debating whether the ISI had created this new fighting force, or as one report suggested, if an alliance of northern Afghan warlords was trying to mount a unified Pashtun opposition against the ISI-backed Hekmatyar. The Saudis had taken an interest in the student movement, American diplomats noted, as had Maulana Fazal-ur Rehman, who ran the Jamiat Ulema-i-Islam (JUI), a leading Pakistani fundamentalist party providing fighters from its chain of madrassas.[7] Probably, the U.S. diplomats concluded, the Taliban enjoyed a combination of backers. All of these groups were in cahoots after all.

Initial cables note that the Taliban's "declared goals were to open up the roads and end the organized banditry of local commanders" and that "all visitors to Kandahar have told us they believe the Taliban must have access to considerable funding."[8] Sources told U.S. diplomats that the Taliban appeared to have built a fighting force of four thousand and was able to pay its troops three times what other Afghan commanders could. After taking control of Kandahar—just months after their initial emergence—the Taliban claimed to have eleven tanks, nine transport helicopters, several MiG fighter jets, and stacks of heavy weaponry and ammunition. They were setting up a police training school and seemed to be educating bureaucrats. When one U.S. contact asked the Taliban about their source of cash, "he was told that funds come from a combination of customs duties and taxes levied on local merchants," the embassy reported in January 2005. "Yet local *bazaaris* deny that the Taliban are taxing them at all."[9]

Two U.S. officials flew to Kandahar in February 1995 to try to pinpoint the Taliban's backers, meeting with the mayor of the provincial capital, Maulavi Abul Abbas, and six other midlevel Taliban. The meeting left the Americans with "more questions than answers," as they cabled back to Washington. The Afghans refused to name members of the Taliban's senior *shura*, or ruling council, or to be lured into discussion over who was supporting them financially. "This cannot be told," Abbas stated flatly. When asked about poppy cultivation, he promptly replied, "Narcotics is prohibited in Islam. This is very clear." The diplomats noted how this statement generated "considerable heated interjection" from other Taliban officials present. Abbas then rephrased his statement, calling poppy an "economic issue" for poor farmers with no alternatives. The Americans concluded that the Taliban had been "coached" but offered no suggestions in their cable to Washington as to who sponsored the group.[10]

Just four days later, the U.S. embassy in Islamabad would get the answer, although it's unclear from declassified cables if anyone in the mission appreciated its significance at the time. On February 17, a Kandahari close to Mullah Omar—probably the Taliban's future foreign minister, Mullah Ghaus—turned up at the embassy in Islamabad to explain the movement's origins.[11] He explained to a U.S. political officer how the Taliban emerged from a small madrassa in Maiwand owned by the "prominent trader" Haji Bashir Noorzai, a former commander who had fought under Yunis Khalis. Noorzai, the visitor revealed, was Mullah Omar's original sponsor as well as a key decision maker and leading member of the ruling council.

Today, Bashir Noorzai resides in a high-security Manhattan jail where he faces ten years to life in prison on charges he conspired to import and distribute more than $50 million worth of heroin into the United States. Although there remains some dispute about whether Noorzai himself was a major drug trader at the outset of the Taliban movement, his clan was certainly well known to American counternarcotics agents. Their 1-million-strong tribe controlled tens of thousands of acres of poppy farmland, as well as the key roadway out of southern Afghanistan. Bashir's late father, Haji Mohammed Issa Noorzai, was a notorious dope smuggler who owned a string of heroin labs.[12] In the mid-1990s, Issa Noorzai was a leading member of the Quetta Alliance, a drug cartel identified in one declassified DEA document as a union of "three interrelated heroin and hashish smuggling groups" that routinely exported "multi-ton shipments of heroin and morphine base."[13] Ironically, the heavily redacted document indicates that the DEA office in Islamabad proposed to designate the Quetta cartel as a "targeted kingpin organization" in 1993, just one year before the Taliban emerged.[14] The designation would have focused U.S. law enforcement on the cartel and given DEA agents in Pakistan access to funds to track the group and build a federal case against it. The TKO designation never came, however.[15] In the years to come, Haji Bashir would actually meet DEA officials in an Islamabad safe house, boldly giving the American agents tips on the smuggling activities of Turkish smugglers who moved heroin through Iran and on to the West.[16]

The Kandahari man who visited the U.S. embassy that day in 1995 was there to cultivate the myth of the Taliban, concealing their real agenda under the cloak of Islam. He told the embassy's political officer: "Mullah Omar went to Haji Bashir and related a vision in which the Prophet Mohammed had appeared to him and told him of the need to bring peace to Afghanistan." Bashir believed Omar, the visitor claimed, and decided to back him. Using family and business connections, Bashir raised 8 million Pakistani rupees (about $250,000) for the effort and donated half a dozen pickup trucks and weapons he had left over from the jihad days. Bashir Noorzai sat alongside Mullah Omar on the eight-member senior *shura*, which made all policy decisions for the Taliban, he said.[17] Incidentally, another *shura* member the visitor listed was Haji Baz Mohammed, who today is also incarcerated in the United States, having pled guilty in 2006 to charges he smuggled heroin for the Taliban.[18]

According to relatives and business associates, Bashir Noorzai in 1993 was only a minor-league trader who could not have birthed the Taliban on his own. "He didn't have that kind of cash," another Noorzai clan member told me. "The original money came from his father." Sources close to Haji Bashir say the initial goal of his movement was to drive badly behaved warlords out of Kandahar, which was his control zone. "By the end, most *muj* had become very crude people," said an Afghan official who closely observed the Taliban's rise.[19] After Mullah Omar's stunning successes in his home district, the Noorzais convinced other partners in the Quetta Alliance, along with other businessmen in the Pashtun trucking mafia, to pitch in more funds.

As the Taliban conquered district after district in Kandahar, they attracted the attention of other warlords with ties to the opium trade. Abdur Ghaffar Akhundzada, the younger brother of Mullah Nasim, who controlled poppy cultivation in neighbouring Helmand, was another early backer, reportedly declaring, "I am a Talib."[20] He later fell out with Mullah Omar when the Taliban chief signed on with a rival, and they battled for two months. In general, however, the Taliban army swept rapidly across Afghanistan. By September

1996, just two years after they emerged, they would roll victorious into Kabul.

As their reputation spread, so did their ability to capture towns without a shot. In areas "where the new movement's moral and religious standing failed to carry the day, generous disbursements of cash usually succeeded," wrote author Anthony Davis.[21] The Taliban's financial backers dished out bribes to regional strongmen as the turbaned fighters advanced on Kabul. Several key tribes agreed to join the cause after Mullah Omar pledged not to crack down on poppy, according to a November 1996 DEA document and western intelligence agents who tracked the movement.[22] Supporting the poppy trade not only garnered the Taliban financial backing. It also won them political support from tribes and the general public, especially in areas where years of warfare had left few viable alternatives for earning a living other than growing and trading narcotics. As a former U.S. counternarcotics official put it: "The Taliban rose to power by co-opting the drug trade."[23]

The Quetta-Kandahar trucking mafia—heavily tied up in both drug smuggling and the U-turn scheme—also poured money into Taliban coffers. Initially Mullah Omar received a monthly retainer from these groups, who came from the same tribes as leading Taliban. As his movement expanded westward, toward Iran, Omar demanded larger and larger payments. In March 1995, witnesses said the Taliban collected $150,000 on a single day at the Chaman border crossing, and $300,000 the following day in Quetta to prepare for an assault on the western Afghan city of Herat, which would open a trading gateway into Iran. For Pashtun smugglers involved in the U-turn scheme, business was suddenly booming, author Ahmed Rashid reported. Pakistan's Central Board of Revenue estimated it lost $275 million during fiscal 1993–94, and a staggering half-billion dollars the following year once the Taliban reopened the highways. The World Bank calculated the total illicit trade in legal goods to be worth $2.5 billion, and the UN estimated the narcotics trade at another $1.25 billion annually. "The cross-border smuggling trade has a long history," Rashid wrote. "But never has it played such an important strategic role as under the Taliban."[24]

Pakistan is often described as the godfather of the Taliban. The truth is more complex. Although Islamabad tried to establish influence over the movement from soon after its inception, the Taliban's original benefactors—and the ones to whom they would remain unfailingly loyal—were smugglers. "Mullah Omar got the traders first and then the ISI behind him," says Mullah Roketi. There's evidence that Pakistan's spy chief at the time, General Javed Ashraf Qazi, initially warned Bhutto against getting in bed with the Taliban. "The general predicted that the Taliban could become a dangerous and uncontrollable force which could harm both Afghanistan—and potentially—Pakistan," reads a 1994 cable from the U.S. embassy in Islamabad.[25] Bhutto had just become prime minister for a second time. She and her interior minister, Naseerullah Babar, an ethnic Pashtun with a taste for intrigue, believed they could capitalize on the Taliban and gain control of regional trade into the former Soviet republics. They enlisted the help of the fundamentalist JUI leader Fazal-ur Rehman, at that time serving in Bhutto's government.

In mid-October 2004, Taliban soldiers attacked a garrison in the Afghan border town of Spin Boldak, taking control of a massive weapons dump. The assault was supported by an artillery barrage from a Pakistani Frontier Corps position and coordinated by

Pakistani officers, according to some accounts. Other reports say the Afghan commander in charge of the base handed over the keys to the arms cache after receiving a payoff from the trucking mafia.[26] As is often the case along the remote Pakistan-Afghanistan border, no disinterested parties were on hand to witness what happened. Observers and historians tend to agree this was the moment when Pakistan threw its chips in with the Taliban. Later that month, a thirty-truck convoy from Pakistan's National Logistics Cell—the same military-owned trucking firm that funnelled arms to the mujahideen and reportedly transported heroin out—set off from Quetta for Turkmenistan carrying medical supplies. The ISI's most experienced Afghan hand, known by the nom de guerre Colonel Imam, led the operation.[27]

Just outside Kandahar, the convoy was stopped by mujahideen commanders each wanting a cut. The Taliban came to the convoy's rescue, buoyed by fighters flooding over the border from JUI madrassas. They wore new uniforms and carried weapons still wrapped in plastic, apparently from the Spin Boldak depot. The Taliban stormed on to Kandahar, triumphantly cutting chains blocking the highway. Most of Kandahar's corrupt warlords either fled or agreed to join the Taliban, reportedly after receiving large payoffs. Babar, Bhutto's interior minister, later took credit for the operation, privately describing the Taliban as "our boys" to Pakistani journalists.[28]

Western officials later characterized Babar's comments as more boastful than accurate. "I don't recall that anybody at the time had the notion the Taliban were Pakistan's creation or that the ISI had a lot of influence over them," says a U.S. official then posted to Islamabad. "I think they were just trying to exploit something they had no control over."[29] Throughout the Taliban's time in power, Islamabad would continue to try to establish influence. Short of funds in those post-Soviet resistance days, Pakistan provided logistical support: posting ISI agents to run the Pakistani consulates in Kandahar and Herat, training Taliban cadets, bussing young Pakistani madrassa students to the front, and allowing the Taliban to import wheat and jet fuel at subsidized rates.[30] "I became slowly, slowly sucked into it," Bhutto admitted later. It began with fuel and machine parts. "Then it became money," she said, direct from Pakistan's treasury.[31]

The Taliban played various factions within Pakistan's federal and provincial establishment against one another, as corrupt officials vied for profit from export permits to Afghanistan.[32] In November 1995, the "well-informed" political counsellor from the Russian embassy in Pakistan, Zamir Kabulov, met U.S. officials, telling them that in Moscow's opinion "most Taliban funding still comes from Afghan traders," not Islamabad. Kabulov described Pakistan's military and financial assistance to the Taliban as "modest but pervasive," and said Islamabad's real boost to the Taliban came from "making no effort to stop the booming smuggling trade."[33] Individuals in Bhutto's government (then ranked the world's second most corrupt after Nigeria by the monitoring group Transparency International) profited enormously from continued chaos in Afghanistan. Bhutto would be thrown out of office a second and final time in 1996 amid charges that she and her husband, Asif Ali Zardari, bilked her country of $1.5 billion.

As it was, Islamabad never established much sway over the Taliban, who Pakistani officers complained were wilful and stubborn. Pakistan's senior generals privately expressed worry to American officials that Islamabad's covert support for the Taliban had gathered a dangerous momentum no one could stop.[34] While the ISI urged Bhutto to support a push on Kabul, the army chief, General Jehangir Karamat, described the Taliban to a U.S. diplomat as "a millstone around our necks."[35]

In the spring of 1996, as Pakistan's generals fretted about how to extract themselves, the Afghan situation became yet more complex. A jet chartered from Afghanistan's state-run Ariana Airlines touched down on the dusty Jalalabad runway carrying a man who would become another key patron to the Taliban: Osama bin Laden. His return to Afghanistan heralded a new chapter in the Taliban chronicle, one that would have a dramatic impact on modern history.

The Saudi exile wasted no time in ingratiating himself with Afghanistan's new masters, helping to bankroll their takeover of Kabul. Bin Laden reportedly put up $3 million from his personal funds to pay off the remaining warlords who stood between the Taliban and the Afghan capital. The cash injection came at a crucial time, and Mullah Omar would never forget it.

In *The Ghost Wars,* author Steve Coll reports that the Taliban also received contributions from the trucking mafia, heroin traders, the ISI, and other Arab donors.[36] Once in control of the capital, the Taliban began issuing archaic decrees—banning girls from school and forcing men to pray five times a day—focusing the world's media on their exacting interpretation of Islam. Amid western outrage over their treatment of women and anxiety about their ties to Arab and Pakistani terrorist groups, the Taliban also came under international pressure to crack down on the poppy trade. On September 10, 1997, the Taliban's foreign ministry responded:

> The Islamic State of Afghanistan informs all compatriots that as [*sic*] the use of heroin and hashish is not permitted in Islam. They are reminded once again that they should strictly refrain from growing, using and trading in hashish and heroin. Anyone who violates this order shall be meted out a punishment in line with the lofty Mohammad and Sharia Law and thus shall not be entitled to launch a complaint.

The ruling was amended by a clarification ten days later outlawing cultivation and trafficking of opium as well.[37] No one paid it much attention. A year earlier, Afghanistan had produced a whopping 2,248 metric tons of opium, according to UNODC. That number climbed to 2,804 tons in 1997, dipping slightly the next year because of widespread drought, and then soaring to a whopping 4,581 metric tons in 1999 (see table).[38] By this time the Taliban controlled most of the country, and Afghanistan's poppy crop represented about 75 percent of global production; 97 percent of it was grown in Taliban-held areas.[39]

Afghan Opium Production
(in metric tons)

	2001	2000	1999	1998	1997	1996
U.S. government	74	3,656	2,861	2,340	2,184	2,099
UNODC	n/a	3,276	4,581	2,102	2,804	2,248

Courtesy of DEA website

Far from making efforts to stamp out poppy, the Taliban started taxing and regulating the trade. They collected a 10 percent tax (*ushr*) from farmers who grew poppy and other produce. *Ushr* was collected in kind at the farm level (as it still is today) and then spent locally, according to Bernard Frahi, a UNODC official.[40] In the south, the Taliban also began collecting a 20 percent *zakat*, an Islamic levy, on truckloads of opium leaving farm areas.[41] Following a law enforcement crackdown in neighbouring Pakistan, heroin refineries based in the tribal areas shifted across the border.[42] The Taliban swiftly began taxing their output as well—charging between $50 and $70 a kilo depending on whether the final product was morphine base or crystal heroin. Zuber, a former lab worker interviewed in a Peshawar rehab centre, reported that the Taliban collected as much as $5,500 a week during peak season from the lab where he bundled morphine base for export. He said there were about twenty-five labs with similar output capacity in the district where he worked.[43]

According to a top-secret 1998 CIA report, recently declassified, Haji Bashir Noorzai apparently forged a deal with the Taliban to pay $230 for each kilo of crystal heroin he exported by plane.[44] The Taliban also charged duties on road exports and handed out tax receipts for truckers driving their wares across the border into Pakistan or Iran. A scan of this receipt is posted on the DEA's website:

> *Gentlemen, the bearer of this letter, who possess 4 kilograms of white good, has paid the custom duty at the Shinwar Custom. It is hoped that the bearer will not be bothered.*

Signed: Incharge [*sic*] of Shinwar Custom Stamp, Nangarhar Province
Shinwar Loy Wolaswa Custom Section

How much the Taliban earned from taxing the drug trade each year was a matter of great debate. "It was very difficult to come by hard data," says Julie Sirrs, a former analyst with the Defense Intelligence Agency (DIA). "They seemed to have more money than what rich Arabs and the Pakistan government were providing them."[45] Estimates of their narcotics earnings ranged from $30 million to $200 million annually, and the real figure was probably higher.

Lower calculations of the Taliban's drug-related revenue generally accounted for just the 10 percent *ushr* collected at the farm level, extrapolating from the total amount of opium produced in their control zones. Higher estimates also took into account that the Taliban taxed trucks leaving southern farm areas and heroin refineries. There was also evidence that top traffickers and traders contributed directly to the regime, but no one knows how much or whether it was regulated. As well, the Taliban received millions of dollars' worth of commodities, including vehicles and weapons, from traffickers, traders, and visiting Arab sheiks. Since the Taliban kept virtually no computer or paper records, it is unlikely that the real figure of drug earnings will ever be accurately tallied. "They were controlling the industry completely," says a former ISI agent who worked in Afghanistan in those days. "Now there are so many people doing it, the profits are spread out. Back then, the Taliban made all the profit."[46]

Massive drug bazaars—with literally hundreds of stalls selling opium—operated in places like Ghani Khel in Nangahar Province, Sangin in Helmand, and Haji Bashir's hometown of Maiwand in Kandahar. In Ghani Khel, one could purchase up to ten tons of opium at a time, along with precursor chemicals like acetic anhydride and calcium carbonate, according to David Macdonald, a former adviser to the UN.[47] "Until the demise of the Taliban . . . the larger factories mirrored the drug bazaars in scale," he wrote in his book *Drugs in Afghanistan.* "They were well-armed with rocket launchers, 5-50 caliber machine guns and AK-47s, had upwards of 30 employees, relied on UHF radio and satellite phone communications and had a daily production capacity of more than 100 kg of morphine base and 100 kg of brown heroin." Meanwhile, in the remote areas where it was grown, opium had literally become a form of currency. Local shopkeepers kept scales in their shops, as opposed to cash boxes or registers. One could purchase groceries with a golf ball-sized chunk of opium, according to Macdonald.[48]

Despite their generally brutal treatment of drug users, Macdonald came across evidence the Taliban had no compunction about making addicts of their enemies. He quotes a Northern Alliance fighter captured by the Taliban in the north. "After some time in jail he was taken to the front lines and promised unlimited hashish," Macdonald writes. But it was unlike anything the soldier had previously inhaled: "When I smoked this hashish, it felt different in my body. It made me feel powerful and fearless." Later on, the fighter discovered the hashish they gave him was laced with heroin. He became quite willing to go and fight against his former comrades in the Northern Alliance if the Taliban would just give him more heroin—which they did.[49]

Although they made public statements to the contrary, Mullah

Omar's ruling *shura* was deeply involved in planning and coordinating Afghanistan's drug output, according to declassified documents and ex-officials. "The Taliban liked to organize the traffickers," said the former ISI agent, who visited Afghanistan and the border region dozens of times during their regime. "Their manipulation of the trade was unquestionable." The 1998 CIA report said the Taliban instructed officials in several Afghan provinces to help increase opium poppy cultivation that year by training farmers:

> In addition, [word excised] Taliban officials authorized the establishment of six new heroin-processing laboratories in Taliban-controlled Helmand, Kandahar and Oruzgan provinces.[50]

There were almost sixty labs functioning in Helmand and Nangarhar provinces alone, the report said, adding that the Taliban instructed the labs to close down briefly during a visit by senior officials from UNODC. The top-secret report concluded:

> The Taliban continues to institutionalize its involvement in narcotics trafficking activities despite their public opposition to narcotics-related activities on religious grounds and pledge to work with the UN Drug Control Program to reduce opium cultivation.[51]

It's probably more accurate to say the drug traffickers who stood behind the Taliban—or who sat on the ruling *shura*, like Bashir Noorzai—were influencing the group's decisions about poppy production and lab permits. "The Taliban was right in the middle of things," said Bob Clark, a former DEA agent posted to Islamabad in the late 1990s. "But the Quetta Alliance was never going to give up control over the industry in the south."[52] As well, it was hard to imagine the ragtag Taliban leaders had enough understanding of market economics to be calling the shots anyway. "I always thought those guys had someone behind them," said Adan Adar, a former UN official then based in Kandahar.[53]

The Taliban's other major patron, who settled himself into a sprawling complex outside Kandahar city, also appears to have invested in Afghanistan's biggest export. Although U.S. counternarcotics officials say they never received direct confirmation of Osama bin Laden's personal role in the drug trade, there was overwhelming circumstantial evidence to suggest that the al Qaeda leader was deeply involved—not least since his terror camps were located in the same districts as heroin labs. "It was more or less just an assumption they were involved, but I don't recall any intelligence that we collected on the matter," says a former CIA official. "We didn't give a damn. The way the bureaucracy works, no one really wants to do narcotics."[54] The British government investigated the matter far more closely since the majority of heroin sold on their streets came from Afghanistan, and they had no doubt who was behind that fact. A spokesman for former prime minister Tony Blair said MI6 believed Mullah Omar and bin Laden each maintained personal opium stockpiles greater than three thousand tons.[55]

Blair told a 2001 gathering of Labour Party officials that bin Laden used drug money to finance Chechen and Uzbek rebels. A separate UN panel in December 2000 concluded: "Funds raised from the production and trade of opium and heroin are used by the Taliban to buy arms and war materials and to finance the training of terrorists and support the operation of extremists in neighbouring countries and beyond."[56] Among pockets of the intelligence community, there was growing alarm that bin Laden wanted to strike in the United States or Europe. Concern mushroomed after the August 1998 attacks on the U.S. embassies in Kenya and Tanzania, and again after the USS *Cole* bombing in October 2000.

As the 1990s progressed, international sanctions against Afghanistan isolated the Taliban regime. There were signs bin Laden's influence over Mullah Omar was growing steadily. Western intelligence agents watched nervously from Pakistan as al Qaeda camps multiplied and drew more trainees. Arab "advisers" were spotted among the Taliban troops. "As the years went on, al Qaeda became their chaperones," the former ISI agent said. Meanwhile, Mullah Omar's pronouncements became ever more arbitrary and fanatic: he banned white socks, kite flying, even toothpaste. "Whether or not he had bought into all of bin Laden's beliefs from the first, Mullah Omar came to share his vision," wrote Daniel Benjamin and Steven Simon, two former officials at the National Security Council.[57]

Although bin Laden's public statements (like those of Mullah Omar) indicated he opposed drug use, the DEA received intelligence that bin Laden tried to recruit chemists to develop a "super heroin," which would have been more addictive, to export to the West. The plan apparently never came to fruition, and some U.S. officials later questioned the accuracy of the report itself.[58] There was stronger evidence that bin Laden served as a middleman between the Taliban and Arab drug smugglers from the United Arab Emirates, Qatar, and Saudi Arabia, using commissions to fund his terror camps.[59] There were persistent reports that hunting trips he organized—and often attended—for rich Saudi and UAE sheiks were a mix of business and pleasure. The sheiks flew in on private jets and military transport planes, touching down at the Kandahar airfield and other smaller airstrips, allegedly to hunt the rare birds known as houbara bustards. U.S. and British intelligence officials came to believe that at least some of those flights transported weapons and material to the Taliban and al Qaeda and flew heroin out.[60] In 2007, accused drug smuggler Haji Bashir Noorzai stated in testimony before a New York court that he brokered a deal for the UAE defence minister, Sheikh Mohammed bin Rashid al Maktoum, who later took over as ruler of Dubai to lease lands outside Kandahar as a "hunting preserve."[61] British and U.S. intelligence and law enforcement officials suspected some Arab sheiks of traveling to southern Afghanistan for more than just its exotic birdlife.[62]

It was widely known these hunting teams brought lavish amounts of equipment including vehicles, rifles, and tents, which they left with the Taliban. A former senior UN official described a visit by Sheikh Mohammed in the late 1990s when he imported one hundred vehicles—all of them four-by-four pickup trucks and Toyota Land Cruisers fitted with radios—which he left for his hosts. Counternarcotics officials were interested in the flight patterns of the bustard-hunting trips: they seemed to be heaviest in the spring planting season and just after the fall harvest.[63] Bin Laden himself was a regular visitor on these hunting trips, moving openly in the Afghan desert. "He would be dead if the [U.S.] government had allowed us to kill him during one of these hunting trips," says a former U.S. official who helped track bin Laden. "But we weren't placed to know what went on in terms of conversations."

Private jets weren't the only planes on U.S. intelligence radar

people"—often came on the flights, recalled Shakur. "They would come off the planes with heavy bags and no one would dare ask them anything."[67] The Taliban appointed their own agent, a baby-faced cleric named Farid Ahmed, to run the Sharjah station, where depending on the season, Ariana flights sometimes landed as many as three times a day.[68] Ahmed badgered other cargo firms populating the white-domed airport with requests to buy millions of dollars' worth of weapons and long-distance cargo planes.[69] Mounting concern that Ariana was moving drugs and terrorists led to the UN sanctioning the Taliban in late 2000, barring Ariana from flying internationally.[70] The Taliban swiftly reacted in anger. On November 12, the day sanctions went into effect, rocket-propelled grenades were fired at the U.S. embassy and a UN office in Kabul.[71]

The Taliban turned to Viktor Bout, the notorious Russian spy-turned-smuggler whose Sharjah-based air cargo empire served as a sort of FedEx to criminals, rebel groups, and banana republics. Bout's initial contact with the Taliban was hardly auspicious, as documented in *Merchant of Death*, a book detailing Bout's smuggling empire from Africa to Asia. In 1995, a Taliban MiG-21 jet intercepted one of his Ilyushin-76 cargo planes ferrying ammunition to the Kabul government (which the Taliban would topple one year later). The Russian crew and plane remained hostages of the Taliban for more than twelve months as Bout, his brother Sergei, and the Russian foreign ministry tried to secure their release. Throughout the negotiations, Bout delivered goods to the Taliban, sometimes as many as six flights a day—TV sets, clothes, Chinese consumer goods—an apparent goodwill gesture that soon turned into a profitable enterprise.[72] "Viktor is completely amoral," says a U.S. official who tracks him. "He'll work with anybody."[73] After a year of negotiations, the Russian crew would fire up the jet and hurtle down the runway on a blistering afternoon while their guards dozed.

It was a daring "escape" Bout himself discounted in a subsequent interview. "Do you really think you can jump in a plane that's been sitting unmaintained on the tarmac for over a year, start up the engines, and just take off?" he asked a 2003 interviewer in Moscow. "They didn't escape. They were extracted." Asked to explain, Bout fell silent. "There are huge forces," was all he would say.[74] A subsequent news report would suggest Afghan traders in the Emirates intercepted on Bout's behalf.[75] And a former Bout associate said Bout's Afghan traffic serviced shadowy clients behind the Taliban. Despite the international embargoes on Afghanistan, Bout always received payments for his Afghan work from Swiss bank accounts, according to his associate, who said: "He flew to the Taliban, not for the Taliban."[76]

Between 1998 and 2001, Bout sold the Taliban twelve air freighters and continued to fly weapons, spare aircraft parts, and other supplies into Afghanistan. U.S. and British officials became highly concerned about the pace of flights into Kandahar, where bin Laden had resettled and built several training camps. Arabs were a constant presence at the Kandahar Airport, and western officials worried flights were ferrying Islamic militants, guns, maybe even WMD.[77] Heroin smuggling was another concern; U.S. and British counternarcotics agents wanted to send an undercover team to Sharjah to swab down the planes, according to several former U.S. officials, who said the plan never passed the proposal phase.[78]

After UN sanctions went into effect, an Emirati charter agency named Flying Dolphin won permission to fly humanitarian supplies and aid workers to Afghanistan. The airline was owned by Sheikh Abdullah bin Zayed bin Saqr al Nahyan, a former UAE ambassador to the United States and member of Abu Dhabi's ruling family.[79] Incredibly, Viktor Bout was Zayed's silent partner.[80] An April 2004 intelligence document shown to the author spelled out the conclusion among western intelligence agents: "Under the Taliban government everyone, including Arabs, was active in the narco-trade. As part of this, flights with narcotics went direct from Helmand to the United Arab Emirates." This continued after the UN sanctions went into effect. "The U.S. government was aware there were Taliban flights breaking the embargo," Julie Sirrs, the former Defense Intelligence Agency analyst, told me. "It was widely believed they were moving drugs on those planes."[81]

Far from being hurt by the sanctions, the Taliban seemed to have a steady supply of weapons and money. There was a lot going on in Afghanistan in those days that was alarming to Washington. As in the 1980s, narcotics were not the priority. "The drug issue was one thing on a long list that we were trying to get the Taliban to move on," says Karl Indurfurth, then the assistant secretary of state for South and Central Asian affairs. "Girls' schools, terrorist camps, women's rights. After the embassy bombings in Africa, Osama went to the top of that list."[82] Between 1996 and 2001, the U.S. government pressed the Taliban on thirty different occasions to expel bin Laden from Afghanistan, according to a State Department document.[83] "The message to the Taliban pre-9/11 was, 'We don't like you, but we are willing to live with you if you give us al Qaeda,'" said Teresita Schaffer, another former assistant secretary of state for South Asia.

U.S. officials raised the counternarcotics issue during infrequent exchanges with the Taliban, but after the 1998 terrorist attacks, no one in Washington thought raising the poppy issue would encourage the Taliban to cough up bin Laden. The UN kept up the pressure over drugs, bringing Taliban officials to Pakistan to consult Islamic legal experts on growing and trading narcotics.[84] The Taliban appeared desperate for international recognition of their regime, and wanted UN sanctions lifted. The executive director of the UN's drug control programme, Pino Arlacchi, offered the Taliban $250 million in alternative livelihood aid if they could eliminate poppy—a promise he would fail spectacularly to keep.[85]

UN efforts appeared to pay off in July 2000. Just before the autumn planting season was to begin, Mullah Omar announced a total ban on poppy cultivation. To everyone's amazement (and despite some protests in Nangarhar, where farmers shaved their beards and played music) the ban held. American satellite photos and UN ground surveys indicated just 8,000 hectares were planted the following spring across Afghanistan—down from more than 82,000 hectares a year earlier. Most of it was growing in areas not controlled by the Taliban. It represented the largest single cutback in illicit drug production ever. Bernard Frahi, who brokered the deal for UNODC, called it "one of the most remarkable successes ever" in the fight against narcotics.[86] But as with so many things in Afghanistan, the truth was murkier.

Almost overnight, the price of opium at Afghanistan's border shot up from an all-time low of about $28 per kilo to between $350 and $400, according to UNODC and DEA accounts. And despite the ban on growing poppy, western authorities noticed that the Taliban made no effort to seize drug stocks or arrest traffickers. On the contrary, opium bazaars continued to do a brisk business, and the Taliban still collected tax—now earning much higher revenues from a product that had increased tenfold in value. Levels of heroin purity dipped slightly in western markets over the coming year, but the street price of heroin remained stable, indicating there was virtually no supply shortage.[87]

The poppy ban, it turned out, was the ultimate insider trading con. The Taliban gambled they could win millions of dollars in international aid—and perhaps even recognition of their government—while top leaders sold off their opium hoards at far higher prices. Just before the ban, top Taliban leaders purchased huge amounts of opium—especially Haji Bashir Noorzai, according to sources close to the movement. "That was when Haji Bashir really broke into the market on his own," says a relative. "It wasn't religion," a smuggler told me in 2003. "It was good business. They bought low, they sold high."

Mullah Omar shifted himself into an enormous and garish new estate on the outskirts of Kandahar. The ornate main palace featured crystal chandeliers and kitschy murals. The compound also boasted a mosque, servant's quarters, and an ample guesthouse.[88] The UN-affiliated Narcotics Control Board concluded that, after four years of bumper crops, stocks of Afghan heroin were high enough to supply the European market for up to four more years.[89] "Everyone close to Mullah Omar benefited," said the former ISI agent. Ahmadullah Alizai, who was the counternarcotics chief in Kandahar after 2001, put it more simply: "They all made millions."

The poppy ban also sparked a humanitarian disaster, from which some Afghan farmers have never recovered. Hundreds of thousands defaulted on loans or were unable to make it through the winter months without credit and fled to the Iranian and Pakistani border areas. Many sold off land and livestock, even trading their unmarried daughters to poppy merchants to settle their arrears.[90] A farmer from Khogiani, in eastern Afghanistan, who took a $400 advance on four kilograms of opium in 2000, did not have the harvested crop to repay his debt. Interviewed in early 2004, the farmer remained heavily indebted to the lender, owing twenty kilograms of opium, then worth $7,200. By giving the trader his daughter, he deducted $3,200 of the loan, and then mortgaged part of his land against the remaining $4,000 owed. He hoped to repay the remainder by growing more opium.[91]

During the 1990s, western aid poured money into anti-narcotics efforts in Pakistan, mainly crop substitution efforts, which succeeded in reducing poppy output from a high of eight hundred tons per year to about two. Pakistan was no longer a heroin producer. Instead it became a major transport route for opiates produced in Taliban-held regions, which utilized the same network built up a decade earlier. As Ahmed Rashid wrote, "The same dealers, truck drivers, madrassa and government contacts and the arms, fuel, and food supply chain that provided the Taliban with its supplies also funnelled drugs—just as the same arms pipeline for the mujahideen had done in the 1980s."[92] Although the poppy fields and the processing labs had shifted into Afghanistan, the command and control of the drug trade remained in Pakistan. "Most of the labs in southern Afghanistan are controlled by or associated with a powerful consortium of traffickers known as the Quetta Alliance," read a joint U.S. intelligence report issued in the year 2000. It described the cartel as the "dominant trafficking organization in Southwest Asia."[93]

Amid rising alarm over exploding addiction rates in Pakistan, counternarcotics police worked to crack down on growing traffic.[94] Powerful smugglers grew more sophisticated. They welded secret compartments inside cargo tanks of fuel trucks and under seats in passenger buses and filled them with morphine base. One former director of Pakistan's Anti Narcotics Force recalled intercepting a shipment of cabbage with an ingenious concealment method. A bag of heroin had been placed inside each bud as it sprouted, he said, and the mature cabbage heads had grown around the drug packets.[95] Heroin shipments became smaller but increased in frequency, making them harder to trace. There were growing signs that international organized crime rings were getting in on the action. The mid-1990s brought a sudden influx of Nigerian visitors to Pakistan, who routinely got caught carrying heroin—usually no more than a few kilos—inside rubber pellets they had ingested, according to former British, U.S., and Pakistani counternarcotics officials. "We'd take them to the hospital, pump them full of laxatives, and watch them lay eggs for days," said the former ANF director. Still today, Nigerians account for almost three-quarters of the heroin carriers arrested in Pakistan.[96]

Islamabad came under pressure to do something about the massive quantities of opiates moving through its territory. However, there remained worrisome signs of collusion between the traffickers and elements of the military and intelligence services. In 1996, Islamabad announced that its anti-drug agents had intercepted two tons of brown sugar, or morphine base, in southwestern Baluchistan. Foreign diplomats were invited to an elaborate ceremony to watch Pakistanis set the drugs ablaze. Before they did, U.S. agents took a sample. It turned out that the huge pile of dirt contained just traces of opium. The Clinton administration angrily denounced the seizure as a "hoax."[97] A year later DEA agents arrested a senior Pakistani air force officer trying to sell two kilograms of heroin in a New York City McDonald's. Islamabad was furious about the bust, believing the officer had been set up by the DEA. But after an investigation, Pakistani authorities arrested another air force officer in a Karachi hotel, claiming the pair were part of a "small drug ring" within the military.[98]

Many believed there to be far wider involvement. Rumours swirled in Islamabad diplomatic circles that the same ISI trucks bringing covert military aid to the Taliban carried heroin out. As the 1990s wore on, the U.S. embassy reported that ISI support for the Taliban appeared to have grown.[99] A pair of raw intelligence reports detail a widening flow of supplies, including "munitions, fuel and food," with one noting that the spy agency used a private trucking company to cover its tracks.[100] By this time it was widely accepted that Pakistan's Pashtun trucking mafia was closely tied to the drug trade. British authorities tracked private jets making frequent night flights between the Persian Gulf and Quetta, according to a former western police official. A Thai diplomat got nabbed trying to enter the UK with two suitcases full of heroin. He told British investigators he picked up the bags at an ISI safe house.[101]

At a time when the West had isolated Pakistan, first over its nuclear efforts and again after General Pervez Musharraf's 1999 coup, there was less and less engagement with Pakistani authorities. It was never clear if the accumulating events were just another sign of Pakistan's massive corruption problem or a covert policy to raise funds through drug trafficking. "We heard about things all the time, and if you hear it enough, it starts to sound credible," said William Milam, who was U.S. ambassador from 1998 to 2001. "But we never had any real proof."[102] Milam's successor, Wendy Chamberlain, would later characterize the ISI's role in the drug trade in the 1990s as "substantial" during testimony before the House of Representatives.[103]Another western official put it this way: "At the end of the day the ISI is no different from any other intelligence agency. They have to get funding for covert operations one way or another."[104]

Another murky web of concern was Islamabad's covert aid to the Taliban and to Pakistani extremist groups operating in Kashmir and training in al Qaeda camps. Washington became alarmed in the year 2000, after Musharraf came to power, that "while Pakistani support for the Taliban has been long-standing, the magnitude of recent support is unprecedented." The State Department issued a bulletin to the Islamabad embassy describing large numbers of Pakistani troops crossing into Afghanistan to support the Taliban's campaign against the dwindling opposition coalition commonly known as the Northern Alliance. The U.S. ambassador was ordered to convey Washington's displeasure over the situation to senior Pakistani officials.[105]

Was support for extremists the state policy in Pakistan or a worrisome sign that the military ruler actually had little control over his own security agencies? For years, there have been numerous reports describing the ISI as a "state within a state," beholden only to its own grand designs. Some historians and diplomats suggest there's a small clique within Pakistan's intelligence community handling black operations like supporting Islamic extremists and developing (and proliferating) nuclear technology. For longtime Pakistan watchers, the debate over the existence of this rogue element has been central to western policy toward the country—driving debate over whether to isolate or engage Islamabad.

In his 2006 autobiography, then President Musharraf claimed his government actually had little sway with Mullah Omar. Contrary to popular belief, he wrote, "our relations with the Taliban were never smooth; in fact they were quite uncomfortable."[106] A U.S. official then on his second posting to Pakistan agreed with the president's assessment, saying that when he returned to Islamabad in the late 1990s, his contacts told him, "al Qaeda replaced us out there. They have the chequebooks." When the Taliban blew up the ancient Buddhas of Bāmiān, even after Islamabad had dispatched its foreign minister to beg them not to, the Americans concluded Islamabad had created a monster it could no longer control. "I can only say I was underwhelmed by their level of influence in Afghanistan," said the U.S. official.[107] The persistent and contradictory indications that elements of the ISI were deeply involved with the Taliban, while other Pakistani officials tried and failed to rein them in, would continue to muddle U.S. policy toward the increasingly complex region.

By spring of 2001, threat reporting related to al Qaeda had surged to a level the U.S. intelligence community had never before seen. Between May and July, the National Security Agency reported at least 33 intercepts indicating a terrorist attack was imminent. The FBI tracked 216 secret threat warnings between January 1 and September 10, 2001. And the Federal Aviation Administration issued 15 separate warnings about possible attacks on American airlines.[108] CIA director George Tenet would later tell the 9/11 Commission: "The system was blinking red."[109] The Bush administration would consider backing the Taliban's opposition—then led by the Tajik commander Ahmed Shah Massood—and arming a Predator drone to assassinate bin Laden. Tenet even travelled secretly to Islamabad to meet with his Pakistani counterpart, ISI director general Mahmoud Ahmed. Among other things, they discussed the possibility of getting to bin Laden through counternarcotics channels.[110] By summer, U.S. spies were scrambling to get a handle on what was coming down the pipeline. Their failure to do so would cost the lives of more than three thousand people on 9/11, and send the United States to war.

On September 11, 2001, the regional price of a kilogram of opium had reached an all-time high of $746. Within weeks, it had dropped to $95 a kilo, according to the DEA, indicating its owners were dumping their stocks in anticipation of the U.S.-led invasion, possibly for hard currency, possibly to trade for weapons.[111] UN officials believed the Taliban, al Qaeda, and allied drug lords possessed more than 2,800 metric tons of opium. Sold on the wholesale market in Pakistan, the opium would fetch more than $1 billion, UN officials worried. If processed into crystal heroin and smuggled to the West, the deadly harvest could keep every addict there high for more than three years.[112]

As the United States ramped up for war, the Joint Chiefs of Staff and top Bush administration officials complained that there were few targets in Afghanistan of military consequence. "We're bombing sand," President Bush said in an interview. "We're pounding sand."[113] CIA sources say the agency prepared a comprehensive list of potential targets, which included twenty-five major drug labs, storage warehouses, and other opium-related facilities.[114] The British government also provided Washington with the locations of about two dozen drugs labs and storage areas, according to former INL chief Bobby Charles.[115]

The California congressman Dana Rohrabacher also put together a team "who knew all the players in Afghanistan." The outspoken Republican lawmaker harbours an obsession with the global drug trade, had a long history with Afghanistan, and openly supported the mujahideen during the Soviet resistance. "I had six guys working for me around the clock," he said later. "We identified four storage areas where we believed the Taliban had a billion dollars' worth of drugs hidden."[116]

However, from the start of military operations in Afghanistan, the Bush administration and the Pentagon would conspicuously avoid taking on opium traders. On October 11, four days after Operation Enduring Freedom began, Bush sat down with his National Security Council, discussing, among other things, the continued search for installations U.S. warplanes could target. Defence secretary Donald Rumsfeld said the Pentagon considered hitting drug labs and heroin storage areas, but didn't because of concerns there would be "collateral damage."[117]

The CIA later concluded that bombing those targets would have slowed down opium production in Afghanistan for more than a year. "The drug targets were big places, like small towns that did nothing but produce heroin," a CIA official said. "The British were screaming for us to bomb those targets because most of the heroin in Britain comes from Afghanistan, but they refused."[118]

When he learned of the decision later, Rohrabacher was infuriated. "I kept telling them, this is going to be used to kill Americans," he said. "At a time when I think they could have disappeared, I think this opium kept the Taliban alive."

4. THE NEW TALIBAN

WHEN THE END CAME FOR THE TALIBAN'S TREASURER, HE was hurtling along an isolated smugglers' trail in a rocky wasteland known as Dasht-e Margo—the "desert of death."

Mullah Akhtar Mohammad Osmani travelled in a four-by-four with a regional Taliban subcommander named Mullah Abdul Zahir. A third passenger was Haji Masooq, one of the biggest heroin smugglers in Helmand Province.[1] It was December 19, 2006. Unbeknown to Osmani, a Royal Air Force R1 monitoring plane had picked up his trail when he spoke earlier on his satellite telephone. According to British officials, the spy plane made contact with a U.S. Special Operations team hunting high-value targets. The RAF also reached out to Task Force Orange, a military intelligence unit tracking terrorists electronically.[2] Once they confirmed they had Osmani on the phone, a U.S. warplane took off from Bagram Air Base and sped to Helmand, launching a precision air strike the moment Osmani's vehicle moved out of a populated area. The four-by-four was obliterated in a flash. Osmani and the others never knew what hit them.

As Mullah Omar's money man and the military commander for six key provinces in the south, Osmani was, at the time, the highest-ranking Taliban official to be eliminated since the U.S.-led coalition invaded Afghanistan in October 2001. Although the U.S. military and the western media hailed his killing, a key circumstance of Osmani's death got little attention: the man in charge of the Taliban's finances got taken out while he was doing a dope deal.

The circumstances surrounding Osmani's death came as no surprise to U.S. and Afghan officials tracking the Taliban's links to the opium trade. By late 2006, the Taliban and its allies were addicted to drugs. As was discussed in Chapter 3, the Taliban always relied heavily on opium for funding. Their level of dependence rose dramatically after the regime fell from power. Opium not only played a crucial role in the movement's resurgence from the brink of extinction; it has transformed the insurgency populating the Pakistan-Afghanistan border into a far more ominous incarnation few longtime Taliban watchers even recognize.

The new Taliban—if it can still even be called the Taliban—is a fragmented, transnational force devoid of many of the group's prior characteristics and political aspirations. "These are not old Taliban," says a senior Afghan security official. "We don't even know who they are anymore."[3] Mullah Omar remains the undisputed leader of the core group; however, the larger umbrella movement now spans both sides of the border and includes fighters loyal to regional warlords and troublemakers who engage in everything from local terrorism and smuggling to kidnapping and racketeering. "We could round up the entire Quetta *shura*," says the Afghan official, referring to Omar's inner circle, "and we would still be no closer to ending the insurgency."

The new Taliban might be found defacing ancient Buddha statues in northwest Pakistan, protecting drug convoys in Helmand, or bombing a police bus in Kabul.[4] In some areas, gangland-style fighters who call themselves Taliban (or who are referred to locally as Taliban) have little contact with or allegiance to Mullah Omar's core group. In fact, they probably interact more frequently with corrupt local officials, and may even fight with local rivals who also call themselves Taliban.

Some offshoots have regional aspirations, like attacking India or wreaking havoc in Uzbekistan, or possess global ambitions and work closely with al Qaeda. In many places, the insurgents' field of vision is just a few, remote districts along the border. To put it simply, there's no way to easily define this blurry mix of bad guys who interact in various different ways across a vast expanse of ungoverned territory.[5] As William Olson, a professor at the National Defense University's Near East and South Asia Center for Strategic Studies, puts it, "It's like the movement of gas molecules in a jar, lots of motion within a confining medium."[6]

That confining medium is an ever-widening swath of territory straddling the Pakistan-Afghanistan border.[7] Whatever their locale and their reach, virtually everywhere you look within this ungoverned zone, the new Taliban interact and behave more like members of a criminal syndicate than a political force. "What is the Taliban?" says a UN official. "They are gone now. What we have now is people working together just to make money."[8] If they operate along existing drug routes, and increasingly even when they don't, the opium trade has been vital to the survival of today's insurgents since the U.S.-led coalition swept into the region.[9]

The 2001 invasion of Afghanistan caused the Taliban and al Qaeda to scatter, but it failed to put down the enemy once and for all. Rather than mounting a nationwide invasion with large numbers of foreign troops, the United States and its allies opted for a "light footprint," relying on local proxies with predictably unfortunate results.

Many al Qaeda and Taliban leaders fled over the border into Pakistan. Most famously, Osama bin Laden escaped the Tora Bora siege down a smugglers' trail, reportedly on the back of a donkey.[10] Many Taliban commanders lay low in Pashtun regions of southwest Afghanistan. Quite a few ended up in the fertile plains of west Kandahar and Helmand that also cultivate poppy. "There was no coordinated effort—they just escaped to places where they knew they'd find safe haven," said journalist Rahimullah Yusufzai.[11] It wasn't hard to melt away and hide. Throughout 2002, there were just 4,500 troops dedicated to the International Security Assistance Force in Afghanistan, all based in the capital, Kabul.

Limited numbers of U.S. forces fanned out around the south and southeast, focusing on hunting down "high-value targets" in al Qaeda, not Taliban. CIA agents and U.S. military officials dished out millions of dollars to anti-Taliban warlords whose questionable records on narcotics and human rights have been documented by historians, journalists, and human rights groups. Gary Schroen, the CIA agent sent to coordinate with the Northern Alliance, wrote about handing $500,000 to its leader, Marshall Fahim, during their first meeting.[12] Gul Agha Sherzai, an allegedly corrupt former governor of Kandahar, received Land Cruisers full of cash to help him reconquer that southern province. "During the march on Kandahar," wrote author Peter Maass, "Gul Agha's wallet was a Toyota."[13]

The Northern Alliance swept into Kabul, installing its people, most of them ethnic Tajiks, in key security posts. To cobble together support for his weak coalition government, the U.S.-appointed leader Hamid Karzai began handing out important positions like they were trophies. Fahim became defence minister.

Eastern warlord Hazrat Ali took control of Nangarhar, a province rich in poppy. Western strongman Ismael Khan reinstalled himself in Herat, where he could tax lucrative cross-border traffic with Iran. The Uzbek warlord Rashid Dostum got Mazar-e Sharif and control of trade to the north. He battled over the spoils with a rival warlord, Mohammed Atta. Sher Mohammed, the young nephew of Nasim Akhundzada, was handed the governorship of Helmand.

U.S. officials privately acknowledged the unsavoury behaviour of various individuals who joined the new government, including allegations that some were tied to drug trafficking, but claimed they were needed in the hunt for al Qaeda. Washington's main concern again took precedence, absolving other problems at hand. As the International Crisis Group put it, "a culture of impunity was allowed to take root in the name of 'stability.'"[14] The following spring, poppy fields again carpeted the Afghan countryside. A year before the U.S.-led invasion, Afghan farmers harvested just 8,000 hectares—mostly in areas outside the Taliban's control, according to UNODC. In 2002, 74,000 hectares of poppies were planted. Overnight, Afghanistan had again become the world's leading opium producer.[15]

Drug bazaars quickly reopened, selling vast reserves squirrelled away by traders and farmers alike. Within days of Kandahar falling to American forces, hundreds of shopkeepers were doing a brisk trade at the Hazrat Ji Baba market, just a few miles from where the U.S. military was setting up a new base. Bob Woodruff, a correspondent for *ABC News*, visited another opium bazaar in nearby Maiwand in December 2001 where traders were scooping the sticky resin onto metal scales. "It was incredible," he said. "They were selling it openly in big plastic sacks."[16]

Across the border, agents from Pakistan's Anti Narcotics Force got a taste of the amount of contraband leaving the region when they ambushed a camel convoy in the windswept outreaches of the Baluchistan Desert. The camels carried nearly a ton of heroin and morphine base on their backs. Worth millions of dollars on the black market, it was one of the biggest drug hauls the world had ever seen.[17]

If the smugglers were quick to get back on their feet, the international community was painfully inefficient. After twenty-five years of war, virtually everything had to be rebuilt from scratch, from the roads to the power grid to the justice system to the police force. "Like so many of its people," wrote Barry Bearak in *The New York Times Magazine*, "the nation is missing limbs."[18] The Bonn Agreement divided the mammoth task of regrowing them between the various donor nations: the British took on drugs; the Italians, the justice system. The United States would build an army; the Germans would craft a police force. Funding was scarce, however, and no mechanism existed to coordinate between donor nations. Disputes arose immediately. "There was always the question of where to start," said General David Barno, who commanded the Afghan coalition from 2003 to 2005. "It was the tyranny of the urgent over the important." As in the mujahideen era, when counternarcotics was considered secondary to fighting the Soviets, in post-9/11 Afghanistan the fight against drugs was deprioritized to the hunt for terrorists. "Right now, we realize our work has to take a backseat to the war on terror," a DEA agent told me in 2003.[19] The first counternarcotics policy—implemented by the British—offered cash handouts to poppy farmers if they agreed to grow something else. Not surprisingly, thousands more enterprising farmers planted poppy, just to get their hands on the easy money. The programme was dropped the following year.[20]

As widespread corruption took root in Kabul, a dangerous security vacuum took root in the Pashtun south. Few foreign troops were posted outside Kandahar, and promised reconstruction projects got underway slowly. The Taliban quietly began to regroup. Cautiously, commanders began reaching out to each other, according to sources close to the movement. One by one, Mullah Omar contacted his deputies and appointed them to organize his fighters, pick up fresh recruits from Pakistani madrassas, locate weapons stashes, and raise funds.[21] Drug smugglers close to the Taliban were some of the first investors, putting up small amounts of cash to help the movement start to rebuild, according to local sources along the border and intelligence reports seen by the author.[22]

Some commanders raised money by selling off opium stores. There were reports that Taliban fugitives tapped into Mullah Omar's legendary opium stockpile of 3,800 tons, which DEA informants believed was buried outside Kandahar. Omar's opium stash is like Blackbeard's treasure—no one knows if it really existed. But western and Afghan counternarcotics officials believe the Taliban leaders did maintain stockpiles, which functioned in effect as their federal reserve (there is much evidence such a system still functions today). "After the invasion, we think they parcelled it out in small chunks and sold it to raise money," one U.S. official told me.[23]

The Taliban built their resources methodically and with a steady patience, giving rise to the adage "Americans have the watches, but the Taliban have time." They started out with low-intensity attacks in 2003, using teams on motorcycles to ambush foreign troops and aid workers. Off and on, they set off small bombs.[24] Over time, cross-border attacks from Pakistan became more frequent. When Washington shifted its focus elsewhere, the Taliban surmised the moment was right. In March 2003, just as the United States was invading Iraq, Yusufzai got a call from Mullah Dadullah Lang, the vicious, one-legged military commander. The Taliban had "regrouped," he announced, and would soon launch a jihad to retake Afghanistan.[25]

Three months later, Mullah Omar appointed a new ten-man *shura* to lead the resistance.[26] He named the legendary mujahideen commander Jalaluddin Haqqani, whose base of operations was North Waziristan in Pakistan's tribal areas, to control the southeastern region. Mullah Dadullah would command the south. In time, the Taliban even mended their relationship with their former rival Gulbuddin Hekmatyar, who would lead the eastern flank from the mountainous provinces of Kunar and Nuristan. It was a loosely grouped alliance, with each region more or less responsible for raising its own funds, according to U.S. and Afghan officials. As mujahideen had done during the Soviet resistance, commanders immediately began taxing farmers in their control zones and charging protection fees to smugglers moving all sorts of contraband, not just opium. It wasn't long before the money started flowing.

Mirwais Yasini, who then headed Afghanistan's Counter Narcotics Directorate, estimates the Taliban and its allies took in as much as $100 million in tax revenue in 2003 alone.[27] There were reports that al Qaeda operatives in Peshawar were taking delivery of 4,400 pounds of processed heroin every two months, which they could have sold on the wholesale market for between $38 million and $59 million annually without even exporting it from Pakistan.[28] A 2004 Congressional fact-finding mission to the border region reported that bin Laden was earning up to $24 million annually from a separate Kandahar heroin network.[29]

In late 2003, a separate pair of incidents gave rise to concerns that al Qaeda was closely tied into moving drugs out of the region—the very point in the trade where the profit margins are greatest.[30] First, a British intelligence report in early December mapped out how Pakistani smugglers would hook up with Middle Eastern syndicates on the high seas. Seen by the author, the report said powerful motorboats packed with heroin and hashish set off from Pakistan's southern Gwadar Port, pursuing a course for "210 degrees on a south-westerly heading, and sailing for seven hours at a speed of 12 knots." Using satellite phones, the speedboats would rendezvous with larger dhows in the Arabian Sea, transfer their cargo, and then return to Pakistan. Money would change hands separately using the informal money transfer network known as *hawala*, the intelligence report said. Speedboats carrying drugs also took off from Qasm in southern Iran, the report said, landing in Port Sha'am in the UAE, where Turkish smugglers took the shipments onward.

According to a western official, information gleaned from this intelligence briefing led directly to three seizures by the coalition in the Arabian Sea at the close of 2003. They would provide key evidence of al Qaeda's role in the drug trade. In the first seizure on December 15, a U.S. Navy team from the guided-missile destroyer USS *Decatur* boarded a dhow carrying two tons of hashish worth an estimated $8 to 10 million. Three of the twelve crew members were found to have links to al Qaeda, according to a U.S. Navy statement.

Three days later, a P-3K maritime patrol aircraft from the Royal New Zealand Air Force picked up the two other suspect dhows on the Arabian Sea. Spy planes from Australia, the UK, and the United States tracked the vessels for forty-eight hours. With an RAF Nimrod patrolling overhead, the USS *Philippine Sea* intercepted the two boats late on December 19. A U.S. Navy boarding team found millions of dollars' worth of heroin and amphetamines onboard, and more low-ranking al Qaeda operatives.[31] U.S. officials worried that they were being moved into position in the west, fundraising for the terror network, or maybe both.[32]

When the 2003 seizures took place, western intelligence was already concerned that al Qaeda was using the high seas to move terror cells and materiel. According to *The Washington Post*, American spies identified approximately fifteen cargo freighters around the globe that they believed were controlled by the terror network or simply used by it to ferry operatives, bombs, or money. Osama bin Laden owned boats for years, the report said, some of which transported legal commodities like cement and seeds for his web of companies. At least one vessel had been tied to terrorism: it delivered the explosives used to bomb the U.S. embassies in Kenya and Tanzania in 1998. In the murky world of ocean transport, where records are few and easily faked, U.S. officials never figured out precisely how most of the terrorist freighters were being used, "except that some are generating profits for al Qaeda," the report said.[33]

Through this period, most senior U.S. officials continued to argue that al Qaeda was not systematically involved in drug smuggling, although they would acknowledge that some low-level fighters got involved now and then to earn money. Afghans, especially those who had fought in the anti-Soviet resistance themselves, were clear on the issue from the start. "Everyone is involved," a former commander from Nangarhar told me. "The top guys won't touch the trade themselves—they consider it dirty. But if it's happening in their region, you can be guaranteed top leaders are making a profit."[34] Using drugs themselves might be *haram*, or forbidden, but selling it to the enemy was considered an act of war. "It is an unholy alliance," says Abdul Ghaus Rasoolzai, the head of eastern Afghanistan's anti-narcotics department. "Al Qaeda is using drugs as a weapon against America and other Western countries. The weapon of drugs does not make a noise. The victim does not bleed and leaves no trace of the killer."[35]

Meanwhile authorities watching the remote tri-border region where Pakistan, Afghanistan, and Iran meet up were observing another blurring of commerce and terrorism. In this case it was growing cooperation between people traffickers, drug traders, and terrorists. Coalition spy planes and an increased Iranian troop presence along the border made it harder for drug traffickers to move their product in massive camel convoys, so they got creative. In 2004, Iranian police found heroin hidden in the bellies of nine sheep and goats being led across the desert. In another case, smugglers in Afghanistan painted their vehicle to look like it belonged to a local demining group.[36]

Top officials and authorities from all three countries said migrant workers trying to get to the West were often used as mules to carry narcotics. Pakistani and Afghan counternarcotics teams found individuals carrying heroin sewn into the cuffs and seams of women's dresses, stuffed into hollowed-out high heels, and even glued into walnuts that had been carefully split and resealed.[37]

"We even found heroin sewn into badges honouring Queen Elizabeth," said Major General Khalid Jaffery, the director general of Pakistan's Anti Narcotics Force. "Thank God she doesn't know."[38]

A July 2004 CIA report, seen by the author, described a human and narcotics smuggling operation run by an ethnic Uzbek who ran a network of buses and hotels to illegally shuttle people to the West.[39] By paying large bribes to police in Afghanistan and Iran, the report said, the trafficker was able to move large amounts of heroin to Turkey. The report said "many [carriers] were illegal immigrants trying to get work in [the] Persian Gulf." It was also known that the trafficker employed terrorists from the Islamic Movement of Uzbekistan (IMU), an al Qaeda-linked group, to ferry heroin. Key to his operation's success, the report said, was the trafficker's ability to "provide photo substituted passports from Pakistan, Afghanistan, Iran and Turkey."

Local officials and western diplomats said there was a sudden flood of reports of this type in 2003–2004, indicating people smugglers, drug traffickers, and terrorists were at least using the same routes and modes of transport, if not always working together actively. "Investigators believe if we could wrap up the people smugglers, we would go a long way toward solving this whole thing," said one western envoy.[40] But U.S. military intelligence and CIA agents who were focused on hunting down terrorists still tried to maintain a separation between the insurgents and the criminals. "I always told them, 'If we pursue these avenues together, you will turn up some of the guys you are looking for,'" a U.S. counternarcotics official posted to the region told me. "I used to have shouting matches about this with the agency guys."[41]

Various U.S. officials told me the U.S. military and the CIA resisted doing "finished analysis" on the raw intelligence, which would have required them to take a stand on the nature of the drug trade. "It allows them deniability," said one official. As in the era of the Soviet resistance, fighting drugs might have distracted from the main task at hand, officials said. "There wasn't an intelligence failure," said a former senior CIA official who resigned in disgust. "It was a failure to analyze the evidence we had."[42]

The U.S. military resisted getting involved in interdiction; however, Britain, the lead nation on counternarcotics in the Bonn Agreement, began developing a top-secret strike team. Known as Task Force 333, it would attack labs processing opium into crystal heroin, the high-end product smuggled to the West.[43] Elite Afghan units were trained and mentored by commandos from Britain's Special Air Service (SAS) regiment, according to a western official. A covert programme, dubbed Operation Headstrong, was launched on January 2, 2004, with a raid on a heroin lab in northern Badakhshan.[44] By mid-2004, Force 333 had two operational units of 150 men each. "It was basically a drop 'em in and shoot it up operation," said a western official who assisted in the operations.[45] One former Force 333 commander said that whenever the group hit a lab in the south, they were guaranteed to get attacked. "One time we went to raid a big lab in the Deshu district of Baramcha," a major centre for heroin production in southern Helmand, he said. "Within twenty minutes there was a massive ambush. Bullets were flying everywhere." The lab owner had called the local Taliban subcommander to come to his rescue. The attack was so vicious the commander had to call in U.S. air support to suppress it.[46]

For years after the 2001 invasion, many U.S. officials, and especially those within the military, acknowledged that the Taliban was collecting taxes on drugs and "taking a cut" of narcotics moving through or processed in their region. But it was generally defined as a passive type of involvement typical to Afghanistan, where every local power broker takes a cut of what passes through his control zone. The ambush on Force 333 in Baramcha was one of the first incidents counternarcotics agents could point to indicating the Taliban was more deeply involved in the opium trade than previously acknowledged. "There's a big difference between getting a cut of the action and getting payment for services performed," said a western official.

In the spring of 2004, DEA agents in Kabul set up a sting operation: a Taliban commander was contracted to buy morphine base in Afghanistan and sell it down the line to DEA informants. "When that worked, we could prove that they were tied into the transport and delivery end of things," said an official close to the case. By 2004, the Taliban and the drug dealers were operating "like brother and sister" across southern Afghanistan, according to the Force 333 commander.

Taliban teams attacked security checkpoints so drug convoys could get past or in some cases launched diversionary strikes to draw western troops away from a major consignment passing through. The Taliban escorted illicit consignments themselves, earning millions of dollars a year in protection fees—often as much as 20 percent a consignment. This transformation in battlefield tactics—from trying to make tactical gains to protecting drug shipments—mirrored similar patterns set by the FARC and other insurgent groups. The Taliban were no longer fighting for Allah, but for the almighty dollar.

Insurgents collaborated with traffickers about farm output as well, distributing "night letters" offering protection to farmers who grew poppy and threatening dire consequences for anyone who didn't. "The one who is not cultivating poppy in their lands and accepting the governor order for destroying their poppy cultivations will be killed by Taliban," said one message with typically poor syntax pinned to a mosque door.[47] Locals said the Taliban do not manage the opium trade themselves, but support poppy cultivation on behalf of drug smugglers, who pay them in the form of four-by-fours and weapons.[48] Major traffickers have launched even more grandiose schemes, with the Taliban's protection. Spy satellites recently captured images of massive irrigation projects underway in the windswept deserts of southern Helmand. "They are trying to create more farmland so they can grow more poppy," said a senior western official.[49]

District-level field commanders use personal contacts to develop information about people in their area, paying as much as $10 a tip to informants, according to local sources. They work over the local community like mafia henchmen, even using the old "good cop, bad cop" routine. In one typical exchange, Haji Bado Khan, a landowner in Kajaki district in northern Helmand, described how a local Taliban field commander, Haji Khan Gul, wanted to start billing him $3,000 a season. Gul showed up late one night at Khan's house with a clutch of armed men. "We know you have been earning a lot of money these days. We hear you're growing your own poppy and buying it from others to trade," Gul said. "You will have to start sharing some regular money with the mujahideen." Being from the same district, the two men had known each other most of their lives. Gul told him, "I am here as your friend, but if you fail to pay this, I'll have to report you to my commander. No matter what I say, I know he will get someone to come after you." Khan bargained the rate down to $1,500, and paid it in the form of two motorcycles.[50]

Gul charges a 5 percent tax on everything moving through his control zone and has skirmished over taxing rights with commanders in neighbouring districts, locals say. Insurgents like Gul routinely seek room and board as they move through the region. One farmer in Sangin district reported having to feed a group of thirty Taliban fighters twice a week. "They came with guns one night and told me to be ready for them," the farmer said. "Sometimes a government official comes by in the daytime and asks me, 'Why are you doing this?'" he said. "Once, I said to the guy, 'You think I want this? If you would just come out here and stay for two hours a day, I won't have to feed them anymore.'"[51]

Under Taliban protection, and in some areas protected by corrupt officials, traffickers sent out armies of poppy merchants, who pre-purchase crops at planting time for prices below what farmers could fetch at harvest. The salaam system provides money poor sharecroppers and small farmers need to buy food for their families throughout the winter, but it's designed to trap them in debt come harvest time. Many get caught in a vicious cycle of owing more and more every year, and appalling tales of farmers selling off their daughters to settle their arrears are on the rise again.[52] The Taliban provide security for farmers, building defensive positions around poppy fields, or planting mines and IEDs ahead of visits by ERAD, the poppy eradication force.[53]

When Afghan villagers are not coerced to support the Taliban, a complex blend of motives appears to inform the villagers' decisions to engage their protection or even take up arms and join them. The

Toronto *Globe and Mail* conducted a video survey of forty-two Taliban foot soldiers in Kandahar in 2007, finding the overwhelming majority were poppy farmers. About half said their poppy fields had been targeted by government-led anti-drug teams, a striking statistic in a province where just 8 percent of the entire poppy crop was eradicated in 2007.[54] "It's a bit of a chicken-and-egg thing," said *Globe* correspondent Graeme Smith in the multimedia report. "Do they join the Taliban because their fields get targeted or do their fields get targeted because they are Taliban?"

This is a crucial question. Some analysts studying Afghanistan's poppy trade believe iniquitous eradication policies benefit rich landowners and tribal federations close to the provincial and federal power structures, dividing communities across the southern poppy belt and driving many poor farmers to join the Taliban.[55] Put simply, tribes allied with the Karzai administration tend to suffer less eradication; rival tribes often get pushed into the arms of the insurgents. "The farmers have never benefited from poppy cultivation," said Haji Mahuddin Khan, a tribal leader in Helmand. "The profits are taken by those [officials] who tell farmers to engage in cultivation but then threaten their crops with eradication. The international mafia is the main benefactor, while we are being held responsible for it and portrayed as criminals."[56]

The number of fighters interviewed in the *Globe and Mail* project is small, but the uncanny similarity of their responses also supports the theory that Taliban leaders—and perhaps their financial backers—play a powerful role in indoctrinating low-level foot soldiers on a number of issues, including poppy cultivation. Almost one-fifth of the respondents said they grew poppy because their mullahs ordered them to, and sixteen said they hoped to make

iban away on their own. The deal fell apart in February 2007, and Taliban swarmed back into Musa Qala, establishing a district government with a governor, police chief, and sharia courts.

Local journalists from the Institute for War and Peace Reporting (IWPR) were invited into Musa Qala to report on life under the Taliban in November 2007.[59] They found schools and hospitals shuttered. Taliban fighters patrolled the streets by the hundreds, driving through town on stolen police trucks, extorting money for the insurgency. One report described a bustling drugs bazaar where buyers piled sacks of opium into trucks.[60] Little of the drug money seemed to benefit ordinary villagers, for whom basic necessities were scarce. One IWPR reporter found as many as 75 percent of the town's residents had fled, and the only shopkeeper still operating reported that business was down by 80 percent.

"The only people left are those who couldn't afford to go. We are in a very bad economic situation," said Haji Nazar Mohammad, a town elder.[61] The reporter, Aziz Ahmad Shafe, said he was followed by an armed guard and believed many people he interviewed were fearful of speaking against the Taliban. Some residents praised them for bringing security, saying corrupt officials from the Kabul administration had performed no better. "If the government wanted to help, why didn't they do anything before the Taliban came?" said Amruddin Kaka, an elderly resident.[62]

When Afghan and international troops retook Musa Qala in December 2007, they found the Taliban had hanged alleged spies in the town square and overseen heroin production at more than fifty heroin labs. The number of labs in operation had expanded while the insurgents were in control, with some employing as many as sixty men. Fariq Khan, a Musa Qala resident who owns a telephone shop, said Taliban collected about $8 from each family every month at the mosque. Trucks passing through paid $50 each and poppy farmers had to turn over 10 percent of their profits, Khan said.[63]

Since the 10 percent opium tithe is routinely collected in kind, Taliban commanders are known to maintain stockpiles where they can deposit and later withdraw quantities of poppy as if using an ATM. In December 2007, when NATO forces retook Musa Qala, they found eleven tons of opium stored in warehouses there.[64]

Repeated, heavy bombardments have flattened homes and businesses in Musa Qala and elsewhere, killed scores of civilians, and hardened people against NATO as well. The high number of civilian casualties will make it much harder for the coalition and the Afghan government to win the hearts and minds of Helmand's people, who spoke of repeated failed promises to deliver aid and development. "I heard the government on the radio saying they'd help us," villager Gul Mohammed told IWPR. "But we don't want their help. We are not going to forget our dead just because they give us a plate of food."[65]

Despite the dangers, the spring harvest in Helmand, Kandahar, and Farah provinces has become so busy and lucrative that migrant workers now come from as far away as Nangarhar Province, Iran, and Pakistan, according to locals and U.S. intelligence documents. Farmer workers can earn as much as a thousand rupees (sixteen dollars) a day, a massive sum for labourers here, and one recent harvest even caused farm labour shortages around Quetta, according to a U.S. intelligence report seen by the author. And just as European authorities have found al Qaeda cells moving drugs to raise cash, foreign fighters in Afghanistan have been captured while moonlighting as farm hands in the poppy fields.[66]

Taliban involvement in the opium trade expanded further by 2007, with major commanders running their own mobile labs. The number of sites turning opium into heroin has climbed from thirty to fifty, many of them operating off the backs of souped-up pickups hurtling across the rocky terrain along the Pakistan border.[67] Commanders have expanded their protection racket into the business realm, charging shop owners and national enterprises for the right to operate safely. When the provincial director of one mobile phone network refused to pay his monthly "tax" in Zabul Province, Taliban fighters blew up three distribution towers in the Shahjoy district, cutting service for a week.[68] Shopkeepers get hit up as well, to the tune of 10 percent of their earnings. The highest fees are extorted on highways, where truckers can expect to get charged by both the Taliban and the notoriously corrupt Highway Police. "Paying both off is the only way to get my trucks through," complained Mohammed Gulab Achakzai, a trader from Kandahar's volatile Panjwayi district.[69]

Many smugglers own cash businesses like money exchange shops, gas stations, import-export firms, and hotels, which also allow them to launder drug money, western officials say. A December 2003 U.S. intelligence report, seen by the author, describes a smuggler named Mohammed Razzaq, once deputy director of Afghanistan's national bank under the Taliban, who "uses profits from the sale of narcotics to provide material support to the Taliban and al Qaeda." Close to the late Mullah Dadullah, Razzaq allegedly ran money exchange shops in Jalalabad, Kandahar, and

Peshawar, the intelligence report said, where Taliban commanders could bring chits to withdraw cash much like a Citibank customer would cash a check.

In a war zone where there's little to buy with hard currency, many Taliban field commanders simply barter their services for commodities like food, fuel, weapons, or motorcycles. Qais Azimy, an al Jazeera journalist who travelled with a group of Taliban fighters in Helmand in 2007, asked them where they got the Toyota Corolla they travelled in. "They said a smuggler gave us this car. And everything we have is based on opium."[70] Often, commanders will demand "top-up" cards that provide prepaid air time on Afghan mobile phones or the Thuraya satellite network, according to local smugglers and Afghan officials. Major traffickers are often contracted to provide a certain number of four-by-fours and Toyota Hilux pickup trucks a year. A few have built Islamic madrassas in neighbouring Pakistan where recruits can be trained or hotels where Taliban fighters can escape for R&R. Major traffickers are asked to pay medical expenses for Taliban injured on the battlefield, and at least one smuggler runs a health clinic in Quetta, reportedly filled up at any given time by wounded fighters.[71]

From the fields of Helmand to the *hawala* stands of Dubai, elaborate mechanisms filter drug money through the Taliban hierarchy, according to dozens of interviews with smugglers, fighters, and Afghan officials. On the district level, each farmer will receive a handwritten receipt for 10 percent tax paid to the local Taliban subcommander. There's no risk of being charged more than once, farmers say, since the Taliban hierarchy is strict when it comes to assigning regions of influence. In several cases farmers have complained to the Taliban hierarchy of being charged twice by rival commanders, and the Taliban leadership responded by punishing the commanders. Each district commander has to kick a percentage of the taxes he collects up to his regional commander; then it goes to the provincial commander, and so on up the food chain.

One thing everyone interviewed agreed on: it's hard to cheat the system. "They are very organized," says an Afghan intelligence official who tracks the drug trade in the south. "Each commander has his own financial representative—the guy who looks after the money side of things. He will have to come to Quetta and deal with the Taliban's finance committee."[72] Money can travel in both directions. Subcommanders from poppy-rich areas might have to pay into the central coffers, while others in strategic regions with less earning potential might collect a monthly stipend for operational expenses. NATO officials estimate the Taliban now pay contract soldiers as much as $150 a month—a solid wage in a country where the average annual income is less than $500 and a local policeman takes home just $60 a month.[73]

Major drug dealers—those who own refineries and traffic in tons of narcotics—pay directly to the top Taliban leaders, often to the tune of millions of dollars, according to contacts on both sides of the border. Sources close to the Taliban say the senior leadership still depends on donations as much as they do on opium cash. "The top guys are not as reliant on drug money for their day-to-day expenses as the commanders out on the battlefield," says an Afghan intelligence official. "They still get donations from rich Arabs in the Gulf and from Pakistan."[74] The poppy may be grown in Afghanistan and processed along the border into opium base or heroin, but the command and control centre, as with the insurgency itself, is in Pakistan, off-limits to NATO troops and law enforcement advisers working with the Kabul government. "The problem is that even if we work hard to stop this in Afghanistan, the money will still move through Quetta, and we can't get to it," an exasperated U.S. official told me in 2007.

Small, nondescript guesthouses in Quetta and Peshawar are routinely used as temporary centres for massive, drug-related financial transactions, which take place roughly every four to six weeks, according to multiple sources on both sides of the border. In some cases, fighters will come for R&R, and during that time they will collect funding and instructions for the next battle. Commanders will also send their financial emissaries to meet the powerful financial committee, which has the power to decide how funds are spent. The committee has tremendous influence over which subcommanders rise or drop in the rankings since fighters will win appointments to more lucrative postings according to their fundraising ability.

"There has always been a healthy competition between the commanders in this regard," observed Rahimullah Yusufzai. As happened during the internecine battles of the Soviet resistance, that "healthy competition" sometimes erupts into violence. In one incident in September 2007, state-run Afghan Television reported that eight people died in Kapisa Province when fighting broke out between two Taliban commanders over who had the right to collect tax in a given district.

There are tantalizing reports indicating that rivalries for cash pervade even the highest echelons of the Taliban movement. The former defence minister Mullah Obaidullah reportedly worked closely with senior smugglers to export drugs and import weapons. He was responsible for coordinating with commanders along smuggling routes, organizing protection for drug shipments, and negotiating payments in money, weapons, and vehicles. Obaidullah allegedly clashed with Dadullah after Dadullah tried to muscle in on profits and resources in the poppy-rich south.[75]

Dadullah, a fiercely independent commander, also ran afoul of Mullah Omar from time to time and struggled for power with the late Mullah Akhtar Osmani. Osmani's patch was Baramcha, the Helmand border town that's a centre for heroin production, where he collected money and other resources for the Taliban. After his death in a December 2006 air strike, there were rumours among insurgent ranks that Mullah Dadullah had passed information about Osmani's whereabouts to NATO authorities in order to wrest control of the lucrative Baramcha market.[76] When Dadullah died in a firefight in Baramcha the following year, there were reports that Obaidullah had tipped off NATO troops to Dadullah's whereabouts. Mistrust among high-level Taliban officials, and internal competition over drug spoils, could provide opportunities for intelligence and law enforcement agents to play Taliban rivals off against one another and weaken the core movement.

The financial system works in much the same way across the other two fronts of the Afghan insurgency: the east and the southeast. In these zones there's clearer evidence that the top commanders—Gulbuddin Hekmatyar and Jalaluddin Haqqani, respectively—work closely with foreign jihadis linked to al Qaeda to move heroin out of the region. Hekmatyar runs a sophisticated network known as the HIG (Hizb-i-Islami Gulbuddin), controlling border areas in Afghanistan's mountainous Kunar and Nuristan provinces.[77] Since the fall of the Taliban regime, this region has been the scene of some of the toughest battles for U.S. troops, including the June 2005 downing of a Chinook MH-47 helicopter that led to the heaviest single-day losses ever for the Navy Seals.

HIG commanders are known to work closely with Arab al Qaeda operatives, according to western and local military officials. Counterterrorism officials believe the number two person in al Qaeda, Ayman al-Zawahiri, and possibly bin Laden himself are hiding out between Kunar, Nuristan, and the Bajaur and Dir districts of Pakistan's tribal area across the border. HIG commanders operate massive schemes to smuggle timber, gemstones, and heroin out of the area, according to local residents and Afghan and western officials. A 2004 U.S. intelligence document seen by the author concluded that commanders from the eastern flank would "cooperate or assist any group that paid them." Western counternarcotics and military officials say the HIG keeps about 50 percent of the funds it earns from heroin smuggling and funnels the other half to allies in the Chechen conflict. "The HIG is a full-fledged narco-terror organization," one senior western counternarcotics official told me.[78]

The southeastern flank, run by the Haqqani group, is also heavily tied to smuggling, moving weapons, ammunition, and opium for the insurgency, according to western, Afghan, and Pakistani officials.[79] Counterterrorism officials describe the aging Jalaluddin Haqqani, who runs a large madrassa in North Waziristan, as a key facilitator between the Taliban, al Qaeda, and the tribal chiefs along the border. "Haqqani has been smuggling weapons—massive amounts of weapons—since the days of the jihad," says a Pakistani official, adding that his network has also long been tied to moving opium grown in Pakistan's tribal areas and across the border in Afghanistan.

His North Waziristan base of operations is considered a major clearinghouse and planning centre both for fighters moving in and out of the region and for illicit goods—one western intelligence official described it to me as the "cesspit of humanity." Before his death, Mullah Dadullah was known to visit the madrassa regularly for purposes of coordination, and the HIG posted a senior commander, Haji Abdul Ghafour, to Wana, in neighbouring South Waziristan, for similar purposes, according to U.S. intelligence and military intelligence documents seen by the author.

The Haqqani group also operates a series of camps in the border districts of Paktia Province—including Jaji and neighbouring Dand Wa Patan, which locals describe as a central station for moving contraband. Local sources and Afghan officials say heroin gets smuggled down from HIG-controlled areas in the east and from labs in Nangarhar, using centuries-old mountain trails long travelled by traffickers and mujahideen. Haqqani's network protects local smugglers—many of whom are from Haqqani's own Zadran tribe—who move the drugs across the porous border into the Waziristan agencies. From there, Pakistani smugglers pick up the consignments for the onward journey.

Smaller loads tend to travel out of Pakistan on flights to the Persian Gulf from the nearby Peshawar Airport. Larger consignments snake west through the tribal areas to Baluchistan, where they are picked up by new couriers and ferried onward to Iran. Local sources, including police, district officials, and intelligence agents, say Jalaluddin and his son Sirajuddin don't involve themselves personally in moving drugs, but play key roles coordinating the protection racket and take a cut of the action.[80]

Jalaluddin himself is known to move back and forth between the tribal areas and the Gulf, maintaining a residence in Dubai, where he has sought medical attention in the past few years, according to Afghan officials. Western intelligence agencies believe he has close ties to Arab smugglers who move opiates to the West. A March 2004 intelligence assessment on his operations, seen by the author, concluded: "The money received from the Arabs who buy the drugs is an important source of funds for the Taliban." Informants to western counternarcotics agencies have reported that al Qaeda operatives routinely "freelance" by moving drug shipments to the Gulf—usually carrying small quantities of just a few kilograms. "You get these drug dealers in private and they think the al Qaeda guys are certifiably insane," said one western official who had interviewed informants. "But when they talk it's like listening to someone from the mafia, 'bidniss is bidniss.' "[81]

The insurgent group with the deepest reach in the drug trade is unquestionably the Islamic Movement of Uzbekistan (IMU). With a network of fighters extending from South Waziristan up through the former Soviet republics, the IMU was cultivated by bin Laden in the 1990s to develop roots in Central Asia. He may have recognized the group's earning potential: Interpol and the DEA report that the IMU controls as much as 70 percent of the multibillion-dollar heroin and opium trade through Central Asia.[82] The group was founded in the late 1990s by the radical mullah Tahir Yuldeshev and Juma Namangani, a former Soviet paratrooper in Afghanistan who defected to the mujahideen.

The pair originally set out to establish an Islamic state in Uzbekistan, an ambition they later widened to creating a Central Asian caliphate. "The IMU was deeply involved in drug smuggling from its inception in the Tajik mountains," says Ahmed Rashid, author of *Jihad*, a book probing extremism in Central Asia. "Since then they have helped expand al Qaeda and Taliban drug smuggling to Central Asia and on to Russia."[83]

Founded in the Fergana Valley, the heartland of Central Asia where Uzbekistan, Tajikistan, and Kyrgyzstan converge, the IMU moved its base to Afghanistan during the Taliban regime. Mullah Omar allowed Uzbek fighters to launch attacks over the border into Central Asia, and the battle-hardened IMU fighters assisted the Taliban in their fight against the Northern Alliance. During those years, Yuldeshev established close links to bin Laden and Mullah Omar and Pakistan's leading spy agency, the ISI, according to Rashid.

The IMU fighters, many of whom had participated in the anti-Soviet jihad, became partners with the Taliban in moving Afghan heroin through Central Asia to the West. Yuldeshev himself grew close to Mullah Dadullah, who then commanded the Taliban's northern region. Together, they developed smuggling routes up through Turkmenistan, buying off a network of corrupt officials. They also moved refined heroin and morphine base from Kunduz Province over the Amu Darya River into Tajikistan.[84] Many IMU incursions into other parts of Central Asia were considered diversionary attacks to allow heroin shipments to move through.

As opium output soared under the Taliban, Namangani and Yuldeshev made various trips to Kandahar to brainstorm with bin Laden and Mullah Omar, Rashid reports in *Jihad*. By the time the Taliban banned poppy cultivation in 2000, the IMU kept a stockpile in northern Afghanistan of more than 240 tons, according to UNODC estimates.[85] That same year, the U.S. government put the IMU on its list of designated terrorist groups after receiving intelligence that its operatives were providing information to al Qaeda about the movements of U.S. diplomats stationed in Central Asia.[86]

After the U.S.-led invasion of Afghanistan, IMU fighters fled over the border and reassembled in South Waziristan, in Pakistan's tribal belt. Counterterrorist officials believe Uzbeks served as bin Laden's outer security perimeter while he was hiding out in South Waziristan, where he was believed to have fled after escaping the siege at Tora Bora.[87] Their fighters are known for never being short on funds, and for carefully paying local villagers for any supplies they use—often in U.S. dollars, according to tribal contacts. The Pakistan military has tried unsuccessfully on several occasions to root the IMU out of the area, most recently in April 2007, when local tribesmen also turned on the Uzbeks, in part because of their rampant illegal activity. At one point, Mullah Dadullah reportedly invited his old friend Yuldeshev to relocate to Helmand Province if he found South Waziristan inhospitable.[88]

The IMU's drug money and their ties with local smugglers have proved essential to their staying power, according to western diplomats and local sources. "Tahir Yuldeshev is encouraging his men to mint money in any way they can," says a Waziristan tribal elder. Locals in the troubled district say Uzbeks organize courier services, moving drug shipments through the tribal areas to Iran and also up through Afghanistan to Central Asia. One U.S. intelligence report seen by the author described a smuggling route snaking up through Afghanistan's northwest provinces of Baghdis, Faryab, and Jowzjan and into Turkmenistan. It was being used as of mid-2004 by "extremists associated with the Taliban, the Islamic

Movement of Uzbekistan and al Qaeda," the report said. Traffickers would move "both heroin and extremists" along the route and "then onwards into other countries in Central Asia," the CIA document said.

Another intelligence report shown to the author discussed cooperation between the IMU and its former comrades in the United Tajik Opposition (the two fought side by side in the 1992–1997 Tajik Civil War) to move people and drugs into Central Asia. It said that Yuldeshev and Dadullah organized a heroin shipment in June 2004 with a UTO field commander named Makhmadrusal Salomov. "They had worked together in Taliban times," the report said. "The IMU operatives acted as couriers for an estimated 300 kilos of heroin, nearly all of which was given to Salomov," the report continued. "Salomov then provided the IMU operatives with a percentage of the cash from the sale of the heroin. This money was used to fund IMU activities in Afghanistan and Tajikistan." The report said the operatives coordinated with corrupt officials in the Afghan police and army, along with forces loyal to Uzbek warlord Rashid Dostum, to move their shipment through the region.

It may seem contradictory that terrorists are working with the very police and army they are simultaneously fighting—not to mention in cahoots with Dostum, a northern warlord who is notoriously anti-Taliban. But it's a pattern repeated over and over. Across Afghanistan, traditional enemies are working together wherever there's a chance to make money. And instability is vital for the drug business, creating a powerful disincentive for Afghan government officials to build a more peaceful country. The Taliban and their allies may be earning hundreds of millions from the drug trade, but one thing almost everyone interviewed for this project agreed on was that crooked members of Hamid Karzai's administration are earning even more.

Brief descriptions of some of the midlevel drug dealers and fighters, compiled from dozens of interviews with security officials, tribal sources, and villagers, illustrate the seemingly erratic nature of the trade. Like consumers shopping on the Internet, growers, smugglers, government officials, and insurgents alike can tap into various links—sometimes repeatedly, sometimes just for a one-time transaction:

- Haji Mullah is allegedly a major trafficker based in the Nawa-I-Barakzayi district of Helmand, bringing opium for his labs from as far away as Badakhshan and Takhar provinces in Afghanistan's northeast, paying off the Highway Police to move his drugs across the country. He also reportedly doles out protection money to the Taliban, using *hawala* shops he runs in Quetta's Pakhtunabad neighbourhood. Until a crackdown by Pakistani authorities, he also ran a hotel on one of Quetta's main streets where Taliban could come and stay for weeks. "When the Taliban need a major cash infusion, they go to him," says an Afghan official. Haji Mullah is also reported to have ties to Baluch smugglers in Iran who move his product as far as Turkey.

- Haji Mohammad Ali Baloch in southwestern Nimroz Province is alleged to move opium base across the border into Iran and covers his illegal business by importing used Toyota Land Cruisers. He's also reported to be involved in the kidnapping of foreign nationals, but stays out of trouble since he pays off provincial officials and the police. He was close to the late Mullah Dadullah and distributes cash to the Taliban using a Kandahari money changer.

- Commander Mullah Mohammad, a local thug who works for the Taliban in the village of Nawa-I-Barakzayi, runs a team of about twenty men, "mostly just thieves and bad guys," says a local. "They lay mines, attack Afghan security forces, and have been involved in beheading people who help the Kabul government." He's buddies with the district police chief, say provincial officials and locals, and and the two men colluded to move drugs through the village.

- Mullah Sharif Anis is a small-time crook in the volatile Andar district of southeastern Ghazni Province who has hooked up with the Taliban more or less on a freelance basis. Locals say he'll launch attacks for the Taliban on a contract basis, but allegedly his real joy in life comes from abducting and sexually abusing young boys. It's said he keeps a handsome eighteen-year-old named Ahmed as his constant companion. "Recently, he raided a house, took all the jewellery, raped the women, and then forced the family to provide food for his men," says a local official.[89]

The ability and willingness to contract thugs-for-hire like Mohammad and Sharif allowed the Taliban to swell in strength to the point that insurgent forces were staging attacks just outside the capital Kabul by late 2007.[90] Many among this new breed are not the same ideological warriors as before. "They have become so completely aligned with the drug traders, you can't even tell the difference," said Karen Tandy, the former DEA chief.[91]

"We have their communiqués. We have intercepts," said an Afghan security official. "What you realize is that most of these guys are not ideological. They are just paid off."[92]

One report on drug-related corruption within the Karzai administration, compiled by the UN and described to the author, mapped out a complex system of kickbacks—very similar to the one existing inside the Taliban. UN researchers identified thirty-six districts across Afghanistan—located either in poppy-producing areas or along smuggling routes—where governorships, customs, and police postings are the most sought after. The report estimated officials who won plum assignments stood to earn hundreds of thousands of dollars a month in dirty money. One indicator: the huge sums they would have to kick upstairs just to hold on to their jobs. According to one researcher who contributed to the report, top police officials in lucrative districts might have to pay as much as $40,000 a month for job security.[93]

The UN researchers who conducted this study concluded that the man at the top of the organizational chain was Ahmed Wali Karzai, the half brother of the president. He's been implicated in multiple U.S. intelligence reports seen by the author as having ties to the drug trade, and western diplomats say NATO has intercepted him reportedly making deals on the telephone.[94] As with other senior officials and insurgent commanders who profit from drugs, "you won't see Ahmed Wali actually touching the trade," says a UN official who worked on the report. "He has influence over who gets what position—and that gives him extraordinary power." The president's sibling has stoutly denied his ties to the drug trade repeatedly in the media. In private, he is less coy. A European envoy who dined with Ahmed Wali at the splendid Kandahar mansion he calls home once asked him, "Where did the money come for this incredible house?" Ahmed Wali smiled and said, "Everything you see here was paid for with drugs."[95]

Corrupt officials and Taliban don't negotiate face to face over drug smuggling. Rather, smugglers act as go-betweens, working out how to move illicit consignments through specific areas. Sadoo Agha, a poppy farmer in Gereshk, said the local Taliban commander there—who has a force of about twenty full-time fighters—works in partnership with a local smuggler to buy all the opium that the farmers there grow. "The Taliban commander has the firepower and the drug dealer has the money," Agha says. They pay off local officials in the district to move the consignments out. "The opium gets transported in police vehicles, or other times I have seen them take opium away in convoys with thirty or more armed men," he said. "You can see that the government officials have secured the route for them, and next week the local police will have new clothes or motorcycles."[96]

Some police officials even cooked up a way to earn money when they have completely lost control of a district they were assigned to protect. "Sometimes, they'll just 'sell' districts to Taliban," complains a senior interior ministry official in Kabul. "They'll tell us that they lost control of the area because they are outgunned, but it will be a case of where there aren't more than ten Taliban in their region, and we have posted a hundred police to that district. We all know the game."[97] The situation is most acute at the frontier. "Along the border, there's an evil mix of government officials, district commissioners, and police chiefs who work with the Taliban," says General Kamal Sadat, Afghanistan's former counternarcotics police chief. "The government officials mostly just take bribes. It's the Taliban and the smugglers who actually move the drugs out."[98]

The corruption doesn't stop at Afghanistan's borders. Iran, which battles one of the world's highest opium addiction rates, has made concerted efforts to stop Afghan opium from entering its territory, spending more than $400 million a year to fight the problem. It has erected massive ramparts along the border to block smugglers, and lost some 3,400 soldiers and police in battles with drug convoys over the past five years.[99]

However, Iran, like Afghanistan and Pakistan, battles a corruption problem. Multiple sources and western intelligence cables seen by the author report corrupt Iranian intelligence agents are helping to move drug shipments in their vehicles, which have special plates and don't get searched by Iran's anti-drug police. Sources along the border identified a handful of major traffickers, mainly ethnic Baluch, who cooperate with Iranian secret agents to coordinate Taliban attacks on NATO troops.

This would suggest that the problem is more than just an issue of corruption, but rather a covert effort within Iran's wider strategy to disrupt NATO—and specifically U.S.—activities in Afghanistan. This phenomenon was linked to U.S. defence secretary Robert Gates's June 2007 accusation that Iran is supplying weapons to the Afghan insurgency, including plastic explosives being used in deadly IED attacks.

Ever since the 9/11 attacks, when President Pervez Musharraf was forced to choose between allying himself with George Bush or

Mullah Omar, there have been questions over whether Pakistan really abandoned its support for the Taliban. Nowhere is this murky issue more troubling than as it relates to the drug trade. To some extent, as in Iran, it's just an issue of corruption. Western officials and people who work in the drug trade alike identify dirty officials within the police, intelligence agencies, military, customs, and the Anti Narcotics Force. Most say levels of drug-related corruption within the Pakistan military and ISI are nowhere near as bad as they were in the days of the Soviet resistance, but there is still a massive graft issue. Pakistan arrests an immense number of people on drug-related offences—more than 34,000 in 2006 alone, for example. The vast majority of them are low-level drug users—young men caught with a couple of joints in their pocket.

Similar to Pakistan's reticence to go after the Taliban, it's rare to hear of high-level drug traffickers getting apprehended. "Not arresting them is a passive form of assistance," says a western diplomat.[100] Many believe cooperation goes much deeper. "Every time I hear that Pakistani authorities have made a one-ton seizure, I assume there are ten tons moving down another highway," says a European counternarcotics official.[101]

As in Iran, elements of Pakistan's ISI help protect the drug trade, according to multiple smugglers who were able to identify specific agents in specific regions, and even knew the sums of money they had been paid. It was never clear if these represented cases of individuals freelancing for profit or evidence of a covert state policy. Former president Pervez Musharraf has admitted "retired" Pakistani secret agents may be supporting the insurgents, and some western officials believe these "retirees" coordinate the drug trade to keep the Taliban and other local jihadi groups funded.

With billions of dollars of drugs moving through Pakistani territory, "it's impossible to imagine that's not happening," says a western official.[102]

A senior Pakistani customs official, interviewed in Quetta, compared the scale of corruption in the western province of Baluchistan to that in neighbouring Afghanistan. "The vast majority of provincial officials are corrupted by the drugs industry," he said. "This is the condition of our state."[103] He said smugglers connected to the highest level of the Pakistani government used armoured vehicles, protected by well-armed guard units, and often wore actual police uniforms they obtained from corrupt officers. "Whenever we arrest someone or seize a drug consignment the traders band together and block the roads," he complained. "Before long, senior authorities order us to let them go free."

This corruption directly costs the lives of NATO troops in Afghanistan, where U.S. soldiers make up the biggest contingent by far. Foreign soldiers working with the Afghan National Army have fought bloody campaigns to clear insurgents out of various strategic regions, like the Panjwayi and Zhari districts of southwest Kandahar, only to have the Taliban regain control of the area when the troops pull out and leave the region to the inept, ill-equipped, and corrupt police.[104]

The strategy is "clear, hold, and build," says Seth Jones, a Rand Corporation analyst. "The problem has been that when you move the troops on into neighbouring districts, you don't have enough to hold what you just cleared."[105] For that reason, a fourth rotation of Canadian troops in 2007 was battling the same ground in Panjwayi that their predecessors had fought and died for in the three years prior. "We essentially have to start from scratch," said Brigadier-

General Guy Laroche, commander of the Joint Task Force Afghanistan until May 2008. "Everything we have done in that regard is not a waste of time, but close to it, I would say."[106]

The level of violence in daily life is spiralling for ordinary Afghans as well, especially those living in areas controlled by the insurgents. Mullah Omar's Taliban were hardly a lovable crowd to start out with: while in power, they were condemned the world over for stoning women in public and lashing men who trimmed their beards. But for all their medieval behaviour, the turbaned force at least brought security to the war-torn Afghan countryside, and for that they were appreciated, at least in some rural areas.

The drug-fuelled new Taliban bring an increased level of brutality—a viciousness seeming far more senseless to many who live under it. "I don't think anyone likes the Taliban anymore," says Shaystah Gul Khan, a farmer from Gereshk district. "The doctors and teachers have fled. They have closed the schools and put mines on the roads. We haven't seen anything but the destruction of our village and our life."[107] Before 2005, suicide attacks were unheard of in Afghanistan and rare in Pakistan. By 2007, they were occurring routinely in both countries.[108] A high-profile attack in Rawalpindi/Islamabad took the life of the former prime minister Benazir Bhutto as she campaigned for general elections on a pledge to stamp out Islamic extremism. Both countries have experienced a bloody campaign to bomb girls' schools in their border areas, while music and video shops have been blown up and barbers get attacked if they trim beards.

The Taliban, which used to ban TV entirely, began releasing videos. In January 2006, we got a first taste of the order of the day with a gruesome film shot in Miramshah, the capital of Pakistan's troubled North Waziristan. The film paid tribute to Pakistani Taliban who had captured and killed a gang of bandits that had been robbing locals at highway checkpoints. The grainy video showed bandits hanged from lampposts in the town square, and their bodies later dragged through the street behind a truck.

In 2007, troops working with the feared Mullah Dadullah produced a grisly video series showing their fighters beheading men they accused of spying for the Americans. It culminated in an April release that featured a knife-wielding child executioner who looked barely twelve years old.[109] There were also reports of Taliban soldiers gouging out eyes or gutting enemies they captured in battle.[110] We heard of troops who would kill members of their own unit who refused to take part in these atrocities. From eastern Afghanistan came word that the Taliban were chopping off the noses and ears of truck drivers who ferried goods for the coalition.[111]

As connections to their ideological roots withered, so did their strict social edicts. "We get taxed by the Taliban for opium just like before, but otherwise there's no functioning government here," says Haji Batoor Khan, age forty-two, from Sangin. "The big change is that now we can play music and have weddings. Even the Taliban love music, dancing, and television. Most of them keep young boys as their companions."[112]

As horrifying as it is to imagine life under the new Taliban, it's even scarier to look at the map and see how their zone of influence is spreading. Just a few years back, the Taliban could lay claim to a few districts along the Pakistan-Afghanistan border and pockets of remote territory in Afghanistan's Pashtun south. Today the insurgency controls most of Helmand, large parts of the Kunar-Nuristan corridor, Kandahar, Uruzgan, Zabul, and Ghazni and has greatly expanded its influence into the southwestern provinces of Farah and Nimroz. There's also widening unrest in Central Asian states to the north—mainly snaking up along trafficking routes. The situation is downright critical in Pakistan's federally administered tribal areas (FATA), where insurgents who support the Taliban now control or virtually control most of the region's seven districts.

The drug trade is not entirely to blame for the insurgents' strength in Pakistan—poor governance in general and a political crisis in Islamabad shifted focus away from security concerns at the border—but local sources say funds earned from drugs and other contraband have been a contributing factor to the rapid spread of the insurgents' power. "New money is a big part of the equation," the International Crisis Group reported in 2006, quoting a local lawyer on the spreading influence of the insurgents.[113] Local sources and western intelligence officials say Pakistani jihadi groups like Jaish-e-Mohammed and Hizbul-Mujahidin, both of which have close ties to al Qaeda, transport drug shipments from FATA to the Pakistani coast. At least one religious scholar in FATA has declared the opium trade *halal*, or legitimate under Islamic law.[114]

The pro-Taliban insurgents broke out of the semiautonomous FATA in 2007, briefly taking control of six districts in the normally peaceful Swat Valley before being cleared out by a force of more than fifteen thousand Pakistani troops. The episode led to concern among western military observers that Pakistan could conceivably lose control of large portions of the North-West Frontier Province, where levels of governance and law enforcement, as in Baluchistan, are ineffective at the best of times. The insurgent fighters consisted mainly of local Taliban, but Pakistani officials as well as locals who fled the area said they were commanded by several hundred foreign

5. THE KINGPIN

"HAJI JUMA KHAN HAS TWO HUNDRED HOUSES," SAID A skinny man outside the gate at a sprawling compound in Quetta, in western Pakistan. "And this is one of them."

I had been trying to track down South Asia's number one drug trafficker, the smuggler behind the Taliban, for more than two years. It hadn't been easy. The man known as HJK among counternarcotics agents is so shadowy that few have ever heard his name, even among regional policymakers. Yet Juma Khan's drug empire, which moves as much as $1 billion worth of opium and heroin a year, forms the backbone of the Taliban.

"He is the centre of gravity for the Taliban drug trade," a western official told me in 2006. "I find it strange he's not a household name." A 2007 assessment by Afghanistan's spy agency, the National Directorate of Security, listed HJK as that country's premier smuggler. He held the same ranking next door in Pakistan and in Iran, according to officials from those nations. "Juma Khan's forces are terrorists. He pays them to protect his drugs," said General Ali Shah Paktiawal, a senior Afghan police official. "Mullah Omar. Tahir Yuldeshev. Osama bin Laden. They all work for him."[1]

I found his Quetta residence down a dusty, nondescript alley lined with piles of rotting garbage. A white Taliban flag fluttered in the breeze outside the compound next door. It hardly seemed an auspicious address for the region's most powerful kingpin. Another man appeared at the gate and introduced himself as Nematullah. "I am his clerk," Nematullah told me. "Inside this house we all work for Juma Khan." I asked if the boss was in residence, and if I could interview him. "He is on the run and we haven't seen him," said Nematullah. "But please come inside and have a cup of tea."

I briefly pondered his invitation, wondering whether I'd ever see my family again. Like the Burmese drug lord Khun Sa, who financed private armies and generated an estimated $200 million every year in gross profits, Haji Juma Khan's immense wealth made him so powerful that he operated with impunity across Afghanistan, Pakistan, and Iran. When I first asked Kamal Sadat, Afghanistan's former anti-drug police chief, about him in 2004, he rolled his eyes. "I can't find anybody in Kabul who wants me to arrest this guy," he said.

Similar to Pablo Escobar, the Colombian kingpin who packed jetliners with cocaine and maintained a private zoo, HJK, fifty-four, was notorious for his colossal drug shipments and his extravagant lifestyle. For a man who embedded himself with the Taliban and al Qaeda, HJK hardly behaved like his fundamentalist compatriots. "He has many sheep, but even more women," a Kabul police official said.[2] "Juma Khan keeps three wives and so many girlfriends," reported an Afghan diplomat, unable to be more specific. "He loves music and dancing."[3] HJK owns palatial residences in at least six different countries, and it is reported that alcohol-drenched parties hosted by Russian and Turkish prostitutes extended late into the night whenever he was in residence.[4]

Eventually, as I stood outside his gate, my curiosity got the better of me and I followed Nematullah inside. We sat cross-legged on Persian carpets, sipping warm orange Fanta. Veiled women and children peeked around the corner, giggled, and then ran off. Nematullah fetched a man he introduced as his boss, Abdul Karim, who promptly fell over himself trying to convince me he had nothing to do with the Taliban kingpin.

"I have never heard of him," claimed Karim, after I asked if he worked with HJK. When I replied that the other two men had already told me the house belonged to Juma Khan, Karim lit up a cigarette and inhaled sharply. "I don't know the guy," he said. "I just rented this place a year ago."

We chatted for a bit and I inquired about Karim's line of work. "Import-export," he said, waving his cigarette.

"What do you export from here?" I asked.

"Oh, you know," he replied, "whatever needs to be exported."

"These guys say you work for Juma Khan," I said, gesturing to the guard and the clerk, now both staring intently at their feet.

"Work for him? No! I haven't even seen him in years," said Karim.

"So you do know him," I said.

"Well, I met him once, maybe, seven years ago," he said, and then his tone turned pleading. "Who are you? Why do you want to make trouble for me?"

I said I was a journalist and I just wanted to interview his boss. Did he by chance know how to reach him? "It is difficult to find Juma Khan these days because he is hiding in the mountains," said Karim.

"So you do know him," I said again.

"Everyone knows Juma Khan," said Karim, breaking into a wide smile. "He is in the opium business. He is the biggest smuggler there is."

It's tough to pin down hard information about HJK. Part of the reason may be that he comes from a region as obscure as his background. He was born, by most accounts, in Afghanistan's Nimroz Province, the desert outpost jutting between Pakistan and Iran that was once capital of the ninth-century Saffarid dynasty.[5] He comes from a modest background, according to those who know him, and possibly worked as a shepherd in his youth. At the height of his power, the six-foot, three-inch drug lord tended a flock of smugglers, ruffians, and business associates extending from windswept Nimroz and across Iran to Turkey, down through Pakistan into the UAE, with tentacles sprouting up into Central Asia. His terrorist ties were central to his business empire, which came to rival that of the ancient Saffarids in size and reach.

HJK hails from the Mohammed-Hasani tribe of the Brahui people, a Sunni Muslim ethnic group nearly 2 million strong spanning the region between eastern Iran, western Afghanistan, and Pakistan. Historians believe Brahuis immigrated to the remote area about three thousand years ago from the populous Indus Valley region. Linguists interpret their distinct language as grammatically derived from ancient Dravidian tongues. Today, territories the Brahui inhabit are as forbidding and isolated as any on earth. Smuggling is the central livelihood in the tri-border area, where physical boundaries between the three countries scarcely exist. As my research assistants and I trolled the region in search of HJK, virtually everyone we found to be associated with him was Brahui. We found it's not an easy clan for outsiders to penetrate.

In a region where power courses down tribal bloodlines, HJK's is an atypical rags-to-riches story that resounds with tales of his cunning and insatiable lust for money. Afghan and Pakistani officials and tribal contacts say HJK personally came from a humble family. "He was not important in his tribe—not even a rich man," says a tribal elder from the border area. "Haji Juma Khan came from nowhere."[6] It's unclear how he became involved in drugs, and details of his childhood and birthday are unknown. "We know he got his start in the late 1980s," says an Afghan official. "And before that he owned some small businesses and a lot of sheep."[7]

Halfway through the Taliban regime, however, Juma Khan's wealth and influence was clearly established. He built a palatial compound in Zaranj, the barren capital of Nimroz that sits aside the Iranian border. HJK's citadel, which was heavily fortified and guarded by dozens of armed men, dwarfed even the provincial governor's mansion across the street. His massive hundred-vehicle convoys across the Iranian desert soon attracted the attention of counternarcotics officials. "Back then, he was one of the most powerful people in terms of money, people, and big drug consignments," said Hashem Zayyem, an Iranian counternarcotics official.[8]

British counternarcotics police regarded HJK as the man who moved the most contraband from Pakistan's Makran coast into the UAE, according to a former officer. HJK ferried opium and hashish along the narrow channel of the Arabian Sea separating Pakistan from the Arabian Peninsula, coming aground on the stretches of empty coastline between Oman and the UAE. "They would land along the remote beaches and bury their shipments in the sand," said the former British officer.[9]

HJK broke into an opium market fiercely protected by the Quetta Alliance. According to the local lore in southwestern Afghanistan, he has mercilessly purged the area of enemies and rivals, having them gunned down or, in a recent instance, poisoned. His authority eventually came to rival that of Haji Bashir Noorzai, and both men worked closely with the Taliban. "Haji Juma Khan was number three in the movement by the end of their regime," said a U.S. official.[10] He also became close to al Qaeda during the 1990s, according to a CIA document seen by the author. The intelligence report said Khan helped hundreds of Arabs flee Afghanistan into Iran when the U.S.-led invasion began in October 2001.

Incredibly, the towering tribesman was detained by U.S. forces in late 2001 near Kandahar, U.S. officials now admit. Although HJK was known to be involved in drug smuggling and tied to the Taliban, U.S. military intelligence believed he was not a significant threat. U.S. officials naïvely bought his promises to help them track down terrorists. "At the time, the Americans were only interested in catching bin Laden and Mullah Omar," said a European counterterrorism expert in Kabul. "Juma Khan walked."[11] It was a decision they would come to regret. Within three years, his operations expanded even further. The colossal size of his drug shipments amazed authorities. A Pakistani counternarcotics official formerly based in Baluchistan said the Anti Narcotics Force once intercepted a drug cache making its way to the Arabian Sea coast with forty metric tons of morphine base, hashish, and crystal heroin.[12]

By 2004, western intelligence agents identified HJK's drug network as a principal source of funding to the Taliban and al Qaeda and a key conduit for their weapons. He ran a massive refinery and maintained huge underground storage depots in Baramcha, the dusty smugglers town straddling the border between Helmand and Baluchistan.[13] NATO combat helicopters struck those sites in April 2005, working in conjunction with Pakistani helicopters across the border, according to locals from the area. It marked one of the few known occasions that the coalition took military action against a drug dealer.

Once Baramcha got too hot, HJK set up refineries in the remote Chahar Borjak district of southern Nimroz and along the mountainous border with Iran, according to Afghan officials. He also maintained large, hidden weapons caches there, they say. After coming under greater scrutiny, he developed mobile labs, often built on the bed of a Toyota Hilux or hastily erected in people's homes.

HJK also maintained a representative in the Girdi Jungle refugee camp, a notorious smuggling hub along the desolate border in Baluchistan, until it was sealed by Pakistani paramilitary troops in 2007. There, he stored opium grown in Helmand in giant underground bunkers. Consignments going to Iran were handled by two men identified in a U.S. intelligence document seen by the author as Haji Khodi Nazar and Haji Abdul Razzaq. They ran Juma Khan's operations in the Iranian border town of Zahedan. The two men reportedly operated a car showroom as cover for their trafficking activities.

"They would hold opiates, usually heroin, in Zahedan until they had enough to put together a large convoy that would cross Iran to Turkey," the report said. HJK also maintained a representative in Turkey to handle his business affairs at the gateway to Europe, the world's most lucrative heroin market. That associate was an ethnic Baluch named Murtaza who originally came from Quetta, the report said. "His men moved morphine base and heroin from Girdi Jungle and Dalbandin to Iran and then on to the Turkish border," said the Pakistani official.

HJK shifted his shipment tactics once western troops moved into southern Afghanistan. His caravans became more compact—just fifteen to twenty SUVs, which were guarded by fighters armed with heavy machine guns and RPGs. "We have tried to intercept his convoys," said a frustrated interior ministry official formerly posted to Nimroz, "but his connections are very good within the government and the police. He'll get a tip-off that we are coming and pass that information on to the Taliban, and they will come out in force."[14] Seven years after the U.S.-led invasion, HJK's highly equipped forces in Helmand were up against fledgling provincial police who remain "outnumbered, outgunned, and mostly untrained," complained another senior Afghan security official.[15]

In addition to working land smuggling routes, HJK continued to expand his maritime smuggling fleet, which a senior Afghan official said was still HJK's preferred method of moving dope. In May 2004, acting on a tip-off, agents in Pakistan turned up evidence he was moving a fleet of cargo ships between the Pakistani port city of Karachi and the Sharjah emirate, where HJK lived for several years after the Taliban government fell. Under pressure from the United States and the UK, Sharjah authorities eventually ejected HJK. Intelligence agents believed the boats carried contraband out of Karachi and returned laden with weapons—including plastic explosives and anti-tank mines. They would unload their cargo secretly and ship it overland to the militants.[16]

Haji Juma Khan also actively took a role in organizing the insurgency, counternarcotics officials say. "For some time, we knew HJK was meeting directly with Taliban officials who would then sit down with al Qaeda about battle plans," a U.S. official told me. Mirwais Yasini, who used to run Afghanistan's Counternarcotics Directorate, said: "There are central linkages among Khan, Mullah Omar, and bin Laden."[17]

In May 2004, for example, the CIA station in Kabul cabled that HJK "arranged to have sixteen al Qaeda-affiliated Arabs moved to Iran through Pakistan via Nawzad," according to a document seen by the author. The intelligence report said the Arabs had been previously shifted into Helmand to assist the Taliban in taking control of the poppy-rich province, where HJK happened to be the dominant smuggler. "Haji Juma Khan supported the Taliban because his business was more lucrative under the former Taliban regime," the report noted. At HJK's bidding, the Taliban pressured farmers to increase output across the southwest, Afghan officials say.[18]

Taliban troops helped protect his drug shipments snaking through southwestern Afghanistan, but Afghan security officials say there was little distinction between the insurgents and his personal army. HJK maintained a force of up to 1,500 armed men, operating in border provinces like Farah and Nimroz, where they were often referred to as Taliban by the locals. "They pretend to be Taliban," said an Afghan police official. "But they are just Juma Khan's thugs."[19] One such "thug" is a commander named Mullah Manaf, according to Afghan security officials. He protected HJK's convoys as they headed west through the desert wasteland of southern Nimroz in return for Toyota Land Cruisers, Thuraya satellite telephones, and weapons.[20]

Using Manaf and other henchmen, Haji Juma Khan also dabbled in kidnapping, people smuggling, and extortion, security officials say. In 2005, for example, his men took two Turkish businessmen hostage in the Iranian border area and brought them to Baramcha, according to General Ali Shah Paktiawal, a senior Kabul police official. HJK demanded 1 million euros each for their release.[21] He was tied to the 2007 kidnapping of two French aid workers in Nimroz, along with three of their local colleagues, according to security officials in Nimroz and Kabul. And a recently unsealed U.S. indictment linked HJK to the January 2008 attack on the Serena Hotel in Kabul, which killed six people.[22] He also funded a large madrassa in Pakistan that schools as many as 1,500 students at a time, according to an intelligence document on his operations seen by the author, which said he uses the school to "talent-spot potential employees or militia members."

Though tied to the Taliban and al Qaeda, HJK maintained an unparalleled Rolodex of corrupt government officials he could call on for help across South Asia and the Persian Gulf. HJK's real strength came not from his ties to terrorists but from his uncanny ability to build networks and corrupt people in power wherever he chose to operate. In Afghanistan, that network included provincial governors, security agents, regional military commanders, and senior officials in the Highway Police, according to western officials and intelligence documents.

A March 2004 British intelligence document seen by the author even suggested his influence extended to President Hamid Karzai's inner circle. The MI6 document said: "HJK had allegedly used Ahmed Wali Karzai as a conduit to bribe both governors to allow narcotics to be processed and transported through their provinces without impediment." The Afghan president and his brother vehemently deny Ahmed Wali's links to heroin. "I was never in the drug business, I never benefited, I never facilitated, I never helped anyone with the transportation of any kind," Ahmed Wali said in June 2006.[23]

Narcotics leaving southwestern Afghanistan follow three general routes. The first goes directly into Iran from Nimroz and Farah provinces. The second dips down into Pakistan's Baluchistan Province and then heads west for Iran. A third smuggles drugs south to Pakistan's Makran Coast and then by boat to the Persian Gulf. Either way, corrupt officials in Iran and Pakistan were essential to HJK's operations. He paid off a wide network of police, border guards, and intelligence agents in both countries, according to smugglers, officials, and western intelligence documents seen by the author.

A British intelligence report titled "Trafficking Network of Haji Juma Khan Mohammad Hasani," shown to the author, identified a "brother" of Haji Juma Khan named Shah Hussein who runs his operations from a nondescript travel agency on Jinnah Road, the main drag through downtown Quetta. I found the office, right where the document said it would be, walked inside, and asked if a man named Shah Hussein worked there. "He runs the place," said an agent who was ringing up a plane ticket for a customer. "He's right through that door."

I sat down with Shah Hussein, and we exchanged the customary pleasantries. He said he was a Brahui from Dalbandin and offered me a cup of tea. I said I was an American journalist and inquired about his travel agency. "Business is down," he said. "The economy is not good." I asked if he was the owner and he said he was a junior partner.

"How interesting," I said, "because I am here looking for one of your partners. I am trying to find Haji Juma Khan."

Shah Hussein then launched into a familiar routine about how he had never heard of or met anyone named Haji Juma Khan. "But everyone says he is your business partner," I said to him.

"I have not seen him for a long time," he said. "Maybe seven years."

"So you do know him," I said.

"Know him? I mean, I have heard of him, maybe we met once, I don't really know," he said, now visibly sweating. "Who are you again?"

"I'd like to meet him," I said. "Do you know how he can be reached?"

"That's not possible," he said, then added quickly, "I mean, I don't know where he is." My local colleague Naqeeb and I pressed him for a few more minutes, and I left my business card with my phone number. "Please ask him to call me if you hear from him," I said.

"I don't know why you are asking me," he said weakly, "I just sell plane tickets."

However, the British intelligence report I saw claimed Hussein paid bribes on HJK's behalf totalling $2 million to Pakistani intelligence officers based in the capital of Baluchistan Province. "The bribes have been given to the MI [Military Intelligence] Corps Commander and the ISID [ISI] Colonel based in Quetta to ensure the safe passage of HJK's narcotics consignments transiting Pakistan," the report said.

As a result of the payoffs, Hussein had received MI and ISI identity cards so vehicles carrying drugs would not have trouble passing checkpoints manned by police and the Anti Narcotics Force, the report claimed. One frustrated Pakistani inspector called the Taliban, the smugglers, and the intelligence agencies an "evil troika," and said five close associates of HJK who had been arrested by police and ANF in Baluchistan were released on orders of the ISI within two weeks.[24]

A smuggler moving opium across the empty stretch of desert in Baluchistan leading to the Iran border explained how the teams operate once they cross out of Afghanistan. "We go on half-moon nights, putting a guy out front on a motorcycle," he said. The spotter will travel three to ten miles ahead of the convoy, helping the caravan choose its route across the shifting sands, and making sure the coast is clear. The spotter will communicate with the caravan using a wireless radio or Thuraya satellite phone. "Normally, our agents have paid off the intelligence officials and the Frontier Corps, so we know where the checkpoints are," he said. "When you hear of a drug package being confiscated by the authorities, you can be sure it was a deal fixed in advance."[25]

A similar system exists in Iran. A June 2004 CIA cable from Kabul reported HJK would move his shipments to the Iranian border in small convoys where it was transferred into vehicles belonging to Iranian intelligence agents, whose cars would not get searched at police and customs checkpoints. The Iranian agents transported the contraband to Tehran or all the way to the Turkish border, the report said. When one of HJK's associates was arrested in early 2004 in Zahedan, the province bordering Nimroz, with more than a ton of hashish and three hundred tons of morphine base, HJK used his connections with the provincial intelligence chief to secure the man's release. The Iranian spy subsequently claimed the drugs to be a "seizure" and "an indication of his service's achievements" in the fight against drugs, the CIA report said.

Family ties matter greatly within HJK's Brahui-run operations. The 2004 British intelligence report detailed his most trusted representatives in Afghanistan, Pakistan, Iran, Turkey, and the UAE. The informant quoted in the report was described as "an established and reliable source with direct access." He identified HJK's two closest deputies as his "brothers" and gives their names only as Torakai and Shah Hussein. The source described Torakai as HJK's "right-hand man, who often travels with HJK and brokered contacts and meetings for him." Shah Hussein, the contact said, was based in Quetta and handled liaisons with Pakistani authorities "designed to protect HJK's illegal business interests." In interviews, Afghan officials have identified HJK's brothers by other names: Haji Sharif and Mohammed Yar. Another intelligence report also mentioned Mohammed Yar, describing him as a close associate but not mentioning family ties.

A "nephew" named Sharafuddin is another key lieutenant mentioned in several intelligence reports who oversees operations in Baramcha and "makes contacts" with Afghan and UAE authorities. The British report and Pakistani officials also identify Haji Hafiz Akhtar as another nephew and chief of operations. "He was responsible for acquiring, processing and dispatching the opiates," the British report said. All his top deputies are relatives, "although it is not strictly clear how," according to the report, which I saw. Unravelling the family tree and discrepancies in names is complex, since many Afghans—especially those who deal in illegal activity—go by various names, nicknames, and honorific titles. "Juma Khan" itself literally translates as "Mr. Friday."

The fact that his corrupt network extended across three countries—and reached down into the UAE as well—gave the organization an unprecedented ability to switch alliances in a region where loyalties shift more often than the sands. Insiders say HJK was close to the ISI during the Taliban regime but appeared to shift away from the Pakistani spy agency when the Musharraf government distanced itself from jihadi groups under post-9/11 pressure from Washington. In the weeks immediately after the fall of the Taliban—during which time HJK was briefly picked up by U.S. authorities—he may even have traded information with CIA and U.S. military intelligence agents to secure his release, a western official says. "It is widely known they worked with people who had the capacity to get them to places. One was HJK, and another was Bashir Noorzai," the official told me. "Many now ask the question: 'When did the U.S. military and the CIA know the two men were involved in drugs?' "[26]

Afghan security officials believe HJK shifted alliances again around 2005, positioning himself as the central link between the Taliban and the subsequent surge of Iranian weapons, including shaped charges used to deadly effect against NATO troops. In June 2007, U.S. defence secretary Robert Gates complained that Iranian-made weapons were increasingly falling into Taliban hands, admitting, "We do not have any information about whether the government of

Iran is supporting this, is behind it, or whether it's smuggling."[27] In fact, Afghan military and intelligence officials have unearthed evidence that HJK set up a meeting between the late Mullah Dadullah and Iranian intelligence agents to organize the flow of weapons to the insurgency. "HJK is the link between Iranian intelligence and the recent rash of IED attacks," an Afghan official told me. "I have been telling the Americans for a year now that Iran has become a bigger worry than Pakistan for us."[28]

Despite the long-established and well-greased routes south and west, officials and smugglers say HJK also expanded northward, building new smuggling routes through the Central Asian states of Uzbekistan and Turkmenistan. That's in part due to a crackdown along the Pakistan border by NATO-led troops in Afghanistan. Pakistani authorities made it riskier to operate in the Girdi Jungle refugee camp. The new northern traffic may also indicate a greater role for the IMU, the Uzbek terrorists controlling much of the trade through the former Soviet republics. Sources say drugs tend to move north in smaller packets—often using human carriers who travel with loads no heavier than five kilograms.

In April 2004, Haji Juma Khan purchased an entire town in Nimroz Province, according to interviews with locals and a western intelligence document shown to the author. The village, known as Rudbar, is strategically located along the desert highway linking Baramcha to the tri-border area known as Rabat-e-Jali, a notorious gateway for smugglers and terrorists moving between Pakistan, Afghanistan, and Iran. The intelligence report shown to the author says HJK planned to "parcel out the land to members of his tribe," and in return they would cultivate poppy and wheat.

Rudbar's location in the forbidding "Desert of Death" did not put off the region's most powerful trafficker, according to locals. He simply ordered the construction of a massive artificial lake and dug irrigation canals. Locals say HJK's desert lair rises out of the desolate moonscape like a mirage, with hundreds of palm trees and twenty-four-hour electricity, wholly supplied by industrial generators.

HJK also maintained homes in Quetta's Satellite Town, the affluent Defence Colony of Karachi, and Wazir Akhbar Khan, the upscale Kabul neighbourhood home to western embassies and NGOs. He owned other residences in Dubai, Sharjah, Iran, and Saudi Arabia, according to western and Afghan officials. He travelled between countries using as many as twelve different passports from Iran, Afghanistan, and Pakistan, which he changed often.[29] "He sometimes dressed in military uniform or wore a western suit rather than traditional Afghan clothing," says an Afghan security agent.[30] Officials and those who know him say that, despite his height, HJK is relatively nondescript-looking and a master at blending in. One contact from Baramcha described a time when he disguised himself as a shepherd—his former trade—to evade authorities.[31]

Accounts of HJK's excesses veer into the realm of hyperbole. "You go into his house on any given night, and a hundred people will be served," one local said breathlessly. "He likes Russian ladies, Iranians, and he keeps the most handsome boys."[32] The excessive lifestyle caught up with him in 2006, when, according to a former senior U.S. counternarcotics official, HJK was diagnosed with skin cancer. At the same time, he reached out to senior Afghan and western authorities and began talking about going straight. "One school of thought was that he believed he had a terminal illness and wanted to make right with his maker before he died," said the official.[33]

Negotiations advanced to a point where the kingpin actually visited the NATO-run Kandahar Air Base for talks with western officials, according to an Afghan official. The offer was that HJK would go clean and write the Kabul government an enormous cheque compensating for his untaxed wealth. After months of negotiations, HJK reneged. Western officials concluded he feared retribution from business partners who stood to lose money, and possibly realized his malignant lesions weren't going to kill him anytime soon. The episode forced HJK underground, according to locals in his area and officials.

However, on October 23, 2008, the Afghan kingpin would resurface again—boarding a flight from Dubai to Indonesia on the mistaken belief that he was about to land a major drug deal. In fact, the men HJK was working with were counternarcotics agents working with the DEA. They lured him to Jakarta, according to sources close to the case, where he was arrested at the airport by Indonesian authorities, swiftly handed over to U.S. authorities, and whisked to New York City. Wearing a white turban, HJK appeared the following day before the Southern District Court of Manhattan, where he told the judge, "I am not guilty."[34] It would be months before his case reached trial. So far, however, Khan's lawyer and the DEA have refused to comment publicly on the nature of his arrest. The Justice Department and the Indonesian government have declined to explain how his extradition, a process that normally takes weeks, rocketed through Indonesia's famously clunky legal system in just a few hours.

Michele M. Leonhart, the acting DEA chief, said in a press release that Khan's capture "disrupts a major line of credit to the Taliban, and will shake the foundation of his drug network that has moved massive quantities of heroin to worldwide drug markets."[35] But even that is unclear. News of his arrest barely caused a ripple inside Afghanistan or out, and months later residents in his main area of operations appeared not to even know the kingpin was behind bars. Rather, the border-straddling town of Baramcha remained in control of Taliban forces, and sources said HJK's key lieutenants, all members of his Mohammed-Hasani tribe, continued to smuggle narcotics as usual, despite the fact that, as one resident put it, "Juma Khan himself has not been seen for months."[36]

Officials and sources on both sides of the border identified Haji Hafiz Akhtar, HJK's nephew and chief of operations, as the man who now runs the business, operating from Baramcha on the Pakistani side of the border. They also identified Sharafuddin as a key player, saying he runs a fabric shop in the bazaar in Dalbandin, which doubles as a legal front for the business and also provides a meeting place for high-level associates.[37] A Pakistani intelligence official identified Shah Hussein, the man who runs the Quetta Travel Agency, as a critical player in coordinating onward movement of drug shipments once they leave Afghanistan.[38] Sources say Sharafuddin and Shah Hussein pay off officials in the Afghan National Army, the Afghan police, as well as Pakistani security officials who man checkpoints in the border areas. Payments are handsome—as high as 50,000–60,000 Pakistani rupees ($600–$800) even to low-level guards—to get drug convoys through.[39] Critically, the sources say there has been little disruption to the network since "Juma Khan was a wise man," one border source said. "He only promoted his most trusted nephews, who never quarrel over the business."[40]

Like many top smugglers, HJK covered his tracks by investing in

6. FOLLOW THE MONEY

WE SAT IN A DUBAI CAFÉ DRINKING CAPPUCCINOS WHILE Riaz explained to me how the boss of South Asia's underworld launders millions of dollars of Afghan drug money.

"Every big player in dirty business will have a dozen guys like me to make their operations look clean," Riaz explained.[1] And he should know. For about a decade, Riaz laundered money for Dawood Ibrahim, the undisputed crime lord of South Asia.

Wanted in India for his role in the 1993 Mumbai blasts that killed over 200 people and accused of smuggling massive narcotics shipments into the UK and Europe, Ibrahim has the dubious distinction of being the only person Washington has designated both a "Global Terrorist Supporter" and a "Foreign Narcotics Kingpin."[2] The son of a police constable, Ibrahim started out as a small-time hood in Mumbai, graduating to extortion, murder for hire, and gold smuggling. He bought off Mumbai's cops, pitted Muslims and Hindus against each other, and dabbled in Bollywood and fixing cricket matches. In 1984, he fled India for Dubai, where he transformed his D-Company gang into a global crime conglomerate. After the 1993 Mumbai blasts, even freewheeling Dubai wouldn't have him anymore. Ibrahim took refuge in Karachi, reportedly under protection of the ISI.[3]

That's when D-Company began working in the region's opium

trade. Ibrahim "travelled in Afghanistan under the protection of the Taliban" in the late 1990s and brokered a financial arrangement to share smuggling routes with "Osama bin Laden and his terrorist network," a U.S. government fact sheet says.[4] "If you want to understand what Osama bin Laden is up to," a former senior CIA official told me, "you have to understand what Dawood Ibrahim is up to."[5]

Today, Ibrahim is believed to play a major role in laundering drug proceeds from the Afghan opium market. Like bin Laden, he remains at large, reportedly spending most of his time behind the high walls of a Karachi mansion. Around the globe, agents from India, Interpol, the CIA, the DEA, and the Treasury Department are building a case against him. "Dawood's involvement in drugs and terrorism is undeniable," a senior U.S. official told me. Proving it won't be easy. As Riaz explained it, moving dirty money is hardly rocket science. D-Company and numerous organizations like it use surprisingly simple techniques to make sure that drug and terror money slips past the notice of authorities.

Two weeks after the 9/11 attacks, President Bush gathered media in the Rose Garden to declare war on al Qaeda's financing. "Money is the lifeblood of terrorist operations," he said. "Today we're asking the world to stop payment."[6] The following month, he launched Operation Green Quest, a law enforcement programme to block terrorist funding. "The same talent pool and expertise that brought down Al Capone," the Treasury Department boasted in a press release, "will now be dedicated to investigating Osama Bin Ladin and his terrorist network."[7] By December, the U.S. government and allied nations had frozen the assets of 150 known terrorists, their organizations, and their bankers in the United States and abroad, blocking about $66 million.[8] However, the trail of terrorist money quickly went cold. As of 2006, bank assets frozen by U.S. authorities climbed to a little more than $300 million.[9] "Compared to what's sloshing around," one federal official complained to me, "that's a pimple on a pig's ass."

Experts in terrorism finance say the U.S. government is no closer to stopping funds reaching terror groups because it's looking for the money in the wrong places. "We look for dirty money in western institutions," says John Cassara, a former U.S. Treasury special agent and author of *Hide and Seek*. "The methods we use to track crime don't translate to what is going on."[10]

It is impossible to overstate how crucial it is to get this right. U.S. authorities so far have focused on catching high-value targets within al Qaeda and the Taliban, rather than going after the system supporting them. As Robert Charles, the former counternarcotics chief at the State Department, puts it: "It's as if we stumbled upon a combustion engine and we are reaching in trying to grab the individual pistons, and forgetting we should just cut the flow of gasoline."[11] Eight years after 9/11, the single greatest failure in the war on terror is not that Osama bin Laden continues to elude capture, or that the Taliban has staged a comeback, or even that al Qaeda is regrouping in Pakistan's tribal areas and probably planning fresh attacks on the West. Rather, it's the spectacular incapacity of western law enforcement to disrupt the flow of money that is keeping their networks afloat.

U.S. financial crime agents have suspected that drug money was helping fund Islamic extremists since the 1990s, but there has been little systematic investigation into the links between drug profits and terrorism. "We have made virtually no progress following that money," says Cassara. "I am beside myself with frustration."

It's easy to become discouraged when you start looking at the scope of the problem. The trading zone that groups Afghanistan, Pakistan, and the UAE is the financial world's Wild West, where there are disincentives to going legal. Corruption is rife, law enforcement shoddy, and tax evasion the norm. The vast majority of payments—even legal ones—for big ticket items like cars and homes are made in cash, sometimes suitcases of it. Walk into any money-changing market from Kabul to Dubai and you will see dozens of *hawaladars* counting knee-high stacks of $100 bills—literally millions of dollars in cash. The *hawaladars* balance their accounts in grimy notebooks, but keep few records of who sent what to whom for authorities to scrutinize. No one has any idea how much they transfer across borders each year, not to mention how much of it is "legal."

Since 2001, the UAE, Pakistan, and Afghanistan have adopted or at least drafted laws banning money laundering and tightened regulations on bank transfers. However, there's been limited success in tracking money flowing outside the banking system, and no effort to go after those appearing to break the law. Most Afghan opium is actually bartered for commodities, including cars and electronic goods, meaning there's virtually no money trail to follow. "None of these countries watch their trade data," an exasperated western official told me, "and more than half of the goods are smuggled anyway." Drug money flows along a different route than the opium, agents say, often bouncing through Russia and South Africa and usually passing through Dubai, the flashy free-trade emirate that's a hub for money laundering and underground banking.

The funding for 9/11 passed through Dubai, and Abdul Qadeer (A.Q.) Khan's network went there to flog nuclear technology. "Whether it's drug smuggling, people trafficking, or money laundering, all roads lead to Dubai," says Cassara. If you are a drug smuggler, it would be hard to find a more accommodating region to launder your money. And what better place to park your dirty cash than a bustling sheikdom in the oil-rich Persian Gulf?

I travelled the region's money markets, ports, stock exchanges, and border crossings to try to map out how drug money was being laundered. Here's a compilation of the most common techniques for moving or hiding dirty money (not just drug cash):

Hawala

For millions of people across the world with no access to bank accounts—most of them migrant workers—the informal money transfer network known as *hawala* is the cheapest, fastest, and easiest way to transfer money.[12] In Afghanistan, where few banks operate outside Kabul, *hawala* is crucial to the legal economy. A 2003 World Bank study calculated that international aid groups funnelled $200 million in emergency, development, and reconstruction money through the *hawala* market after the fall of the Taliban, for example.[13] The informal transfer system is also heavily penetrated by drug dealers, criminals, and Islamic extremists, officials say.

Riaz, who used to move payments from D-Company's gold-smuggling proceeds, says, "Now all they do is launder drug money." No matter what the proceeds pay for, the system works the same. Say Riaz wanted to transfer $100,000 from India to Dubai to pay off a gold shipment. Through trusted *hawala* agents he would locate a group of Indian labourers in Dubai who wanted to send their salaries back home to their families. Once the agent had put together $100,000 worth of wages, plus his 20 percent commission, he would coordinate a "transfer" with another agent in India, and the two would simply zero their balance sheets. No money would ever cross borders, making it virtually untraceable.

The Indian migrant workers never knew they were tied to an illegal deal—not that records were kept anyway. *Hawala* operates on a basis of trust: the agents on either side of the transaction simply select a confirmation number, and the clients present that number to collect their cash. Just a decade ago, *hawala* agents would give their clients an open receipt, often in the form of a bank note, which had to be presented at the other end to get the cash. The serial number on the bill served as the confirmation number. "Back then," Riaz said, "the entire process took about a week. Now they just send the number by text message on their cell phones, and the whole transfer happens in seconds."

Estimates vary wildly as to how much money is pumped annually through the global *hawala* network. Economists put the total figure at about $100 billion and say most transfers are above suspicion. "Our challenge is separating the good from the bad," Noorullah Delawari, the governor of Afghanistan's Central Bank, told me.

It won't be easy, but it is critically important. The World Bank and UN calculate that *hawala* dealers in Helmand and Kandahar alone move more than $1 billion in drug money every year. Surveyors identified no less than fifty-four *hawaladars* in those provinces as "specialists" in laundering opium money. Pinpointing how much of that money benefits insurgents is impossible, with no regulatory framework in place. Most traded almost exclusively in Pakistani rupees (as opposed to the afghani, which is the currency in Afghanistan), indicating that "the large bulk of drug payments arrive in Afghanistan via Pakistan."[14]

Officials and bankers I interviewed in Pakistan are concerned, too. They believe that as much as one-third of Pakistan's overall *hawala* trade is related to drug traffic, and the sums moving back and forth are staggering. In 2002, *Forbes* reported that $8 billion was being remitted to Pakistan through the *hawala* system, more than eight times what was being transferred into the country through banks. More important, government leaders said $100 billion in capital had flowed out of Pakistan.[15]

Both Afghanistan and Pakistan have launched comprehensive programmes to register *hawaladars* and establish cost-free mechanisms to identify the senders and the receivers. U.S. agents investigating *hawala* transfers praised Islamabad for its efforts to regulate informal cash flows. "Pakistan is leaps and bounds ahead of other countries in the region," one told me. "They are literally seizing bags of cash as they cross the border." However, some Pakistani officials remain frustrated. "It's proving a tough nut to crack," complained Major General Jaffery of the Anti Narcotics Force.

What has Islamabad irritated is the enormous flow of legal goods that are smuggled illegally. That old standby, the U-turn scheme, not only continues to cost Pakistan hundreds of millions of dollars in lost customs revenue, but the cross-border trade is also used to hide drug money.

Commodity Barter

Major drug traffickers in Afghanistan simply barter the opium they export for commodities. This simple con is attractive to the Afghan market, which is desperate for basic goods like vehicles, electronics, and construction materials. Take a stroll along the aptly named Smugglers Creek in Dubai, and you'll see hundreds of dhows being loaded with commodities as they prepare to sail for Pakistan. Walk through the teeming Karachi port, where tiny rowboats unload goods from larger vessels, and then visit the chaotic Chaman border crossing where brightly painted trucks from the town's 3,500 import-export firms stream into Afghanistan, and you begin to understand the complexity of trying to regulate regional trade.

The drugs-for-commodities scam provides smugglers with a "legal" front for their activities. Haji Juma Khan, for example, imported Land Cruisers to southern Afghanistan and also owns an electronics import-export firm in the UAE, according to authorities. Haji Bashir Noorzai was Afghanistan's largest tyre importer until he landed himself in a U.S. jail. It is said that an empty truck never passes over the rugged Durand Line, the disputed border between Pakistan and Afghanistan. "The Pakistanis often complain about the Afghan Transit Trade Agreement," says Cassara. "Basically, it is drugs going out and commodities going in."

Trade-Based Money Laundering

A related trick of the trade is known as trade-based money laundering: two traders agree to misprice a deal so that extra money sneaks past the authorities. Say you want to move $50,000 of drug money. You just transfer $200,000 of widgets and put their value as $250,000. "All you need is a willing buyer and a willing seller," says Raymond Baker, a Brookings scholar and author of *Capitalism's Achilles Heel.* "You can misprice anything by 10 to 20 percent and no one will notice."[16]

While he worked at the U.S. Treasury Department, Cassara proposed working with the Pakistanis and Afghans to harmonize customs duties and collection points (thus reducing the incentive to smuggle legal goods). He also wanted to establish trade transparency units, or TTUs. These computer-based stations identify mispriced trades by spotting anomalies in the cost of commodities between point A and point B. The United States has helped establish TTUs in South America, where Colombian and Mexican smugglers use similar techniques to move cocaine money, Cassara says, but to this day, there's not a single TTU operational between South Asia and the Middle East. "All the construction materials, pipes, wiring, and cement going into Afghanistan—no one is looking at this stuff," he says. "It's not sexy, but we need to start thinking like our adversaries do."

Shell Companies and Real Estate

Key to making your illegal barter scheme work is having a front company in the UAE. That's where men like Riaz come in. He established dozens of fake enterprises for the D-Company: first registering the firm, then getting an employment visa for the "director" and opening an account where the boss supposedly would receive a generous salary. For less than $20,000, Riaz said, he could set up a "totally fabricated" company to move millions of dollars in dirty money into the UAE every year. Then he'd take the firm's "earnings" and pump them into the stock market, where they come out "clean."

Shahbaz Khan, a Pakistani arrested in 2007 in Sharjah and slapped with a life sentence for drug trafficking and money laundering, operated thirteen front companies to disguise his operations, according to the U.S. government.[17] In an interview in Peshawar, Khan's son Gulbaz told me his father was an "innocent businessman" who exported cigarettes and renovated buildings in Sharjah.[18]

U.S. counternarcotics agents have taken note of the property boom across Pakistan, Afghanistan, and the UAE. Property values soared in Afghanistan following the fall of the Taliban—although some of that climb is related to the rush of aid workers and foreign embassies to procure residences and office space. Real estate prices also mushroomed next door in Pakistan. Meanwhile, somewhere between 15 and 24 percent of the world's high-tower cranes are at work at any given time in Dubai, where skyscrapers are popping up like weeds.[19] "With just a thousand real estate transactions, you can recycle $800 million," a western official told me, and none of the countries in this region regulate real estate sales. No one suggests the property explosion in any of these countries is entirely fuelled by drug money, but real estate provides a handy place to park large sums of dirty cash.

The World's Most Volatile Stock Market

The Karachi Stock Exchange (KSE) is whispered to be another good place to hide your black money. The unregulated, volatile, and highly speculative Pakistani bourse has grown by an astounding 200 percent since 2002, despite market collapses that have become almost an annual event. The turnover is sky high, making analysts speculate it's being used by money launderers. More than $120 billion pumped through the KSE in 2006, a year when the country's entire economy totalled only about $130 billion, according to bankers and former Pakistani officials.[20] What makes observers most suspicious is the emergence of a handful of brokers in the last five years who now control almost 40 percent of the daily trading volume. "Their meteoric growth is hard to explain by legal means," a former senior Pakistani finance official told me.

Many wonder whose cash they are trading. "I can't prove it is drug money," said Tariq Hassan, the outspoken former chairman of Pakistan's Securities and Exchange Commission (SECP), "but there is definitely money laundering going on there."[21] Hassan lost his job after he launched an investigation into the March 2005 KSE collapse, which cost small investors $13 billion. He claims he was shown the door after he presented the Pakistani government with irrefutable evidence that a dozen major stockbrokers had deliberately triggered the crash and then reaped in billions in profits by devouring cheap shares.[22]

As the KSE swelled in the past five years, these dominant brokers raised eyebrows by expanding their operations into private banking, real estate, and even oil and gas exploration. Some observers suspect that elaborate business frameworks are laundering money, comparing the setup to the infamous Bank of Credit and Commerce International (BCCI). "These men are now power brokers in Pakistan, not just stockbrokers," Hassan said, adding that he believed top officials in the Islamabad government receive handsome payoffs to look the other way.

In April 2007, I flew to Karachi to meet Aqeel Karim Dhedhi, Pakistan's biggest stockbroker, whose firm, according to his company's website, controls about 8 percent of the KSE's daily trading volume.[23] By all accounts Dhedhi wields considerable influence in the country's political and economic circles. It has been reported in the local media, for example, that the SECP chairman who replaced Tariq Hassan used to work for him.[24] Dhedhi told me his father started the AKD brokerage house, which other bankers and Pakistani officials said was unknown until a few years ago.

Today, Dhedhi runs a multibillion-dollar empire from a nondescript office on a Karachi backstreet, where his English-speaking CEO, Nadeem Naqvi, patiently swatted away my questions about their client base.[25] Even though Pakistani law didn't require it, "AKD has a very strict 'Know Your Customer' policy," Naqvi said. "As a house we have tightened up." The firm now scrutinizes all large-volume trades, records traders' telephone calls, and employs a full-time compliance officer, he said. Still, AKD's client profile could raise eyebrows: according to records Naqvi and Dhedhi showed me, the house has only 1,500 active clients, most of whom make trades of about $2,000. That suggests only a handful of clients account for the majority of their gargantuan daily trading volume.

Since Pakistan doesn't regulate its stock trades, it's impossible to know if any of the KSE funds are tied to the Taliban or the drug traders who back them. But U.S. officials worry that brokerage houses are moving staggering sums through the KSE and that this deserves closer scrutiny. Some financial analysts believe the KSE could mark one of the financial gateways where dirty money flows into the legitimate banking system. After all, says Baker, the Brookings scholar, "once cash has been traded through a stock market, it comes out clean."

It's important to recognize that none of the money-laundering mechanisms being used in South Asia and the Gulf are the least bit unusual. The International Monetary Fund estimates that about $1.8 trillion of dirty money is laundered globally every year, mainly by moving it through informal markets or posing it as legitimate business. Financial crime experts say the *hawala* transfer system is equivalent to the Black Market Peso Exchange, which moves cocaine money in Latin America. In the mid-1990s, the Cali cartel was believed to recycle as much as half of its $7 billion a year in cocaine revenues using trade-based money laundering.[26]

Meanwhile, shell companies exist in tax havens across the globe, from Switzerland to the Cayman Islands. And the KSE is hardly the only financial market that appears riddled with dirty money. A 2001 report for the French parliament identified forty banks and individuals working out of Britain's City of London that were believed to maintain direct or indirect relations with bin Laden.[27] "Drug kingpins and terrorist financiers did not create this system," says Baker, who is pushing for nothing less than a global revamp of the free-market system. "They simply stepped into the mechanisms we have created to make it easy to shift money across borders." Osama bin Laden once told an interviewer that his people were as "aware of the cracks inside the Western financial system as they are aware of the lines in their hands."[28] For western law enforcement, the challenge will be closing those gaps.

To this day, surprisingly little is known about al Qaeda's financial structure: how much money the group raises through donations versus business ventures, what its annual budget is, and who decides how it gets spent. Authorities aren't entirely sure about the way in which money is shared between its network of allies, like the Taliban, the IMU, and the Pakistani jihadi groups, although some recent intelligence indicates a greater level of cooperation between them.[29] As discussed in Chapter 1, there is evidence al Qaeda cells in the West are turning to crime to raise money. As well, it's clear that the Taliban and the IMU profit from Afghanistan's booming opium trade. Yet debate continues over where Osama bin Laden stands on narcotics smuggling. According to U.S. officials, captured al Qaeda operatives have told interrogators that bin Laden banned his fighters from getting involved in the drug trade, fearing that narcotics could corrupt his movement.[30]

In its "Monograph on Terrorist Finance," the 9/11 Commission overturned the widespread belief that bin Laden funded al Qaeda from a $300 million fortune he allegedly inherited. In fact, the commission concluded, bin Laden received an annual stipend of around $1 million from his family, hardly small change but not enough to fund his terrorist ambitions. In fact, when bin Laden returned to Afghanistan in 1996 from Sudan, where he had set up construction projects and ran farms, some evidence suggests he was nearly broke.[31] What allowed him and his network to survive, U.S. investigators concluded, was his unparalleled ability to raise funds and reinvent his organization.

"Unlike other terrorist leaders, bin Laden was not a military hero, nor a religious authority, nor an obvious representative of the downtrodden and disillusioned," testified Lee Wolosky, the former director of transnational threats at the NSC. "He was a rich *financier*... distinguished by his ability to organize an effective network."[32]

The 9/11 Commission later concluded that donations from rich Arabs and Muslim charities contributed the bulk of al Qaeda's funding. "We have seen no substantial evidence," the panel added, "that al Qaeda played a major role in the drug trade or relied on it as an important source of revenue either before or after 9/11." To this day, there's still no smoking gun to prove bin Laden's link to the opium trade, officials say. "There is fragmentary evidence of their use of the criminal infrastructure," says a senior western official. "But not much more."[33] However, there is widespread evidence Uzbek insurgents linked to al Qaeda are heavily tied to drug smuggling and control as much as 70 percent of the multibillion-dollar heroin and opium trade through Central Asia.[34] Other incidents prove low-level Arab al Qaeda operatives have engaged in trafficking, including the two maritime seizures in late 2003.

There's no shortage of evidence that al Qaeda engaged in smuggling—both before and after bin Laden relocated to Afghanistan. A former operative named Jamal al Fadl testified before a U.S. court that he ferried suitcases of cash and coordinated deliveries of weapons to operatives around the globe.[35] The former *Washington Post* reporter Douglas Farah uncovered evidence that al Qaeda operatives struck a deal to purchase diamonds from rebels in Sierra Leone.[36] Farah also later reported that al Qaeda and the Taliban smuggled millions of dollars' worth of gold and bundles of U.S. currency out of Afghanistan in the wake of the 9/11 attacks. The treasure was sent via *hawala* to Dubai, where it was laundered and subsequently scattered around the globe.[37] After the U.S.-led invasion of Afghanistan, coalition troops would find an al Qaeda manual that explained how to smuggle gold on small boats and conceal it on the body.[38]

The structure of bin Laden's network, which always blended

business and terrorism, was similar to large, successful criminal organizations: flexible, diversified, decentralized, and compartmentalized. While in Sudan, bin Laden ran construction businesses, imported sugar and soap, and exported sesame seeds, palm oil, and sunflower seeds. He purchased farms, some of them enormous, which grew corn and peanuts and also served as training camps.[39] In Afghanistan, he expanded his terrorist empire, allowing him to take his ambitions global. One French intelligence report compared al Qaeda's financial architecture to the disgraced BCCI, which forged a complex decentralized structure of overlapping shell companies to launder drug money, hide terrorist funds, and funnel weapons to the mujahideen. "The financial network of bin Laden, as well as his network of investments, is similar to the network put in place in the 1980s by BCCI for its fraudulent operations, often with the same people (former directors and cadres of the bank and its affiliates, arms merchants, oil merchants, Saudi investors)," the seventy-page report said. "The dominant trait of bin Laden's operations is that of a terrorist network backed up by a vast financial structure."[40]

Time and time again, as I and the local reporters who helped research this book looked for bin Laden's ties to the drug trade, our contacts suggested we would never establish clear links. The people who benefit most from the drug trade in this region never actually touch the drugs, they said. I believe that bin Laden, as well as Mullah Omar, don't sully themselves in the opium trade, but they have created an environment that has transformed Afghanistan into the world's leading supplier of opiates. Even if the Afghan opium drug trade grew without their approval or indirect involvement—an idea I find ludicrous—terrorists and insurgents are at the very least fellow travellers on the same black market circuit. "God forbid there is another major terrorist attack on the United States," says Baker, "it will absolutely use the same illicit financial structure that moves narcotics."

7. MISSION CREEP

IN OCTOBER 2006, AFTER AFGHANISTAN HARVESTED 6,100 metric tons of opium, two U.S. congressmen sat down to draft a letter. They had a bone to pick with Donald Rumsfeld.

"We all know that drugs fuel the violence and insurgency," wrote Henry Hyde and Mark Kirk, "and now we need new policy that addresses both the drugs and related terror simultaneously."[1] The U.S. lawmakers knew better than to ask the cantankerous defence secretary to take on the fight against opium. Rumsfeld had repeatedly expressed concern that Afghanistan could turn into another costly drug war like Colombia and rejected proposed engagement in counternarcotics activities as "mission creep." Five years into the war in Afghanistan, with most of Washington distracted by Iraq, the Pentagon continued to insist that the Afghan insurgency was the military's responsibility, defining the opium trade as a problem for law enforcement.

Kirk and Hyde, who chaired the Foreign Relations Committee, were receiving disturbing information from Afghanistan, however: U.S. military units would not disrupt opium bazaars, rarely stopped drug shipments moving toward the borders, and routinely rejected DEA requests to provide backup to their missions.[2] In their letter, the lawmakers suggested ways the military and the DEA could harmonize their efforts. They wanted DEA agents to ride along on military missions when there was a likelihood that drugs would be found, and urged the military to notify counternarcotics agents when they came across opium caches. "We must find a way to merge your counter insurgency mission with that of the DEA's drug-fighting mission," Hyde and Kirk wrote.

The congressmen waited almost two months to get a response from the Pentagon. The tepid reply noted that Britain, not the United States, was the lead nation on counternarcotics issues within the coalition. The U.S. government did support the British-run initiative, but that was handled by the State Department, the letter added. "Regarding your specific recommendations for DoD [Department of Defense], the Secretary has already taken such action," wrote Eric Edelman, Rumsfeld's undersecretary.[3] For frustrated counternarcotics officials and lawmakers in Washington, who felt Afghanistan drug policy was seriously adrift, the letter reflected the Pentagon's unaccommodating attitude. A congressional study found that the DEA had requested military airlifts on twenty-six occasions in 2005 and these requests were denied in all but three cases. The Pentagon improved its record in 2006, approving twelve of fourteen DEA air support requests.[4]

DoD policy itself was ambiguous: official guidance sent to commanding officers said they "could" destroy drug shipments they intercepted, but didn't say they had to.[5] Some U.S. commanders supported counternarcotics efforts, seizing and destroying drug shipments and communicating with counternarcotics agents. Others seemed to deliberately ignore them. One Green Beret complained that he had been ordered to disregard opium and heroin stashes when he came across them on patrol.[6] Contrary to what Edelman's letter said, there seemed to be no clear directive from the top to accommodate the DEA, or at least there was little awareness of it on the ground. Seth Jones, a Rand analyst travelling with U.S. Special Forces in 2006, was on hand when the elite troops obtained "actionable intelligence" that narco-traffickers were crossing from Pakistan. "Their attitude was, 'We're not getting involved,'" Jones told me.

In other cases, senior military officials discarded intelligence, or said the fragmentary evidence didn't prove the Taliban was systematically exploiting the poppy trade (just as U.S. officials had said about the mujahideen in the 1980s). "We had camera work and GPS locations about the Taliban moving huge levels of opium and pocketing the cash," said a U.S. counternarcotics official posted to Kabul. "The army would just tell us, 'Oh, they just happen to hold power in that area so they take a cut.'"[7] U.S. military officials often denied there was any clear proof of a link between the Taliban and the drug trade. As one U.S. official complained to me: "You would have to find Mullah Omar on the phone trying to sell drugs and use that cash to buy weapons with which he planned to kill Americans. Only then would they believe it."

As much as anything, senior U.S. military commanders justifiably felt they already had enough on their plate. The initial number of foreign troops deployed to Afghanistan—just four thousand peacekeepers in Kabul and another eight thousand U.S. troops focused on capturing or killing Taliban and al Qaeda members—was tiny in comparison to the country's size and population. After the 2003 Iraq invasion, U.S. forces in Afghanistan were stretched even thinner. The Pentagon's hesitancy to take on the growing drug problem stemmed from three concerns. U.S. commanders feared that taking on poppy farmers would conflict with their campaign to win hearts and minds, especially in the southern countryside where the Taliban was active. An estimated 12 percent of the Afghan population is tied to the poppy industry—with much heavier population concentrations in the south and the east.

Plus, opium makes up between 30 and 50 percent of Afghanistan's GDP, and it's not just the insurgents profiting.[8] Complicating the picture is the fact that key allies in the CIA and U.S. military-led effort to hunt down al Qaeda and Taliban are themselves known to run massive drug rings. It is clear that senior officials in the Karzai administration are involved as well, though efforts to fight corruption have stalled badly. The Afghan president raised eyebrows in 2007 when he appointed Izzatullah Wasifi as his anticorruption tsar. Wasifi was convicted two decades ago for trying to sell $2 million worth of heroin to an undercover officer in Caesar's Palace, Las Vegas. Wasifi called the bust a youthful indiscretion.[9]

There were worse cases. In June 2004, counternarcotics agents raided the offices of the twenty-something Helmand governor Sher Mohammed Akhundzada, where they found nine metric tons of opium.[10] He was removed as governor soon after, but Karzai swiftly appointed him as a member of parliament, and he never faced an investigation, much less any charges against him. Other senior Afghan officials and warlords with known ties to narcotics remain in business, according to U.S. military intelligence documents seen by the author. A number of them still work closely with the U.S. military and the CIA.

"This is the Afghan equivalent of failing to deal with looting in Baghdad," said Andre D. Hollis, a former deputy assistant secretary of defence for counternarcotics. "If you are not dealing with those who are threatened by security and who undermine security, namely drug traffickers, all your other grandiose plans will come to naught."[11]

The third issue, according to U.S. officials familiar with the Pentagon's mind-set, is an unspoken concern that individual American units deployed to drug-producing areas or along trafficking routes could become corrupted. "There's just too much money sloshing around out there," a senior Republican aide who works closely on drugs matters told me. The Pentagon's attitude infuriated counternarcotics officials, not least since it gave many Afghans the impression that Washington is unopposed to the poppy trade, and may even condone or partake in it. Besides, no one was asking the U.S. military to take on the drug trade itself—just to support operations by the DEA, the British-led Task Force 333, and the Afghan counternarcotics police. "In the war environment, you don't get from point A to point B without military assistance," says a Washington-based official. Adds Jack Lawn, the former DEA chief: "You can't drop a team into a troubled area without military backup."

Part of the problem was systemic: efforts to fight drugs in post-Taliban Afghanistan were divided among donor nations with no framework for coordination. From the start, levels of commitment were highly skewed and priorities conflicted. Washington pledged more than $4 billion in equipment alone for the new Afghan National Army, for example, while Germany sent just forty police trainers who trained cadets in a Kabul police academy. Tens of thousands of Afghan police in the countryside got no training until 2004, when the United States opened seven regional training centres.[12] Washington's commitment to Afghanistan was greater than any of the other foreign donors', but it still paled in comparison to the funds dedicated to rebuilding Iraq (which wasn't half as destroyed). The United States allocated $909 million in reconstruction assistance to Afghanistan in 2002, compared to $20 billion for postwar Iraq.[13] Aid money was slow to arrive in Afghanistan in general, and very little trickled out to remote areas like Helmand and Nimroz.

Within the newly reopened U.S. embassy in Kabul, fighting narcotics was secondary to hunting terrorists, just as it had been during the Soviet resistance. Beverly Eighmy, who had worked for USAID in Pakistan and Afghanistan during the 1980s, was brought out of retirement in late 2001 to serve as the crime and narcotics adviser on a six-month contract. "That was the length of the tour," she said. "It was pretty brutal, seven days a week, fourteen hours a day—the hardest job I ever loved. And it was just me."[14] When the spring 2002 planting season began, it quickly became apparent that the opium crop was going to be enormous. "I kept telling people at the embassy: 'At some point, somebody has got to get serious on this,'" she said. But for another three years, there would only be one counternarcotics officer posted to the Kabul embassy at any given time, all of them on temporary duty contracts. The DEA didn't open an office in Afghanistan until 2004, and even then most agents were on temporary duty rotations.[15]

Back home in Washington, Rand Beers, who ran the State Department's Bureau of International Narcotics and Law (INL), was tasked to come up with ideas for fighting the opium problem. In autumn 2002, he sat down with British counterparts and they hammered out a plan blending forced eradication of poppy fields, interdiction of traffickers, and alternative livelihood programmes to wean farmers off poppy. "The British said they would be responsible if we gave them some forms of support, including military airlift for drug operations," he said. "This was the most prominent thing we did not agree to 100 percent, but in principle, we agreed to it whenever possible."[16]

Beers drafted a cable that got signed off by the relevant officials in Washington—including the Pentagon. "Then I dispatched a senior counternarcotics Foreign Service officer to Kabul with the paper in hand, and the United States military told him they had never heard of it," Beers told me. "It would appear Central Command sat on it, whether on their own or with orders from the Pentagon. Effectively, they put a stop to the programme then and there."

Unable to pursue its plans to wipe out the poppy crop or arrest drug traffickers, the British government instead launched a three-year, $140 million crop substitution programme that would amount to a spectacular and costly failure. As more farmers planted poppy to receive the easy money, opium production skyrocketed past three thousand metric tons. "It was well-intentioned," a western official based in Kabul told me. "But the Brits got snookered. The Afghans took them to the cleaners." The programme, hastily dropped after its first year, was a major embarrassment for the British government and built friction with U.S. officials, who wanted to use crop dusters to spray herbicide on the poppy fields. Privately, both sniped about each other's proposals.

Publicly, the Bush administration continued to tout Afghanistan as a major success story. On May 1, 2003, just a day before President Bush made his historic tailhook landing onto the USS *Abraham Lincoln* and declared Iraq "mission accomplished," Rumsfeld travelled to Kabul, where he announced an end to major combat operations there as well. Acknowledging that "pockets of resistance" continued to make trouble along the Pakistan border, the defence secretary said, "The bulk of this country today is permissive. It's secure."[17] Girls were back in school, aid groups were pouring into Kabul, and a nationwide vote the following year would choose Hamid Karzai, an American client, as Afghanistan's first democratically elected president. Behind the scenes, however, a handful of U.S. officials had begun to worry the opium trade would soon wash away any successes. By 2004, raw intelligence reports flowing into the embassy indicated the insurgency was profiting heavily from the booming opium trade, as poppy cultivation exploded across Taliban-dominated regions in the south.

The Pentagon continued to refuse to target drug labs, even as counternarcotics officials became more and more convinced it would weaken the Taliban. In January 2004, a U.S. Air Force A-10 bomber was called in to support a British Special Forces team that was locked in a firefight at a major drug lab. Within days, opium prices nationwide climbed by 15 percent.[18] "We found that if we had a successful raid in Nangarhar [in eastern Afghanistan], within twenty-four hours our snitches in the south would tell us that the price had shot up," a U.S. official told me. "Opium prices were phenomenally sensitive."

After the 2003 harvest produced 3,600 tons of opium, even the Pentagon couldn't avoid the problem entirely any longer. It dedicated $73 million to anti-drug efforts in 2004, up from nothing in 2003. The State Department, meanwhile, increased its funding from $30 million to $50 million.[19]

In 2004, President Karzai told American diplomats he feared Afghanistan "had only two or three years to solve the [drug] problem or risk dissolving into a classic narco-state."[20] According to a cable sent by the U.S. embassy in Kabul in March 2004 and seen by the author, Karzai believed Pakistan was encouraging the Taliban to get involved in the opium trade. He charged that Islamabad was "using profits from the drug trade to finance armed opposition" to his government. Some former U.S. officials believe Karzai's reticence to go after tribal allies who engage in drug trafficking stems from a belief that he needs to compete with his Taliban rivals, who are backed by Pakistan. The same year, the outgoing CIA station chief in Kabul dispatched a message home warning of the growing link between the Taliban and the drug trade. "His cable said there was a direct causal link between insurgent funding and the opium trade," according to a U.S. official who saw the document. "If we do not do something about this, he wrote, we will win the battle and lose the war."[21]

Back home in Washington, Robert Charles, who had replaced Rand Beers as INL chief, got nicknamed "Cassandra" in his office for his routine tirades about the Afghan drug problem. When he delivered downbeat testimony on the matter to Congress, a White House official warned he was becoming "inconvenient."[22] Charles wanted to launch an aggressive spraying campaign across the south, matched with alternative livelihood packages for farmers, and he believed he could get the Afghan government to sign on. Charles put together a team of experts and scientists whom he planned to accompany to Kabul to pitch their case to President Karzai. U.S. ambassador Zalmay Khalilzad, an Afghan American envoy known to his colleagues as Zal, denied Charles country clearance, even though as INL chief he had assistant secretary of state status. "I had a knock-down drag-out with Zal over this," Charles said. "I said,

'Zal, I know all the great things you are doing, but if you do not tackle this dragon it will ultimately consume you."[23]

Khalilzad opposed the aggressive programme Charles was advocating, but the U.S. envoy was nonetheless pushing for stronger measures on the narcotics front. He characterized the British approach to fighting drugs as "inadequate both conceptually and operationally" in an April 2004 cable classified secret and titled: "Counternarcotics: Rethinking our Strategy."[24] Asking Washington to increase the number of staff dedicated to counternarcotics matters, Khalilzad warned: "There is a growing danger that the rapidly growing illegal drug industry will sweep away all the other things we are doing to rebuild Afghanistan." There was evidence that "money from the illegal drug industry finds its way into the coffers of the Taliban and other terrorist groups. Disrupting this connection should be our first priority in the counternarcotics area," he wrote.

There may have been growing consensus within the U.S. embassy that Afghanistan's opium trade urgently needed to be tackled, but by 2004 there was considerable friction between the Americans, the British, and the Karzai administration over how to approach the problem. The British and Afghan governments vehemently opposed U.S. proposals to spray the crops. They wanted the focus put on arresting "bad guys," not targeting poor Afghan farmers, according to British and Afghan officials. Interdiction was easier said than done, however, especially in a country where there was no functioning police force or judicial system. Extraditing Afghan drug lords was tricky, too. Britain does not have extraterritorial drug laws, meaning their agents couldn't arrest an individual for committing narcotics crimes outside British territory. The DEA had similar legal limitations developing cases against Afghan smugglers, because they had to prove their product ended up on U.S. streets, which it rarely did. Eventually, diplomats and counternarcotics agents came up with a target everyone could agree on. "Zal wanted to find a superficial solution that was high-profile and made everyone happy," a former embassy official told me. "That ended up being the arrest of Haji Bashir Noorzai."

When the almanac of great criminal investigations gets written, don't expect to find a chapter on the case against the man counternarcotics agents call HBN. Haji Bashir Noorzai's path from Taliban financier to inmate at a Manhattan correctional facility is less a tale of legal triumph than one of missed opportunities, conflicting interests among rival U.S. government agencies, and a private contracting firm operating under murky authority. Bashir Noorzai long walked a fine line with the U.S. government, simultaneously serving as an asset to U.S. agents while doing business with Washington's archenemies. His case highlights the complexities U.S. law enforcement faces in building cases against the shadowy drug networks working with the Taliban and al Qaeda.

As I detailed in Chapter 3, the powerful Noorzai tribe has been known to the U.S. government since the 1990s, when DEA agents began tracking Bashir's father, Mohammed Issa, a leading member of the Quetta Alliance of smugglers. Bashir himself became a DEA informant, providing U.S. agents with information about Turkish smugglers. He also worked with CIA agents to recover Stinger missiles after the Soviet army withdrew. In his 2007 sworn deposition before the court of the Southern District of New York, Noorzai testified he recovered about a dozen missiles working with two agents he knew as Mike and Sam. The agency paid him approximately $50,000 for his work, he said.[25]

The State Department was aware of Bashir Noorzai's role in founding the Taliban; and the CIA reported on deals he brokered with Mullah Omar to export crystal heroin.[26] Federal agents believe Bashir Noorzai reached the pinnacle of his smuggling days under Taliban rule. The DEA says Noorzai processed opium into heroin in labs along the Pakistan border and shipped the narcotics, hidden in suitcases, to New York.[27] By 1990, he allegedly ran a network of distributors in Manhattan.[28] His sealed indictment says he shipped fifty-seven kilograms of heroin to New York City in 1997.[29] After the 9/11 attacks, he was placed on a list of high-value military targets by the U.S. military.[30] The burly tribesman would have surely known U.S. drug agents were on his tail, not that he let such trifles worry him. Ever the opportunist, Noorzai promptly made contact with American troops after they invaded Kandahar and told them he wanted to help form the new Afghan government. "I am a tribal leader," he said, according to his testimony. "And I want to bring stability to Afghanistan."

American officials held Noorzai in custody in Kandahar for six days, interrogating him about the whereabouts of Mullah Omar and the Taliban's financial setup, according to Noorzai's testimony and U.S. officials familiar with the meetings. He offered to bring his 1-million-strong tribe—traditional allies of the Taliban—into the new political order and to collect weapons the Taliban had stashed in his territory. The soldiers let him go, and two weeks later he had lived up to his word. Noorzai returned to the American base with more than a dozen trucks piled with weapons, including four hundred antiaircraft missiles.

Within months, foreign journalists based in Kandahar were describing Noorzai as a major power broker in the new regime. Mark Corcoran, a correspondent for the Australian Broadcasting Corporation, reported on his luxurious mansion and his twelve-thousand-man private army.[31] "He's the most powerful drug lord in southern Afghanistan," Corcoran reported. "With each new administration that comes to Kandahar, they have to face the choice of either taking Haji Bashar [Bashir] on or making a deal with him." The U.S.-appointed provincial governor, Gul Agha Sherzai, had moved into Noorzai's mansion, the story said, and even U.S. forces appeared to be working with him. "The Americans, for their part, received intelligence on a level that I do not believe they had been receiving before," said Michael Ware, then a reporter for *Time* magazine, interviewed in Corcoran's story. "Haji Bashar intimately knows senior members of the Taliban. He, more than anyone, has information on where these leaders went and how they got away, and he is now proving pivotal in negotiating the surrenders of countless Taliban commanders."

Within several months, Noorzai's dealings with the Americans would sour. He convinced the former foreign minister Wakil Ahmed Muttawakil to come out of hiding, and the Americans promptly shipped the senior Taliban official off to Guantánamo Bay. Noorzai then tried to secure the surrender of Haji Birqet Khan, another Kandahari close to the Taliban. U.S. warplanes attacked Birqet's home shortly after the pair met, having apparently received information they were hatching a plan to attack U.S. troops. Noorzai later claimed the Americans had bad information. Regardless, the air strike killed Birqet, one of his wives, and two of his grandsons.[32] Fearing he, too, would be killed, either by the

Americans or in a revenge attack, Noorzai fled to Pakistan, according to his own testimony.

There, the DEA believes he swiftly returned to the heroin trade, reportedly with the help of Pakistani intelligence agents who gave him a new passport.[33] According to a 2004 U.S. intelligence report seen by the author, Noorzai travelled between Pakistan and the Gulf—mainly Dubai—but stayed away from Afghanistan. Business was as brisk as ever. The 2004 intelligence report said Noorzai maintained eighteen refineries in Registan, a desert district in southern Kandahar.

According to testimony given to the House International Relations Committee, he was smuggling two tons of heroin out of Kandahar Province every eight weeks and moving it west with the help of al Qaeda operatives based in Pakistan.[34] Nonetheless, American authorities reached out to Noorzai again, dispatching President Karzai's brother Ahmed Wali (a curious choice given Ahmed Wali's alleged ties to smuggling) and Khalid Pashtun, a Kandahar parliamentarian, to Quetta to ask him to meet U.S. officials. Noorzai agreed, and in August 2004 he flew to Dubai for talks with two American investigators, identified in court documents as Mike and Brian.[35] Those talks would continue in Peshawar, Pakistan, the following month.

Mike identified himself to Noorzai as an employee of the Defense Intelligence Agency and said that Brian was from the Federal Bureau of Investigation, according to Noorzai's deposition. Close scrutiny of the exchange reveals Noorzai provided Mike and Brian little information. He repeatedly denied his own involvement in what he called the powder trade. "I have told you about my father, that he was involved, did you understand? But I have not done this work," he said at one point. Noorzai claimed not to know the whereabouts of people Mike and Brian sought, but did offer to help find them. "I do not want enmity with you people," he kept saying. When pressed about how much drug money went to finance al Qaeda, Noorzai replied, "None." Mike said: "But the entire world says the opposite." Noorzai stood his ground. "I do not believe it," he replied.

Instead Noorzai tried to convince the two Americans he was a well-intentioned friend of the United States who had been double-crossed by the very emissaries they had dispatched to invite him to Dubai. "He is a thief," Noorzai said of Khalid Pashtun, adding later that "I can line up not ten but twenty people in front of you that Karzai's brother [Ahmed Wali] and Khalid [Pashtun] took money from." Noorzai also claimed then Kandahar governor Gul Agha Sherzai was spreading lies about him. Noorzai's accusations deserve analysis, because he had personal and tribal issues with all three men, whose past history also warrants inspection. Whether they realized it or not, Mike and Brian stepped into the middle of a centuries-old rivalry between the Panjpai and Zirak branches of Kandahar's Durrani tribes.[36] Struggles for power and money between the rival Panjpai and Zirak Durranis have long created strife in Kandahar.

There was also the personal rivalry at issue. When the Taliban took over Kandahar city in 1994 (an operation Noorzai helped bankroll), they ousted Gul Agha, then the leading mujahideen commander. It was the excesses of Gul Agha's men that reportedly prompted Mullah Omar's initial rise against Kandahari mujahideen. The toppling of the Taliban in 2001 not only allowed the Zirak Durrani tribes to regain dominance in Kandahar, it once again put

Gul Agha at the helm. U.S. forces bankrolled Gul Agha's return—literally with carloads of hard currency—and appointed him governor of Kandahar.[37] Khalid Pashtun, a former taxi driver, served as Gul Agha's interpreter and spokesman. When Hamid Karzai became president, his brother Ahmed Wali was appointed to a senior provincial position in Kandahar. Human rights groups have accused Gul Agha of human rights abuses and Ahmed Wali Karzai of ties to the drug trade, accusations backed up by U.S. government documents seen by the author.[38]

Noorzai offered forth details of a recent drug bust he linked to Ahmed Wali Karzai. He also fingered Arif Noorzai, then the minister for border and tribal affairs, as a partner in Ahmed Wali's narcotics network. "All of them work in this fuckin' business," he said. This, too, was perhaps a revelation with a purpose, according to another member of the Noorzai clan. There is an intense rivalry between Bashir Noorzai and Arif Noorzai. Since Bashir was a patron of the Taliban leader Mullah Omar, he controlled the lucrative trade corridor out of Kandahar (straddled by the Noorzai tribe) during the Taliban era. When the U.S. forces rolled into Afghanistan, Arif leapt closer to the centre of power because he was married into the Karzai family.[39] Arif not only sidelined Bashir after 9/11, says the relative, he may have poisoned Bashir's reputation with the Americans. "This is all about family and money," said the relative. "It's like a soap opera."[40]

The two American investigators appeared to have only a passing interest in the drug trade anyway. Throughout hundreds of documents reviewed by the author, covering four separate meetings in August and September 2004, their line of questioning with Noorzai focuses on "our money flow of funds project," as Mike called it. The Americans appear to be trying to identify how *hawala* traders sent money to al Qaeda and wanted Noorzai to secure them meetings with prominent money changers close to the terror group. "These are people who can give us information and educate us on how money moves," Mike said at one point, appearing to refer to a diagram linking al Qaeda to specific *hawaladars.* "The prominent *hawala* dealers, the prominent moneychangers, the people who can help us understand how monies are being diverted to these guys up here [al Qaeda]." From their first encounter, Mike and Brian told Noorzai they had access to high-level U.S. officials and tried to convince him that if he came to the United States to meet their superiors, he would have nothing to fear from the long arm of the law.

An exchange between Brian and Babar, the translator, during an August 9 meeting is representative:

Brian: Listen, I want Haji Bashar to understand that over the next two months, let's say OK, we're gonna probably need to get together again.

Babar: Definitely.[41]

Brian: OK.

Babar: Ahem.

Brian: And we can do it just like this or we can do it in Pakistan or he can do it wherever he wants to do it.

Babar: Right.

Brian: But, umm, the first point I wanna make is that we're gonna have to come together again and this can't be the last time that we . . .

Babar: (in Pashto) He says that this is obvious that it will take a month, it will take three weeks or it will take a month and a half, but we will meet once again. Our meeting will not end by this gathering. We said this that morning too, all right?

Noorzai: (In Pashto) Only if they make it so that we become free and people don't capture us.

Babar: (In English) At least get me relieved that no one . . . *(mixed voices)* rest everything [*sic*] is you know I should not be caught.

Brian: Listen, after this meeting, OK . . .

Unknown person: (In Pashto) He says after this meeting . . .

Brian: After this meeting, umm, I believe the, the, the, the, this position of his affairs as they relate to the U.S. government and the immediate threat to apprehend him . . .

Babar: Uh huh.

Brian: Will be diminished.

Unknown person: (In Pashto) They won't do anything to you.

Babar: (In Pashto) He says.

Mike: But there's gonna be a . . .

Brian: There's gonna be a window there where . . .

(Mixed voices)

Unknown person: (In Pashto) He says that you are standing in the door.

Brian: It's going to take us time to explain this to the right people and we can't do it from here. It has to be done in person over a couple of days, so there's going to be a window where nothing is diminished. Everything's gonna be the same. I want him to know that we are gonna go back and we're gonna explain it to the right people and we will get it diminished I hope.

Babar: OK.

Babar: (In Pashto) He says he will talk to our important people there seriously and will take guarantee and will end your sudden capturing. For example, they follow you and whenever you are found they will suddenly capture you, we will remove you from that list. But to completely prove you innocent, that will take time. But now we will talk to the right people, and through them we will do this that they will not capture you; they will not follow and find you.

Unknown: (In Pashto) Did you understand?

Babar: (In Pashto) Did you understand? After that . . .

Unknown: (In Pashto) You are standing in the door.

Babar: (In Pashto) You have arrived at the door. Now we will take you inside that we can clear you completely, systematically.

Appalling translation aside, the investigators' tactics reflect standard interrogation strategy: they convinced their subject they believed him and that he could trust them. After four meetings where this message was systematically repeated, Bashir Noorzai could be forgiven for thinking it would be okay to "take a vacation," as Mike put it, to the United States. In their final session on September 16, 2004, Mike said his superiors wanted to sit down with Noorzai in New York:

> It would be like a vacation. He would be interviewed. He would be talked to about a lot of subjects, but the goal would be to position him very appropriately to assist us with opening dialogues with some of the people there. Then he is coming back here, like he was just away for a couple of weeks on vacation. . . . The goal of the trip would be that no one will really know that he made the trip to the United States. It will be

> kept very, very quiet.... I think quite frankly the way our government prefers to do it is to take him quietly to the U.S.

Much to the surprise of everyone involved, the man that DEA agents have since labelled the "Pablo Escobar of Afghanistan" agreed to make the trip. A passport and U.S. visa were hastily arranged, and on April 13, 2005, Noorzai landed in New York City, where he was met at the airport by DEA special agents.[42] Unbeknown to Noorzai, a grand jury had issued a sealed indictment against him three and a half months earlier.[43] Noorzai would have saved himself a lot of trouble had he checked the DEA's website before he boarded the plane. His name had been added to Washington's list of the world's top ten targeted drug kingpins. The U.S. government's changing perspective on Noorzai—from dubious ally to wanted criminal—had less to do with Noorzai himself than shifting priorities in Washington. Afghanistan had just harvested 4,200 metric tons of opium, and the insurgency was gaining ground. To demonstrate it was getting tough on drugs, Washington needed a high-profile arrest.

Nonetheless, the Bush administration was so startled that Noorzai had agreed to come to New York, officials weren't sure at first what to do with him.[44] Noorzai was put up at the Embassy Suites Hotel in lower Manhattan for thirteen days, where he was grilled by DEA and FBI agents. Noorzai said later he wondered why they told him he had a right to a lawyer and the right to remain silent at the start of each meeting, but didn't comprehend the significance of these statements until the day he tried to return home.[45] The moment a DEA agent present told him he was under arrest, Noorzai demanded they provide legal counsel. U.S. officials first presented him with a defence attorney named Steven Goldenberg. "Goldenberg allowed Bashir to meet with U.S. officials, and the government's version of those meetings is not helpful to the case," said his current attorney, Ivan Fisher.

In one of those unrecorded meetings, the DEA note takers reported that Noorzai agreed he owned land where poppy was cultivated, processed into heroin, and exported to the United States.[46] In court, Noorzai's lawyer tried to argue that those conversations were poorly translated, like the ones in Peshawar and Dubai, and that Noorzai did not understand the questions he was answering. Around this time, Noorzai also must have realized he wasn't being well represented. One of my local colleagues in Afghanistan, who comes from the same region as the Noorzais, received a phone call one day from Bashir's cousin. "You work with Americans," he said. "Can you ask if they know a good lawyer in New York?"

In the end, the Noorzais turned to a more sympathetic ear for help. Bashir would retain Ivan Fisher, one of New York's leading defence attorneys, through Haji Ayub Afridi, the drug baron from Pakistan's Khyber Pass who was extradited to the United States in 1995. Fisher's client list reads like a who's who of smugglers, crime bosses, and other ne'er-do-wells. As a young lawyer, he defended Jack Henry Abbott against murder charges, arguing that the bestselling author of *In the Belly of the Beast* stabbed an actor in a moment of "extreme emotional disturbance." In addition to representing Afridi, Fisher also worked on the "French Connection" case, served as lead counsel for mafioso Salvatore Catalano in the "Pizza Connection Trial," and represented Michele Sindona, an

Italian financier dubbed "the Vatican's banker," whose financial empire collapsed amid charges of fraud, bribery, and murder. He told me Noorzai is his most interesting case yet.

It won't be his easiest. In September 2008, a federal jury found Noorzai guilty of manufacturing and conspiring to import and distribute heroin to the United States. "Noorzai's decades-long criminal career has finally ended, and one of Afghanistan's most prolific heroin exporters now faces a potential life sentence to be served in a U.S. prison," said Michael Garcia, the United States Attorney for the Southern District of New York. Fisher has appealed the case, saying it is almost impossible for an American jury to give a defendant who has such close ties to top Taliban officials a fair trial.[47]

Fisher has sought dismissal of the trial on evidence Mike and Brian were actually private contractors with no known authority to offer HBN immunity.[48] The court threw out that argument, though jurors later told *The New York Times* they believed Noorzai had been "tricked."[49] Fisher also argues that since Noorzai willingly travelled to and was arrested in U.S. territory, his Miranda rights were violated by U.S. agents who did not make it clear he was under indictment when he landed in New York. "As a matter of U.S. law, their conduct was reprehensible," he said.

U.S. officials hoped that snaring Haji Bashir Noorzai would demonstrate Washington's determination to get tough on traffickers linked to the Taliban and al Qaeda. If the verdict is overturned on appeal, his trial may prove a lengthy and costly embarrassment, drawing attention to the tremendous legal challenges to stopping Afghanistan's multibillion-dollar opium trade.

More than anything, it illustrates how DEA and other federal agents must operate in convoluted legal territory to bring Afghan traffickers to the United States, since Afghanistan has no extradition laws.[50] In October 2005, Haji Baz Mohammed, allegedly a partner in Noorzai's operation, became the first Afghan trafficker "extradited" to the United States. He pled guilty the following year, according to a DEA statement.[51] In 2007, the DEA apprehended Mohammad Essa, another alleged smuggler with alleged links to the Taliban, charged with conspiring to smuggle $25 million of heroin into the United States.[52] Essa "consented to his removal to the United States," a DEA statement said.[53]

Legal experts close to the process say the two men were convinced they would be more comfortable in a U.S. jail than an Afghan one, and smugglers apprehended in the future will also have to be convinced of the benefits of facing trial under U.S. law until Afghanistan's Wolesi Jirga (National Assembly) approves an extradition treaty.[54] Given that corruption plagues the Afghan justice system, some foreign law enforcement officials are frustrated that such legal hurdles continue to slow down U.S. law enforcement efforts there. "With the Afghan justice system the way it is, we should be extraditing twelve or more of these guys every month," said a former U.S. counternarcotics official.[55]

There have been some success stories. Under pressure from western nations, Shahbaz Khan, a major Pakistani trafficker, was jailed in Sharjah and $90 million of his drug profits seized.[56] Three other smugglers were convicted and sentenced under new Afghan narcotics laws.[57] Under the auspices of Operation Containment, heroin seizures increased 2,826 percent by 2006 and a U.S.-trained interdiction unit within the Afghan police was working with DEA paramilitary foreign-deployed advisory support (FAST) teams on law enforcement operations.[58] Similar programmes were developed in Pakistan and Central Asian states bordering Afghanistan.[59] In public, former DEA administrator Karen Tandy praised the Pentagon for its support of her agency, noting that the Department of Defense was building a base camp for the FAST teams and providing the Afghan Interior Ministry with eight Mi-17 helicopters to support counternarcotics operations.[60] However, delays meant only two helicopters had arrived by 2006, and they were just used for training. Meanwhile, the U.S. military still won't support DEA operations in Helmand, Kandahar, and Nimroz provinces, the main regions where the poppy trade benefits the insurgency.

Behind the scenes, U.S. officials said Tandy fought hard for more support. "Without the helicopters, we can't move," complained a DEA agent. "We're sure not going to go out in caravans with a couple of pistols."[61] Tandy touched on the issue in June 2006 testimony before the House of Representatives. "The key challenge," she said, "is force protection for our DEA agents and [Afghan] counterparts."[62] A bipartisan group of U.S. lawmakers continued to hound the Pentagon on the issue, passing a 2007 appropriations bill authorizing $2.1 billion in spending on counternarcotics and development, which aimed at pushing the Pentagon to better support the DEA.

The sheer size of Afghanistan's problem—versus the lack of resources—slowed progress. When I visited Ahmadullah Alizai, the Kandahar counternarcotics police chief, in 2004, his entire force comprised himself and a rusty motorcycle. "I have made a request for a police force," he told me shrugging. "We need at least two to three hundred well-trained anti-drug police for this province alone." Four years later, the DEA was importing Colombian counternarcotics police who used mock AK-47s made of wood to instruct

Afghanistan's fledgling anti-drug force. "This is kindergarten," said Vincent Balbo, the DEA chief in Kabul. "This is Narcotics 101." Another DEA agent added: "We are at a stage now of telling these recruits, 'This is a handgun, this is a bullet.' "[63]

The biggest problem facing law enforcement efforts is widespread corruption and lack of capacity in the Afghan government, judiciary, and police. Almost eight years since 9/11, amid fresh calls to build a bigger Afghan army, what the nation really needs is a functioning police and judiciary. The Afghan National Police remain largely untrained, underequipped, poorly funded, and riddled with graft. Regional warlords who stepped into rural power vacuums often installed their private militias as the provincial police. The international community, with Germany as the lead nation on police reform, got off to a slow start transforming these ragtag groups into a 62,000-strong national force.

In 2004, Washington accelerated the effort with a $1.1 billion programme, contracted in part to Virginia-based DynCorp International, to put provincial police through eight-week crash courses, using retired American police as trainers. Even this massive investment failed to make much of a difference, however, in part because there were so few trainers per province, and eight weeks was not nearly enough time to turn militia fighters—70 percent of them illiterate—into respectable, trusted law enforcement officers.

A joint 2006 report by the Pentagon and the State Department found most of the programme's graduates were incapable of carrying out even routine law enforcement work.[64] The initiative was also chronically mismanaged. Two years into the initiative, its directors couldn't say how many police were on duty or locate thousands of vehicles and other equipment the programme had purchased.[65] Police commanders were widely known to put "ghost" employees on the payroll, while their forces reportedly worked with smugglers and extorted money from truckers and local businessmen.

Some of the most insecure regions received the fewest trainers. DynCorp initially sent two former sheriff's deputies to Lashkar Gah, the capital of Helmand, to train the entire province's three thousand police. Security was so poor the two Americans couldn't visit any of the districts, however. They described their students as eager to learn, but pitifully underequipped. In one class, forty police officers shared just fifteen rifles.[66] In the volatile south, U.S. and Afghan officials estimate police are dying at a rate six times that of the Afghan National Army. "The police down south are outgunned, outnumbered, and outfinanced," a senior Afghan security official complained. "And it's going to be like that for years."[67] The U.S. military is now implementing a $2.5 billion overhaul of the Afghan police that aims to retrain the country's entire 72,000-member force and embed 2,350 American and European advisers in police stations across the country. Entire police units are to be pulled from districts, retrained as a group for eight weeks, and then sent back in a "top-to-bottom" effort to eliminate corruption.[68]

A top-to-bottom overhaul of the interior ministry will also be critical. A UN study found drugs corruption has penetrated the highest levels of the ministry, with senior officials and police commanders earning tens of thousands of dollars every month in kickbacks and bribes. The study found senior officers "purchase" plum positions along lucrative drug smuggling routes, and then pay monthly fees to their seniors not to get fired.[69] Delays in training judges and prosecutors for Afghanistan's faltering judicial system have slowed progress in convicting drug criminals, and so far courts have mainly only gone after small-time crooks and drug addicts.[70] Meanwhile, a gleaming new $4.4 million prison, built with British funds to house major smugglers, sits virtually empty on the outskirts of Kabul.[71] At least four convicts already escaped, prompting UNODC chief Antonio Maria Costa to remark that the prison's greatest weakness was its front door.[72]

Perhaps most troubling of all, in the light of President Karzai's notorious reluctance to take on the drug trade, are persistent reports that his immediate family members are taking an active role in coordinating it, and that members of his Popalzai tribe, his half brother and other cronies, have been posted to positions along trafficking routes around Afghanistan. In May 2005, American diplomats cabled back to Washington that Karzai "has been unwilling to assert strong leadership" on the narcotics issue "even in his home province of Kandahar."[73] Afghan technocrats who populated the Karzai regime at the outset of his government had mostly resigned or been sacked. Regional warlords and tribal chiefs with dubious records on drugs continue to populate the administration. "Karzai's record with counternarcotics is even worse than his record of going after corruption," a western official complained to me. Widespread graft within the Kabul administration is what gives the insurgency space to grow. "Afghanistan's biggest problem isn't drugs," said Doug Wankal, a former DEA agent who later ran the Counternarcotics Task Force at the U.S. embassy in Kabul. "It's corruption."[74]

Major campaigns to wean Helmand's farmers off of poppy have been expensive failures. A sizable portion of Washington's $600 million Afghan counternarcotics effort is now spent on "alternative livelihood" programmes. More than $200 million in U.S. and British funding was designated for Helmand in 2007, a year when poppy output there still increased by 45 percent.[75] In early 2008, the World Bank estimated donor nations would need to invest more than $2 billion in irrigation, roads, and other development projects to entice Afghan farmers away from poppy cultivation.[76] That will be challenging logistically to implement in the south, given NATO and the Kabul government's inability to quell the violence there. A number of facilities built with aid money already sit empty and crumbling. One western-funded school on the edge of Lashkar Gah was turned into a poppy field after it closed in a shower of Taliban threats.[77]

In other cases, projects have been unsustainable or just plain pointless. In 2006, I visited a cash-for-work project to build a cobblestone road between Lashkar Gah and the ancient fortress of Qala-e-Bost on the outskirts of the provincial capital. I was accompanied to the worksite, where half a dozen Afghans hammered stones into the earth, by four Humvees each full of U.S. soldiers and bodyguards from the security contracting firm Global. I pointed out to the USAID organizers that the last thing Afghanistan needed was more bumpy roads. They agreed, but said the project was "labour-intensive," and that cobblestone roads lasted centuries. It looked more security-intensive to me, and the stone workers who lined up to tell me they had given up the poppy habit seemed disingenuous. On the way back into town, a British bodyguard in my armoured vehicle confirmed my suspicions. "Come back in six weeks and you won't see any of these workers here," he said. "They'll all be off harvesting poppy."

Aid projects were built to suit U.S. deadlines and values—including political time lines and priorities in Washington—

rather than meeting the needs and realities of poor Afghan farming families. Despite poor roads, a shortage of electricity, and deteriorating security, USAID planned to launch an apricot and raisin industry, a flour mill, Internet cafés, and a dairy-processing plant. One aid worker I met was doing a feasibility study for an industrial park. A separate plan would have Helmand's produce exported by plane, despite rising fuel costs.[78] Although I believe these groups are genuinely trying to help, most plans I have come across have been utterly unrealistic.

In 2007, aid worker Joel Hafvenstein, contracted by USAID to help set up Helmand's cash-for-work programme, published his memoirs, *Opium Season.* His vivid account of his treacherous year in southern Afghanistan revealed the pressure his team came under from the Bush administration to meet arbitrary quotas they set. Washington dispatched advisers—hired by the Defense Department but answerable to the State Department—to get Afghanistan's faltering reconstruction effort off the ground. The advisers ordered Hafvenstein's team to create 2.5 million workdays in Helmand during their first year, a Herculean task that meant employing thousands of people. They appeared to be unconcerned about the nature of the work, but worried about accusations that too much USAID money went to pay high-priced foreign advisers. The advisers wanted 70 percent of the cash to be spent on Afghans. "Condoleezza Rice will be getting weekly updates on this project," one of the advisers told Hafvenstein, who wondered to what extent the targets were for "Condi's benefit," as he put it, and not based on on-the-ground realities.[79]

Ultimately, none of Washington's goals would be met. Hafvenstein and his colleagues fled Helmand after pro-Taliban assailants killed eleven of their local colleagues and guards. Hafvenstein's experience, while tragic, nonetheless evokes the old adage that the U.S. government is the world's last communist institution, with five-year plans, risk aversion, and targets everyone pretends to meet. Planned economies are doomed to failure when their goals are shaped to meet the political priorities of their planners instead of the needs of the people who live under them.

Deteriorating security and the day-to-day pressures it brought, coupled with the demanding work schedule and Afghanistan's general lack of comfort, has made it hard to keep aid programmes and embassies staffed. The country's complex environment presented a steep learning curve for even the most highly dedicated people, especially when tours of duty for diplomats, aid workers, and foreign troops rarely lasted more than one year. As often as not, former officials have complained to me, short-termers tended to bury problems rather than try to solve them. It was a policy the former INL chief Robert Charles dubbed "not-on-my-watchism."

The most spectacular case of this phenomenon came in 2003, when President Bush and Donald Rumsfeld, under domestic pressure to show they were bringing U.S. troops back home, handed the Afghan conflict over to NATO. The changing of command, which came months after the U.S. invasion of Iraq, led many officials in Pakistan and Afghanistan—not to mention the Taliban—to conclude that the United States was looking for an exit strategy. "This decision was made for political impact back home," a former senior U.S. commander in Afghanistan told me. "It reinforced everyone's opinion in the region that we were unreliable."

Afghanistan is the most complex mission NATO has ever taken on, and the first outside the Euro-Atlantic region. Cracks in the twenty-six-nation alliance began to appear immediately. European nations bickered over every troop and aircraft deployment, while lawmakers in Germany, Italy, and Spain have refused to deploy soldiers to dangerous southern regions. American, Dutch, Canadian, and British soldiers do most of the heavy fighting, and have sustained by far the most casualties. Some national forces only take part in combat missions once they have permission from home, making it hard for commanders in Kabul to react rapidly. Some fear the NATO alliance itself may be crumbling. Washington is now seeking a total revamp in strategy, and boosting its forces with thousands of Marines. Canada briefly threatened to pull out of the coalition.[80]

Within the shaky coalition, the fight against the opium trade remains one of the most divisive issues of all. Washington finally "got religion" on the Taliban's ties to the drug trade, according to senior U.S. officials, but convincing the Europeans they have to help fight it has been a tougher sell. "Diplomatically, my biggest challenge is finding unity," said Thomas Schweich, who formerly led the State Department's efforts to address Afghanistan's opium problem. "I spend far more time in Europe than I do in Afghanistan."[81]

Washington put forward a five-pillar strategy to fight the opium trade in 2007, with a focus on aerial eradication, alternative livelihoods, interdiction and law enforcement, justice reform, and public information.[82] The Kabul government and most European nations rejected it as too heavily focused on aerial eradication using the herbicide glyphosate, which is commonly sold in the United States under the trade name Roundup. Senior U.S. officials insist their real priority is arresting opium kingpins but admit that the policy also creates divisions since it will mean going after top officials in the Karzai administration.

"I'm a spray man myself," quipped President Bush, summing up his depth of understanding of the controversial and complex issue in two meetings with stunned Afghan officials. U.S. ambassador to Afghanistan William Wood was far less flippant in his messages to Afghan officials, threatening to cut off aid from Washington if they didn't agree to allow crop dusters to wipe out the 2008 harvest.[83] When the 2007 opium harvest soared past $4 billion in value, even the normally impartial UN issued a call for alliance members to take military action against the problem. "Destroy the drug trade and you cut off the Taliban's main funding source," said UNODC director Antonio Maria Costa in an open letter to NATO.[84]

At the end of the day, the biggest problem in coalition building may come not from NATO but from across the border. Counternarcotics officials publicly praise Pakistan's efforts, but privately gripe that Islamabad has done little to shut down the command and control centres for the Afghan drug trade, which are in Baluchistan Province and the southern port city of Karachi. In 2007, Pakistan was quietly slipped onto the State Department's list of major trafficking countries, a designation that in the past could have cut off millions of dollars of aid to Islamabad. "No matter what we do in Afghanistan, we won't touch the problem if we can't get to Pakistan," one senior U.S. official told me. "What keeps me up at night," said a senior western envoy, "is that I don't see a way out of this."[85]

8. ZERO-SUM GAME

IT'S EASY TO TRACE HOW WE GOT TO WHERE WE ARE IN Afghanistan, and to finger who is responsible. It's a lot tougher to formulate a way forward.

After reading the data that field researchers compiled for this book, readers could almost be forgiven for concluding (as the U.S. government has) that the best way forward is to launch an aggressive aerial spraying campaign to wipe out Afghanistan's poppy crop. That way we deny the insurgents and terrorists much-needed funds, right?

Wrong. Wiping out poppy fields would actually drive up poppy prices and put *more* money in the pockets of drug dealers and terrorists. It's basic economics (the Taliban used it themselves when they banned poppy in 2000). When supplies go down, prices go up. Poppy prices have been dropping for several years now, to the point one actually hears opium smugglers saying they *hope* the United States will launch an aggressive spraying campaign: "I'll be very happy if the eradicators are successful," said a Helmand trafficker in 2007. "I have lots of poppy stored. If they don't destroy it, I'm afraid the price will come down."[1]

Moreover, the eradication strategy proposed by the U.S. government would be economically devastating to Afghanistan. No nation has ever been as dependent on its drug income. In Colombia, the cocaine crop never reached more than 5 percent of GDP. Today in Afghanistan, it represents an astounding 30 percent of GDP. According to the U.S. State Department's annual report, as much as 12 percent of the Afghan population lives off the poppy trade.[2] Destroying their livelihoods overnight—before providing alternatives—would not only create a humanitarian disaster, it would turn more Afghans against the United States and create an international public relations nightmare. The poppy farmers are already victims of the opium trade. We shouldn't add to their troubles.

I'm not suggesting we go soft on this issue. Quite the contrary. I recommend wide-ranging military action against top smugglers. But the goal should be to cut or eliminate profits for smugglers and financiers at the top of the narcotics trade and to stem the flow of drug money to Taliban insurgents and terrorist groups who are in their pay.

The coalition, working with local and international law enforcement agents, should arrest or kill the kingpins and midlevel smugglers, tracking and targeting them as they do senior Taliban and al Qaeda functionaries. The coalition should also target the small number of chemists able to cook opium into heroin (many counternarcotics agents estimate there are fewer than twenty-four in the entire country). That would put a significant dent in heroin production very quickly. Warplanes should bomb heroin labs and launch air strikes against drug convoys making their way toward the Iranian and Pakistani borders. Drug convoys don't travel down the highways, so there's less chance of collateral damage and civilian casualties. In 2005, I flew with a U.S.-funded air wing in western Pakistan that patrols for drug convoys using forward-looking infrared (FLIR) cameras. The $35-million-a-year programme is effectively impotent in Pakistan since pilots who track drug convoys have to count on Pakistani authorities on the ground to chase down smugglers (which they don't). We ought to shift those planes over the border, where NATO warplanes can target the convoys spotted carrying opium or heroin.

We have to remember that people don't go into the drug business because they enjoy gardening. They do it to make money—lots of money. The more we make it hard for those at the top to profit, the greater our chances of beating them. But we must shift the focus away from strategies that would affect ordinary Afghans.

The kind of campaign I recommend would target "bad guys," and not victimize debt-ridden Afghan farmers. I believe that if military and law enforcement efforts against smugglers took place in conjunction with aid programmes to help farmers establish legal alternatives (more on this later), we would have a greater chance of winning the "hearts and minds" of poor Afghans whose lives have been torn apart by the criminal opium economy.

Currently, the West and the Taliban are fighting a zero-sum game: The West wants to wipe out the insurgents and their al Qaeda allies. The Taliban want to drive foreign non-Muslims out of Afghanistan. The best strategy against the Taliban is not to fight them but to make them irrelevant. We are not losing Afghanistan because Afghans like the Taliban (they don't). The coalition is failing because it hasn't offered Afghans a better alternative. Fixing Afghanistan—and the greater region—is going to be costly and slow-going and require an enormous amount of manpower. There is no silver bullet. Since the Bush administration failed to complete the job in 2001, defeating the insurgency and the drug trade will now take years—maybe decades—of sustained investment and effort. The cost of not implementing the following recommendations could be unthinkably high.

A complete strategy would combine nine pillars (not just five): diplomatic initiatives for regional peace and free trade; a properly equipped and implemented counterinsurgency strategy; blended intelligence and law enforcement efforts; military strikes against drug lords, labs, and opium convoys; the creation of a farm support network; a public relations campaign; the isolation and disruption of drug and terror funds; and an alternative-livelihood programme. Eradication, which comes first on the U.S. government's list, would be used in extremely limited cases, and only when all the other efforts have failed.

Precious time is being wasted in Washington and Europe arguing about where to begin and which programme gets precedence. A successful policy would resemble the drug cocktail administered to HIV patients: it would mount a simultaneous, multipronged attack. The effort should be holistic, not prioritized. The Bush administration was wary of nation building. In fact, this problem requires *region building*. As the biggest donor, with the largest number of troops deployed to Afghanistan, the United States should take the lead in revitalizing strategy.

Support Regional Peace

Afghanistan was centre stage in the nineteenth century for the "Great Game" between tsarist Russia and the British Empire. In the 1980s, it was the final battleground of the cold war. Now on the front line in the war on terror, Afghanistan again finds itself the victim of regional and global power plays having little to do with Afghans themselves. Overcoming the India-Pakistan rivalry as well as finding common ground between the United States and Iran are among numerous regional barriers preventing sustainable peace in Afghanistan. At first glance, these issues seem totally unrelated to the poppy problem, but boundary disputes and global geopolitics are at the heart of the region's security and trade problems.

Poppy cultivation may be increasingly concentrated in southern provinces where the insurgency holds sway, and the opium harvested there may be processed into morphine base or heroin in unstable border areas, but command and control of the southern Afghanistan drug trade—just like the insurgency itself—is mainly located in Pakistan.[3] Profits from the southern drug trade are laundered between Quetta and Dubai, often ending up in western banking institutions. Precursor chemicals are smuggled in from Pakistan, China, and India. Iran appears to be supporting insurgents, possibly using opium smugglers as conduits. A successful strategy must take into account the regional nature of the opium trade and its financing, and accommodate the conflicting international and regional interests of the nations playing host to it.

It will be critical to get the India-Pakistan peace process back on track. It's not inconceivable that U.S. authorities could sit down with Iranians over Afghanistan, as they did in Iraq. Former U.S. envoy Peter Tomsen suggests a Helsinki-style peace conference to address broader regional peace goals. "Bold creativity and thinking big could produce lasting benefits," Tomsen said.[4] At least in this region, every nation has a common interest: stopping the flow of the opiates that are addicting vast numbers of their citizens.

Support Regional Trade

Southwest Asia remains one of the few parts of the world without a free-trade grouping like NAFTA, ASEAN, or Mercusur. A free-trade zone could one day expand to include the isolated Central Asian states. Opening markets and surmounting border, ethnic, and religious divides plaguing the region since the British colonialists departed would bring stability and increase prosperity—two factors vital to easing the dependence on smuggling illegal drugs. Afghanistan must have access to Pakistan's seaports, and should harmonize its customs duties with Pakistan to cut down on the smuggling of legal goods. Pakistan loses an estimated $2 billion a year in tax revenues because of the U-turn scheme, according to Sardar Shaukat Popalzai, president of the Baluchistan Economic Forum. Afghanistan, for its part, has one of the lowest tax bases on the globe. Helping both countries harmonize and better regulate customs collection would weaken smuggling groups and strengthen both federal governments.

To support my first two proposals the United States should launch a diplomatic surge to the region, host peace talks, and encourage dialogue between the various players. Leading by example, Washington should first sit down with Tehran to mull mutually beneficial programmes to fight the opium trade.

Launch a Proper Counterinsurgency Effort

It's commonly referred to as the "ink-spot strategy." Small military units deployed across a wide, hostile territory, establishing safe havens where they build the locals' confidence, launch development programmes, and improve governance. Slowly extending control, they spread their influence just as an ink spot spreads across fabric. First used by the British in Malaya half a century ago, this strategy can't be applied piecemeal, as it has been in many parts of southern Afghanistan, with too few troops forcing commanders to rely on air assaults that result in heavy civilian casualties. Experts who have studied modern counterinsurgencies say the standard rule of thumb is to deploy at least twenty reliable and trusted soldiers or law enforcement officers for every thousand inhabitants (meaning there should be fifteen thousand in Helmand alone, for example). There should be less attention paid to how many insurgents are killed in battle. Kill ratios make little difference when the local population despises you.

It's crucial that the three pillars—security, progress, and good governance—are implemented simultaneously, while thorough intelligence on each district is vital *before* foreign troops arrive. As more U.S. troops deploy across poppy-producing regions of the south, applying the strategy correctly will contribute to force protection and the programme's success. Leo Docherty, a former British officer stationed in Helmand, called his country's initial intervention "a blundering catastrophe," saying soldiers had little information about local communities they entered and no plans to bring immediate improvement to their lives.[5] Dozens of British troops died in heavy fighting throughout Helmand, along with hundreds of Afghan National Army troops and Afghan National Police.

Dutch troops have had somewhat more success employing the ink-spot technique in central Uruzgan Province, another hotbed of Taliban activity. Unlike U.S. and British soldiers who inhabit fortresses looped with razor wire, the Dutch soldiers operate from small, mud-walled compounds known as *qalas* (*qala* is the Pashto word for "house"), which have a visitor's room where locals can come for impromptu meetings. The soldiers make house calls in the region they patrol, making sure the locals' needs are met.[6] Their setup follows the number one rule in counterinsurgency: troops are actually safer with less hard security. As is to be expected, the Dutch have encountered push-back from the Taliban, especially along strategic drug-smuggling routes.[7] The ink-spot technique works slowly and there will be setbacks. Interaction with the locals is vital to building trust. This is especially true in Afghanistan, where personal trust forms the basis of all relationships—whether in business, in politics, or elsewhere. "You have to hunker down with the Afghan people to get stuff done," says Beverly Eighmy, former counternarcotics official. "You have to have credibility. You can't go out there with seventy-five bodyguards looking confrontational."

There are benefits to providing security, according to a 2007 *ABC News* poll. The national survey found that Afghans rated U.S. efforts twice as high in areas where they described security as "very good." Meanwhile, in areas where there was heavy U.S. troop deployment, 73 percent of respondents held positive views of America as a nation and 67 percent said they thought U.S. soldiers had done a good job.[8] U.S.-led counterinsurgency programmes in Afghanistan's east, where violence levels dropped by 40 percent, have begun to show success.

Seth Jones, a Rand Corporation analyst who visited programmes in Khost Province, where suicide attacks have dropped from once a week in 2006 to once a month in 2007, credits the turnaround to the increased U.S. focus on "soft power." This proves the old counterinsurgency adage: the best weapons don't shoot. U.S. military officers communicate with locals about their needs, and then provide them, making sure jobs go to locals, as opposed to imported, highly paid consultants.[9] In Kunar Province, job-training centres have succeeded in luring unemployed young men away from insurgent recruiters.[10] It's important to acknowledge that violence has dropped in eastern Afghanistan in part since insurgents have refocused their efforts on Pakistan. But they may have done so in part because they find eastern Afghan soil less fertile (unlike southern Afghanistan, where violence has spiked). Expanding "soft power" programmes will not only help rebuild war-shattered Afghanistan; it will eventually reduce violence.

This strategy may offer a way around the caveats some European nations have placed on their troops, barring them from participating in combat missions. Italy, Spain, and Germany could redeploy their forces as "peacekeepers" into areas where security has been partially established, but where the presence of foreign troops remains necessary to support newly trained police forces and budding provincial regimes. Combat-willing forces could continue to contain insurgents in areas outside the ink spots, while supporting counternarcotics paramilitary forces like the DEA's FAST teams and the British-run Task Force 333 who attack heroin labs and smugglers' lairs.

Blend Counterinsurgency and Counternarcotics Efforts

In the wake of 9/11, it became painfully clear that better cooperation between U.S. intelligence and law enforcement agencies might have prevented those attacks. Yet seven years later, these agencies seem no closer to reaching a state of harmony between spies, soldiers, and law enforcement agents. Levels of hostility remain appalling: there are reports of agents from different U.S. departments not even taking each other's phone calls.[11] As a U.S. military official put it, "We get so wrapped around the axle about who has what responsibility: Is this for the military, the DEA, or law enforcement? The terrorist doesn't worry about any of that. You never hear him say, 'I'm not working with that guy, he's a drug dealer.'"[12]

Better cooperation would improve overall security. Since December 2005, DEA agents have provided actionable intelligence deterring or preventing hostile attacks in Afghanistan on nineteen occasions.[13] It would be possible to prevent incidents every month if agents worked in unison. If U.S. agents in the region can't cooperate on their own, then at best their bosses in the United States should mandate weekly, even daily, sessions to share information. Typically, calls for improved cooperation result in Washington appointing another high-level official—a new drug tsar or a director of national intelligence—however, better interagency synchronization is needed in the field offices rather than among political appointees in Washington.

U.S. lawmakers should continue their efforts to force the Pentagon to embed counternarcotics agents on military missions in poppy-rich areas. U.S. troops shouldn't be expected to run counternarcotics missions, but they should support them. A criminal investigation is different from a military intelligence mission, but the two can be complementary. Counternarcotics intelligence will be especially crucial to U.S. Marines deployed in southern Helmand. To effectively wage war against the Taliban, they should have counternarcotics agents working alongside them, gathering criminal evidence to apprehend or disrupt traffickers.

Just as the U.S. military must shift to accommodate the DEA, the DEA should also reshape its mission in Afghanistan. The counternarcotics agency has always focused on stopping the flow of illicit drugs to the U.S. market and building strong cases against traffickers for U.S. prosecution. Neither of these pursuits is particularly relevant to the current situation. Only a small percentage of the Afghan opium crop ever reaches U.S. shores, yet it is as vital as ever that DEA agents and the military disrupt the trade. DEA agents can and should play a crucial role in collecting intelligence about the traffickers linked to the insurgency, but their efforts need to support the war strategy: disrupting the trade, not necessarily developing cases for a U.S. court of law.

The top ten traffickers working with the Taliban and al Qaeda within Afghanistan should be targeted—just as top terrorists themselves get targeted—by NATO. As I said earlier, aircraft equipped with forward-looking infrared (FLIR) cameras (also used along the U.S.-Mexico border and in western Pakistan) should take to the skies over southern Afghanistan, to help warplanes track and target drug convoys heading for the Pakistan and Iran borders. An increased level of risk would serve as a powerful disincentive for traffickers to work with—and therefore provide profits to—the insurgency. Intelligence activity must support interdiction efforts.

Target Criminals, Not Farmers

UNODC and counternarcotics officials estimate that about twelve people control the majority of the Afghan opium market. "Everyone knows who they are and where they are," complains a western official. "Why aren't they being arrested?"[14] In a region where corruption is rife and political will almost nonexistent, the capture and prosecution of major traffickers is not as simple as it sounds, especially since the masterminds of the opium trade related to the insurgency reside in Pakistan or the UAE. Neither country has a positive track record for apprehending powerful crime lords, but such individuals can be named and sanctioned by the international community. As UNODC and the Center on International Cooperation have argued, UN member states could add top traffickers who work with the insurgency to the Security Council's list of al Qaeda and Taliban members, "in order to seize their assets, ban their travel and facilitate their extradition."[15] President Karzai's administration, which has been reluctant to go after big traffickers, claims to support a "naming and shaming" campaign as well.[16]

Efforts to shift Afghan poppy farmers to other crops have failed in part because so many individuals within the Kabul government are also profiting from drugs. The fact that interdiction has never been a priority has created the impression that U.S. leaders actually condone the opium trade and sparked widespread rumours that U.S. agents are even participating in it, or helping their allies within the Karzai regime get rich. A few major arrests would help change that impression, and they should not just focus on traffickers linked to the insurgency.

Foreign and Afghan law enforcement officials working in Kabul should jointly and thoroughly investigate claims that high-level officials in the Karzai administration, including the president's brother, are tied to the opium trade. They should present Karzai and the Afghan National Assembly with finished evidence, not just rumours, and press for prompt judicial action when necessary. There should be stepped-up efforts—and greater funding—to reform Afghanistan's interior ministry, judiciary, and national police. The international community should establish a fund to pay police and judges better wages, and put as much focus on these sectors as the Pentagon has put into building the Afghan National Army.

Create a Farm Support Network

Albeit achieved through intimidation and violence, the Taliban and drug traffickers have managed to succeed at something the international aid community has failed to do: creating a sustained farm support network in one of the world's most remote, underdeveloped places and integrating their agricultural product into the global economy. Naturally, opium would succeed where others would fail—chiefly because of the price it fetches and the fact that it doesn't rot, allowing stockpiles to be kept. Any plan to rid Afghanistan of its drug crisis will fail until the Afghan government and international donors can come up with a farm support network for legal alternatives.

There has been much talk of legalizing Afghanistan's poppy crop and selling the opium for medicinal purposes to poor countries. The proposal, however, fails to account for certain realities: no country, aid group, or pharmaceutical firm has actually expressed interest in buying Afghan poppy to make morphine, and the International Narcotics Control Board has said that current legal poppy stocks are more than sufficient to meet world demand.[17] Afghan poppy is not harvested hygienically, meaning few if any nations would allow its use in legal medicines. As well, it would be nearly impossible in the current security vacuum to account for the poppy's legal distribution. India grants licenses to more than seventy thousand farmers to grow opium for medicinal purposes, and monitors their activities using smart identity cards, farm patrols, and satellite imagery. Despite Delhi's efforts, it is estimated that a third of its poppy crop is sold illegally, since drug traffickers pay five times as much for opium. If poppy were legalized, Afghan farmers would not make much more than if they grew wheat.[18]

Why not subsidize *legal* crops? The establishment of a team inside Afghanistan's commerce ministry to source regional buyers and form partnerships with international produce firms could yield positive results. By determining what subsidies are needed to make crops viable for farmers and buyers alike, a farm support plan based on market needs and in consultation with Afghan tribal councils would benefit locals rather than arbitrary targets set by policymakers in Washington. William Byrd, a World Bank expert on Afghan poppy, suggests donors invest in fruit and nut orchards instead of annual crops like wheat and rice. Pomegranate, orange, and grape orchards take longer to mature, meaning there would have to be a sizable initial investment on the part of international donors, but once orchards were planted, it would become harder for farmers to shift back to poppy.

There should be focus on identifying and gaining entrance to new markets. This will be challenging and expensive. Experts suggest that an effective agricultural replacement strategy will cost $1 billion a year over the next five years.[19] "This would have to start in noninsurgent areas and then grow," says Byrd. "And you have to assume that half of the projects or more are going to fail."[20] It's not beyond the realm of possibility that Afghans could turn away from drug crops. Before the Soviet invasion, Afghanistan was not only self-reliant; it exported farm products, earning $100 million a year.[21]

Personal trust plays a vital role in all business deals in Afghanistan. Farm support programmes working closely with tribes and local leaders—trying to meet their needs and connect them with international or regional investors—would have a better chance at winning public support. "It has to be a one-to-one thing with the Afghans," said Eighmy, who negotiated alternative crop programmes with tribal leaders in Nangarhar in the late 1980s. "They knew me, so I could go out to the countryside and I could sit down with the tribal elders and say, 'We can do this and this, but I cannot see any poppy come next spring.' And I would get their personal guarantee and it worked." As the number of NATO troops expands across the poppy-rich south, there is a need to deploy agricultural experts and commerce ministry teams to negotiate new markets. The idea, as another U.S. official puts it, is "to come upon enemies and leave behind friends."[22]

Improve the Public Relations Campaign

Ninety-five percent of the people surveyed for this project opposed the poppy trade, and virtually every farmer interviewed by local researchers expressed an urgent desire to grow something else. Afghan people in poppy-growing and opium-refining areas loathe the insurgents and traffickers, but they don't hold the Afghan government or NATO in high esteem, either. A successful public relations campaign would convince the Afghan public that the Kabul government and the international community are trying to make their lives better. This campaign will only succeed if it occurs in conjunction with the other eight pillars of this strategy, in particular the anti-corruption drive.

Using radio and local television will be pivotal to creating awareness about the policies of NATO troops and alternative livelihoods on offer for the Afghan people. The Koran can be an ally in the war on drugs, as Islam forbids the use, cultivation, and traffic of narcotics. Islamic law experts and Muslim clerics supporting a call to stamp out poppy could prove useful in broadcast media.[23] Moreover, NATO and the Afghan government should go public with their knowledge of the links between insurgents and the drug trade and reveal the sinister motives behind their veneer of piety and religion. Aid workers say Afghans also respond to messages from doctors that heroin addiction—an increasingly common affliction there—is not curable.

Isolate and Obstruct Drug Money

Afghanistan has created a financial supervision unit within its central bank to monitor money transfers in and out of the country's financial institutions. Any transfer above $20,000 must be reported, and suspicious activity is investigated with cooperation from more than twenty countries with which Afghanistan has signed protocols. Finance agents say there are suspicious amounts of funds bouncing between Afghanistan, Russia, the UAE, and South Africa, but they are starting to develop the ability to separate the good from the bad. "We are ahead of the game," says Noorullah Delawari, governor of the Central Bank, "because we have to be. We are in the front line in both the wars on terror and drugs."

Since the majority of money transfers through Pakistan and Afghanistan pass through the informal *hawala* system, better efforts must also be made to separate the minority of dirty money from the majority of innocent funds. In Afghanistan, there is already a programme underway to license the *hawaladars* and instal a cost-free reporting system, allowing financial agents to track money flows and identify who is sending what where. It has already helped isolate various money traders who appear to be tied to dirty money. Financial experts say it would be unfeasible—not to mention pointless—to transfer a U.S.-style regulatory system onto Afghanistan.

Donor nations should support, even subsidize, efforts to help Afghanistan and Pakistan establish cost-free reporting mechanisms for the *hawala* network and use the vast data bank of information the *hawaladars* have to help fight crime, rather than move criminal money. Benefits must be offered for individuals who regulate and work within the legal market. "Only when we can make the regulated systems more attractive to customers than the unregulated will we win," said a western official. NATO governments should press the UAE to implement such programmes as well.

Regulating the region's trade is of even greater importance. Afghanistan and Pakistan should be encouraged to harmonize their customs duties and to collect the taxes together at the Karachi port. This would increase badly needed tax revenue for both countries and reduce the smuggling of legal commodities that is closely tied to the export of opiates. The establishment of trade transparency units between Afghanistan, Pakistan, and the UAE would monitor commodity flows and isolate cases of trade-based money laundering. Eventually, this system could be expanded to include Central Asian states.

John Cassara believes a small team of specially trained financial agents could target major Afghan traffickers—not to mention insurgent cash flows—and interrupt them relatively quickly. If it becomes difficult to make money in the Afghan region, traffickers will move elsewhere. That won't necessarily slow narcotics supplies to the West, but it may break their ties to the Taliban and al Qaeda in this region.

Stamping out the drug trade could weaken the Afghan economy in the short run, and that is something the donor community must prepare for financially. Once drugs are replaced with legal commerce, exactly the opposite is true. The export value of the 2007 opium harvest was $3.1 billion, with approximately 25 percent of the opium's value, or $755 million, paid to Afghan farmers and the remainder going to traffickers who mainly live outside of Afghanistan. "Drugs drain money from a country, and they don't bring the profits back home," says Raymond Baker, author of *Capitalism's Achilles Heel.* Delawari, at Afghanistan's Central Bank, put it another way: "We get called a narco-state and the money ends up outside the country."[24] The net outflow of drug money offsets inflows of investment and aid, making it impossible to drag Afghanistan out of poverty. One often hears the argument that fighting the drug trade will create instability. I believe there is no way to build a stable Afghanistan until the criminal economy is dismantled and replaced.

Alternative Livelihoods Before Eradication

The use of crop dusters to wipe out Afghanistan's poppy crop remains a hotly disputed issue. It has soured relations between Washington (which wants to spray) and the Karzai regime (which does not) and heightened tensions between the United States and Britain over how to operate in Helmand, where most of Afghanistan's opium crop is grown. Is it morally acceptable to destroy the crops of already impoverished farmers if it prevents another terrorist attack or reduces NATO casualties? Or will it actually spark further violence by sending millions of farmers into the arms of the insurgents? NATO officials don't want to see more NATO casualties and western governments are afraid that there could be another al Qaeda attack paid for by Afghan heroin profits. Patience is nonetheless vital.

There are a few instances where eradication would not disrupt peace-building strategies. Spy satellites have sent images of desert reclamation projects in southern Helmand where farmland is being created to grow more poppy. There are massive land holdings by traffickers like Haji Juma Khan. These fields do not benefit poor farmers, and eradicating these crops would not disrupt efforts to build peace and win public support. But these are very rare cases. In general, U.S. funds earmarked for eradication could be better spent on alternative-livelihood programmes and efforts to build Afghanistan's domestic security and law enforcement capability.

Zero-Sum Game

Criminal and terrorist groups take root and flourish everywhere there is an absence of good governance and security. We must stop thinking about Afghanistan's drug and insurgency problems as isolated issues and understand that this country—and the region as a whole—will remain a problem until a comprehensive, holistic strategy is adopted. The nexus of terrorists and traffickers is as much a threat to the West as it is to South and Central Asia. The campaign against it must be global in scope, reach, and purpose. The ultimate goal should not be the end of the Taliban and al Qaeda, but the creation of prosperity and stability in Afghanistan and the greater region. We owe it to the citizens of Afghanistan and it will make the West safer, too.

AFTERWORD

On December 22, 2008, a U.S. district judge in Washington, D.C., sentenced Khan Mohammed, a Taliban commander convicted of drug trafficking and terrorism, to life in prison. Eight years, two months, and eighteen days after the U.S.-led invasion of Afghanistan, it was the first time a Taliban fighter was put away on narcoterrorism charges.

Mohammed was brought down in an elaborate sting operation in which an Afghan farmer, secretly working with U.S. federal agents, used a hidden camera to record Mohammed conspiring to smuggle opium to the West and also launch attacks on foreign "infidels."[1] Mohammed's conviction is certainly reason for hope: It's this kind of blending of law enforcement and counterinsurgency strategies that, I believe, will help turn the tide in a war that is currently not going our way. Afghanistan is today as much a war on drugs as it is a war on terror. Just as the insurgents and drug traffickers have blended their activities and objectives, we must also merge our strategies to weaken them both.

Many Afghanistan watchers applauded when the 2008 United Nations farm survey showed a 19 percent decline in the country's poppy crop. "[Afghanistan's] opium flood waters," the UNODC boldly declared, ". . . have started to recede."[2] Yet in fact, a close inspection of the figures should have raised alarm. It's true there were significant declines in poppy output in non-Taliban areas in the north.[3] But 98 percent of Afghanistan's still massive 157,000 hectare poppy crop was cultivated in areas controlled by the insurgency (a whopping two-thirds in Helmand alone, where the area planted with poppy declined only marginally).[4] In addition to trafficking drugs, insurgents on both sides of the Pakistan-Afghanistan border smuggled people, weapons, timber, gemstones, and antiquities, some dating back to the era of Alexander the Great. They took to kidnapping foreign journalists, contractors, and diplomats, whom they swapped for high-level Taliban prisoners or hefty ransoms. They "taxed," looted, or simply destroyed trucks carrying NATO supplies through the Khyber Pass, multiplying the cost of supplying foreign troops in Afghanistan and forcing the alliance to seek more costly supply routes through Central Asia. The Taliban extorted fees from local businesses in areas where they held sway, such as a marble quarry in the Mohmand agency of Pakistan's tribal areas, where they collected about $500 a day off trucks loaded with gleaming white stone.[5]

As criminality spread, casualty figures have soared on both sides of the border. A record 151 U.S. soldiers lost their lives in Afghanistan in 2008, with an average of 21 American deaths per month during the May–October fighting season.[6] U.S. missile strikes and bloody fighting between Pakistani troops and insurgents turned the FATA into a war zone, while the Pakistani Taliban made gains outside the tribal belt, securing control of the Swat Valley and bombing Islamabad's Marriott Hotel, killing 54. The proportion of ungoverned territory grew wider on both sides of the frontier, with insurgents and criminals operating more brazenly than ever. I watched Taliban soldiers loading pickup trucks full of supplies in the heart of a bustling Quetta bazaar in July of 2008. Pakistani police standing near me also watched them, but made no move to arrest them. "Since Musharraf was ousted, the Taliban operate openly here," a friend in Quetta told me.

As the administration of President Barack Obama sends thousands more U.S. troops to the Afghan theatre, there seems to be consensus that fighting the opium trade will be critical. But there's no consensus on how to do so. NATO finally approved proposals to take military action against drug labs and to go after traffickers, but so far plans have been hobbled by member nations who refuse to let their troops engage in counternarcotics activities.[7] Ironically, these objections come mainly from European nations like Italy, Germany, and Spain, which are central destinations for Afghan heroin.

While the United States trudges through a credit crisis and the worst financial turmoil since the Great Depression, business has clearly been strong for America's enemies. And unlike the United States, they appear to be squirrelling away nuts for the future. UN and law enforcement officials began to notice in late 2008 that Afghanistan had been producing about twice the amount of opium that the world's addicts smoke, eat, or shoot for several years now. So where is all that extra dope? UN officials estimate the Taliban and the smugglers they work with have stockpiled as much as 8,000 tons of opium—enough to supply the world's heroin addicts for two years.[8] "These stockpiles are a time bomb for public health and global security," said Antonio Maria Costa, the head of the UNODC.[9] He has appealed to NATO forces and western intelligence agencies to track it down.

Perhaps the Taliban are still hoping the Obama administration will go ahead with an aerial spraying campaign. Or maybe they plan to ban opium themselves. After all, prices have been dropping steadily for four years (22 percent between 2007 and 2008), just like they did in the years leading up to the ban in 2000. Afghans working for the UN in southern Afghanistan have found notices posted by the Taliban advising farmers not to grow opium in 2009. It could be they want to pave the way for peace talks, while simultaneously manipulating world opium prices.

Suddenly, it has become the rage to offer talks to the Taliban, especially after the publication of a Rand study noting that 43 percent of insurgencies end when fighters are brought into the political process.[10] Yet widespread talk of negotiating with the Taliban—by U.S. officials, NATO leaders, the British, and even President Karzai himself—has never spelled out precisely *which* Taliban they plan to engage, not to mention how they would accommodate their murderous and criminal behaviour.

Mullah Omar himself has stoutly rejected peace talks.[11] And regardless, it's not entirely clear whether he speaks for Gulbuddin Hekmatyar, the Haqqani group, or Pakistan's Taliban movement, not to mention the myriad criminal gangs who also call themselves Taliban. The situation along the border is now so complex and messy that it is hard to imagine one blanket peace process that would bring concord to the entire Afghan theatre. Any solution must deal with the fact that there are many loosely affiliated insurgents and criminal groups wreaking violence along the border, and it will take an assortment of nuanced settlements to pacify and/or decriminalize all of them. Since returning to the United States, I have held meetings with American military planners and intelligence analysts. I tell them: Treat each village as its own campaign. Start small. Think big. This won't be easy, but in every area, there is a solution.

NOTES

1. The New Axis of Evil

1. Interview with Ahmadullah Alizai, Kandahar, July 2004.
2. U.S. Central Command, "Coalition Forces Make Second Major Drug Seizure in Five Days," news release, NNS031220-01, December 20, 2003; U.S. Central Command, "USS Decatur Captures Possible Al-Qaida Associated Drug-Smuggling Dhow in Arabian Gulf," news release, NNS031219-09, December 19, 2003.
3. Interview with western official, Kabul, March 2004.
4. Peters, "Hostilities Flare Again in America's Other War."
5. Nick Meo, "The Spoils of War: Hate and Heroin," *Sydney Morning Herald*, November 21, 2004.
6. Interview with western official, Kabul, March 2004.
7. Drug traders with links to the Northern Alliance and other regional warlords are another major cause for instability in Afghanistan. So are corruption and drug trafficking by officials in Hamid Karzai's administration. These problems warrant a book of their own, not just this note.
8. Jason Straziuso, "U.S. General Expects Record Poppy Crop in Afghanistan, Promises to Step Up Anti-Drug Effort," Associated Press, January 2, 2008; Richard Beeston, "Exclusive: Afghanistan Is the Bad War; Iraq the Good, Says U.S. Commander," *Times* (London), January 24, 2008.
9. Jonathan Karl and Luis Martinez, "Afghanistan Now Most Dangerous for U.S. Troops," November 30, 2007, ABC News, http://abcnews.go.com/International/story?id=3937323&page=1; David Morgan, "Iraq 'More Stable' than Afghanistan," Reuters, March 25, 2007.
10. Molly Moore, "NATO Confronts Surprisingly Fierce Taliban," *Washington Post*, February 26, 2008.
11. Interview with western official, Kabul, March 2004.
12. Interview with Ali Jalali, former interior minister of Afghanistan, Washington, D.C., May 2007.

13. Aziz Ahmad Shafe, "Taleban Ghost Town," Institute for War and Peace Reporting, ARR no. 275, November 27, 2007, http://www.iwpr.net/?p=arr&s=f&o=340968&apc_state=henfarr340973; Khan, "Taliban Collected Taxes, Ran Heroin Labs, Had Own Judge in Afghan Town"; Khan, "Taliban Hang Three Alleged Afghan Informers."
14. See, for example, "U.S. Counternarcotics Strategy for Afghanistan 2007," http://www.state.gov/documents/organization/90671.pdf, and UNODC, *Annual Drug Survey 2007*, http://www.unodc.org/pdf/research/AFG07_ExSum_web.pdf; see also Jon Hemming, "Poverty Not Biggest Factor Driving Afghan Drug Crop," Reuters, March 15, 2008.
15. Interview with senior UNODC official, Kabul, October 30, 2006.
16. David Mansfield and Adam Pain, "Evidence from the Field: Understanding Changing Levels of Opium Cultivation in Afghanistan," Afghanistan Research and Evaluation Unit, Briefing Paper Series, November 2007, 14, http://www.comw.org/warreport/fulltext/0711mansfield.pdf.
17. Institute for War and Peace Reporting, "Helmand Heads for Record Poppy Harvest," ARR no. 241, February 9, 2007, http://www.iwpr.net/?apc_state=hpsparr&l=en&s=f&o=333474.
18. See Hafvestein, *Opium Season.*
19. Interview by research assistant 2 with Dastoor Khan, farmer, Musa Qala, July 2007.
20. Asia Foundation, *Afghanistan in 2006: A Survey of the Afghan People* (San Francisco: Asia Foundation, 2006), 13. http://asiafoundation.org/resources/pdfs/AGsurvey06.pdf.
21. Thomas Johnson, "On the Edge of the Big Muddy: The Taliban Resurgence in Afghanistan." *China and Eurasia Forum Quarterly* 5, no. 2 (2007): 92–129, http://www.silkroadstudies.org/new/docs/CEF/Quarterly/May_2007/Johnson.pdf.
22. Hersh, "The Other War: Why Bush's Afghanistan Problem Won't Go Away."
23. James Risen, "Poppy Fields Are Now a Front Line in Afghan War," *New York Times*, May 16, 2007; interview with former INL chief Robert Charles, Washington, D.C., June 2007.
24. Telephone interview with a U.S. official, May 2005.
25. Nita Colaco, "The Candidates Must Address the Conflict in Afghanistan," *Richmond Times-Dispatch*, February 10, 2008.
26. Jason Straziuso, "Afghan Aid Money Spent on High Salaries," Associated Press, March 26, 2008.
27. Rubin, *The Road to Ruin*, 6.
28. Interview with Marvin Weinbaum, Scholar in Residence, Middle East Institute, Washington, D.C., April 2007.

29. Telephone interview with DEA spokespersons Garrison Courtney and Mary Cooper, August 30, 2007.
30. Braun, "U.S. Counternarcotics Policy in Afghanistan: Time for Leadership," 27.
31. Cilluffo, "Threat Posed by the Convergence of Organized Crime, Drug Trafficking, and Terrorism."
32. Kaplan, "Paying for Terror."
33. For example, see Haseeb Humayoon, "The Iraqization of Insurgency in Afghanistan," Kabul: Center for Conflict and Peace Studies, July 12, 2007.
34. Interview with a senior U.S. official, Islamabad, February 5, 2008.
35. Telephone interview with Seth Jones, Rand Corporation, November 20, 2006.
36. Charles, *Narcotics and Terrorism*, 43.
37. Interview with a U.S. military official, Kabul, March 2006.
38. Interviews with U.S. officials, April 2006 and April 2007.
39. David Rohde, "Second Record Level for Afghan Opium Crop," *New York Times*, August 28, 2007; multiple interviews. The figure of $133 million is based on an assumption that 80 percent of the opium also gets refined in Taliban-dominated territory.
40. Interview with a UNODC official, Kabul, March 4, 2008.
41. Multiple interviews by the author and research assistants.
42. For details, see Lawrence, ed., *Messages to the World*, 98, 167.
43. Glassner and Pincus, "Seized Letter Outlines al Qaeda Goals in Iraq." Stephen Ulph, a scholar at the conservative Jamestown Foundation, suggested the letter was a fake. For details, see http://www.turkishweekly.net/comments.php?id=1794.
44. I believe a significant portion of the funds flowing from the Persian Gulf are in fact *payments* for drugs shipments, not *donations*; I discuss this further in Chapter 3.
45. Interview with a senior U.S. counternarcotics official, Washington, D.C., June 18, 2007.
46. Tenet, "Worldwide Threat in 2000: Global Realities of Our National Security," statement, Select Committee on Intelligence.
47. Beers, "Narco-Terror: The Worldwide Connection Between Drugs and Terrorism."
48. Asa Hutchinson, "Narco-Terror: The International Connection Between Drugs and Terror," lecture to the Institute for International Studies, Washington, D.C.: Heritage Foundation, April 2, 2002, http://www.heritage.org/Research/HomelandSecurity/HL751.cfm.
49. Interview with Robert Charles, Washington, D.C., May 23, 2007.
50. Telephone interview with a senior Republican aide, June 7, 2007.

51. Telephone interview with Jack C. Lawn, former DEA administrator, July 27, 2007.
52. Hsu and Pincus, "U.S. Warns of Stronger al Qaeda"; Office of the Director of National Intelligence, "The Terrorist Threat to the U.S. Homeland," news release, July 17, 2007, http://www.dni.gov/press_releases/20070717_release.pdf.
53. Telephone interview with a U.S. official, June 7, 2007.
54. Interview with a counternarcotics official, Kabul, March 2004.
55. Kaplan, "Paying for Terror."
56. Kaplan, "Paying for Terror"; Paul Haven, "Madrid Bombings Show No al Qaeda Ties," Associated Press, March 9, 2006; Paul Haven and Mar Roman, "Madrid Bomb Suspects Face 40 Years in Jail," *Scotsman*, February 14, 2007.
57. Kaplan, "Paying for Terror."
58. Ibid.
59. Interviews with western and Afghan officials, March 2004, October 2006, and March 2007.
60. Tenet, "Converging Dangers in a Post 9/11 World," testimony, Select Committee on Intelligence; Tenet, "Challenges in a Changing Global Context," testimony, Select Committee on Intelligence.
61. Mark John, "Pressure for Tougher Afghan Anti-Drugs Drive," Reuters, September 5, 2007.
62. Schweich, "Is Afghanistan a Narco-State?"
63. UN Office on Drugs and Crime, "UN Drugs Chief Calls for Extra Recourses to Help NATO Target Afghan Opium," news release, Brussels, September 12, 2006; telephone interview with Antonio Maria Costa, Executive Director, UNODC, September 12, 2006.
64. From http://www.drugpolicy.org.
65. Telephone interview with a UNODC official, January 30, 2007.

2. Operation Jihad

1. This segment is drawn from interviews conducted in Washington, D.C., with former DEA administrator Jack C. Lawn, retired DEA special agent Richard Fiano, and former CIA chief of station Milton Bearden on July 19 and October 4, 2007. Retired special agent Charles Carter was interviewed by telephone on May 25.
2. Or at least the longest anyone will admit to. I interviewed various former intelligence officials and diplomats, as well as Fiano and Carter, on the subject.
3. Information from this paragraph compiled from http://www.opiods.com/timeline/index.html; Macdonald, *Drugs in Afghanistan*; Booth, *Opium*.

4. See, for example, "GOP Begins Cleanup of Smugglers Den at Sohrab Goth," U.S. State Department cable.
5. Lowinson and Musto, "Drug Crisis and Strategy."
6. It's important to note two external factors simultaneously contributed to a rise in opium production in Afghanistan. First, counternarcotics efforts in the Golden Triangle, which includes Thailand, Laos, and Burma, started to show a decline in production from that region. As well, the new Khomeini regime in neighboring Iran banned all forms of narcotics production and usage, thus shifting a lively economy over the border into Pakistan and Afghanistan.
7. See "National Narcotics Intelligence Consumers Committee Report for 1985–1986."
8. Bonner, "Afghan Rebel's Victory Garden: Opium."
9. Ibid.
10. Ibid.
11. Ibid.
12. Telephone interview with a former U.S. official, July 28, 2007.
13. For more information, see Rubin, *The Fragmentation of Afghanistan*; Coll, *The Ghost Wars*; and Yousaf and Adkin, *The Bear Trap*.
14. Akhundzada was a member of the Revolutionary Islamic Movement, one of the less centralized mujahideen parties. Some former U.S. officials believe he turned to the opium trade for spare cash because there was no organized mechanism within his party to distribute funds received in Peshawar.
15. Telephone interview with Peter Tomsen, former U.S. special envoy, July 28, 2007.
16. Rubin, *The Fragmentation of Afghanistan*, 263.
17. Ibid.
18. Griffin, *Reaping the Whirlwind*, 148.
19. Macdonald, *Drugs in Afghanistan*, 89.
20. The original Hizb-i-Islami split in 1979. Today Hekmatyar's faction is known as Hizb-i-Islami Gulbuddin, or HIG, and is considered a terrorist organization and trafficking group by coalition forces in Afghanistan.
21. Rupert and Coll, "U.S. Declines to Probe Afghan Drug Trade; Rebels, Pakistani Officers Implicated."
22. Rubin, *The Fragmentation of Afghanistan*, 257.
23. Telephone interview with Edmund McWilliams, May 3, 2007.
24. Telephone interview with a former U.S. official, July 28, 2007.
25. Lifschultz, "The Death Toll of Educated Afghans in Peshawar Is Now More Than One Thousand," 61.

26. Macdonald, *Drugs in Afghanistan*, 88.
27. Griffin, *Reaping the Whirlwind*, 142.
28. Interview with a U.S. military official, Bagram Air Base, August 2006.
29. In another case of history repeating itself, the supply line bringing weapons to the Afghan National Army, which the U.S. military is training and equipping, also appears riddled with graft. One weapons supplier with a $300 million contract was sending aged munitions made in China and the former Soviet bloc and working with a middleman on a U.S. federal list suspected of illegal arms trafficking. For details, see C. J. Chivers, "Supplier Under Scrutiny on Aging Arms for Afghans," *New York Times*, March 27, 2008. So far, however, no one has publicly accused any U.S. suppliers of also smuggling drugs.
30. Lawrence Lifschultz, "Pakistan, the Empire of Heroin," in McCoy and Block, eds., *War on Drugs*, 320; Lifschultz, "Heroin Empire," 71–72.
31. Yousaf and Adkin, *The Bear Trap*, 100.
32. Hussein, "Narco Power," 15; Rupert and Coll, "U.S. Declines to Probe Afghan Drug Trade; Rebels, Pakistani Officers Implicated."
33. Information for this passage comes from Hussein, "Narco Power," 14, and Lifschultz, "Inside the Kingdom of Heroin," 495.
34. "Narcotics Trafficking and the Military," Near East and South Asia briefs, CIA.
35. Rupert and Coll, "U.S. Declines to Probe Afghan Drug Trade; Rebels, Pakistani Officers Implicated." Bugti remained in opposition for decades, leading a resistance against the government of President Pervez Musharraf. He was assassinated in an air strike in August 2006.
36. For examples, see Lifschultz, "Inside the Kingdom of Heroin," and Rupert and Coll, "U.S. Declines to Probe Afghan Drug Trade; Rebels, Pakistani Officers Implicated."
37. Lawrence Lifschultz, "Pakistan, the Empire of Heroin," in McCoy and Block, eds., *War on Drugs*, 321.
38. Telephone interview with Edmund McWilliams, May 3, 2007.
39. Sciolino, "U.S. Urging Afghan Rebels to Limit Opium."
40. Telephone interview with William Piekney, former CIA agent, September 24, 2007.
41. "HFAC International Narcotics Control Task Force Hearings, May 22," U.S. State Department document.
42. "UN Striving for Tact in Its Fight on Drugs," *New York Times*, July 25, 1987.
43. Telephone interview with a former CIA official, September 5, 2008.
44. Until the war began in Afghanistan, most of the opium produced there was exported to Iran. Opium grown in Pakistan, meanwhile, was more likely to be

processed into heroin and smuggled to the West, according to former DEA officials and declassified government documents.

45. "Pakistan's Narcotics Control Program," letter from Edward Fox, Asst Secretary of Legislative and Intergovernmental Affairs, to the Chairman of the Foreign Affairs Committee, U.S. House of Representatives.
46. Interview with Teresita Schaffer, Washington, D.C., May 11, 2007; also see http://www.csis.org.
47. "Pakistan: Countering an Expanding Drug Industry," Intelligence assessment, CIA.
48. "Daily Muslim Article on Balochistan Heroin Seizure," U.S. Embassy (Islamabad) cable. The tribes running the Quetta Alliance were the Noorzai, the Rigi, and the Notezai, according to counternarcotics officials and local media reports from the time.
49. "Afghanistan, Iran, Pakistan Country Profiles," Office of Intelligence Drug Enforcement Administration.
50. "Visit of INM Assistant Secretary Wrobleski: Meeting with President Zia."
51. Lifschultz, "Inside the Kingdom of Heroin," 495; Haq, *Drugs in South Asia*, 200–201.
52. Alexiev, "Inside the Soviet Army in Afghanistan," 49. Another passage from this report reveals the lengths Soviet soldiers would go to create intoxicants: "You cannot imagine what they drink. They will drink shaving lotions and cologne. That's the good stuff. Then they will drink toothpaste. The best one is the Bulgarian Pomorian brand. They will simply squeeze four or five tubes in a jar, dilute it with water and drink it. They also drank truck antifreeze, glue and brake fluid. The brake fluid, they used to heat up and put some nails in it for some reason. I don't know why. They will also take shoe polish and smear it on a piece of bread and leave it in the sun until the alcohol separates from the shoe polish. Then you eat the bread and get drunk."
53. Bonner, "Afghanistan's Other Front: A World of Drugs."
54. Information and quotes in this paragraph come from Cooley, *Unholy Wars*, 128–129, and Sancton, "Dispatches."
55. Interview with Mohammed Yousaf, Wah Cantonment, October 2006.
56. Telephone interview with William Piekney, September 24, 2007.
57. Coll, *The Ghost Wars*, 103–105.
58. Yousaf and Adkin, *The Bear Trap*, 102. Corruption along the pipeline was reportedly rife. The Federation for American Afghan Action, a support group for the resistance, concluded that 70 percent of the $342 million appropriated by Congress for weapons between the fiscal years 1980 and 1984 had never reached the mujahideen in the field.

59. Coll, *The Ghost Wars*, 105.
60. Interview with Zamir Kabulov, Russian ambassador to Afghanistan, Kabul, March 4, 2008.
61. Telephone interview with a former CIA agent, October 3, 2007.
62. Interview with a former CIA agent, Washington, D.C., May 21, 2007.
63. Telephone interview with a former CIA agent, October 2, 2007.
64. Telephone interview with Robert Oakley, May 21, 2007.
65. Frederick Hitz, "Obscuring Properiety? The CIA and Drugs," *International Journal of Intelligence and Counter-Intelligence* 15, no. 4 (November 2002): 565–579.
66. Interview with Richard Fiano, former DEA agent, Washington, D.C., June 2007.
67. Telephone interview with Larry Crandall, former USAID official, September 20, 2007.
68. "Narcotics and the New Government," U.S. Embassy (Islamabad) cable.
69. "Heroin, Guns and the War in Pakistan," U.S. Embassy (Islamabad) cable.
70. The main highway from Baluchistan also snakes into Sohrab Goth, passing right by the Karachi office of the NLC before entering into the port. To this day, the road is crowded with colorfully painted trucks, many of them festooned with the Afghan flag, lumbering into the seaside slum. There appear to be no authorities checking their contents.
71. "Pakistan: Countering an Expanding Drug Industry."
72. Coll, *The Ghost Wars*, 182–183.
73. Interview with Milton Beardon, former CIA agent, Washington, D.C., July 19, 2007.
74. Coll, *The Ghost Wars*, 180–183; Rubin, *The Fragmentation of Afghanistan*, 182–183.
75. Rubin, *The Fragmentation of Afghanistan*, 183.
76. "Narcotics Trafficking from Afghanistan," U.S. Embassy (Islamabad) cable.
77. Sciolino, "U.S. Urging Afghan Rebels to Limit Opium"; telephone interview with Peter Tomsen, July 28, 2007.
78. Alfred McCoy, "Fallout: The Interplay of CIA Covert Warfare and the Global Narcotics Traffic," paper delivered at the Institute for African Studies, Columbia University, November 14, 2002, 19.
79. "Request for Afghan Opium Crop Figures," U.S. Embassy (Islamabad) cable.
80. "Narcotics Production/Trafficking in Northern Helmand," U.S. Embassy (Islamabad) cable.
81. Telephone interview with a former U.S. official, July 28, 2007.
82. Telephone interview with Robert Oakley, former U.S. diplomat, May 21, 2007.

83. Rubin, *The Fragmentation of Afghanistan*, 264. USAID's program in Nangarhar suffered a similar fate. Then governor Haji Abdul Qadir accepted a $200,000 USAID program to cut production in half, but when U.S. funds disappeared, he ordered farmers to grow crops again, according to former U.S. officials.
84. David B. Ottaway, "GAO Asked to Probe Alleged Diversion of Afghan Rebel Aid," *Washington Post*, March 13, 1987; Tolchin, "CIA Admits It Failed to Tell Fed About BCCI."
85. Lifschultz, "Pakistan, the Empire of Heroin," 350.
86. Rubin, *The Fragmentation of Afghanistan*, 182–183.
87. Ibid.
88. Interview with a former CIA officer, Washington, D.C., August 18, 2007.
89. Griffin, *Reaping the Whirlwind*. After the Taliban took over Kabul in 1996, they hanged Najibullah in Kabul's Ariana Square.
90. "Request for Afghan Opium Crop Figures."
91. "Afghanistan: U.S. Interests and U.S. Aid," letter to U.S. State Department.
92. For more on this, see Napoleoni, *Terror Incorporated*, 119–120.
93. Ibid., 119.
94. Griffin, *Reaping the Whirlwind*, 142.
95. McCoy, *The Politics of Heroin*, 483.
96. Hussein, "Narco Power."
97. That Afridi worked with Zia's government comes from "Heroin in Pakistan: Sowing the Wind," a CIA report leaked to Pakistan's *Friday Times*, which published it in full on September 3, 1993.
98. Zahid Hussein, "Three Major Drug Syndicates in Pakistan," *Newsline*, May 1993.
99. Haq, *Pakistan*, 34–35.
100. "Pakistan." DEA country analysis.
101. "The Narcotics Issue and Contacts with Politicians." U.S. State Department letter to U.S. Embassy (Islamabad).
102. "Request for Afghan Opium Crop Figures." U.S. State Department cable to U.S. Embassy (Islamabad).
103. "Narcotics—FY 90 Budget." Robert Oakley, U.S. Embassy (Islamabad) cable.
104. Coll, *The Ghost Wars*, 220–221.
105. Interview with a former U.S. official, Washington, D.C., July 18, 2007.
106. "Heroin in Pakistan: Sowing the Wind," CIA report.
107. Knut Royce, "Country Run on Drugs: CIA Report Says Heroin Is Pakistan's Lifeblood," *Newsday*, February 23, 1993.

108. John Ward Anderson and Kamran Khan, "Heroin Plan by Top Pakistanis Alleged," *Washington Post*, September 12, 1994.
109. Interviews of former airport workers by research assistant 1, Jalalabad, June 2007.
110. Interview with a Pakistani police official, Islamabad, June 2007.
111. "Interview with Zbigniew Brzezinski," *Nouvel Observateur*, January 15, 1998.

3. Narco-Terror State

1. Peters, "Taliban Stamping Out Hashish but Opium Production Continues to Flourish."
2. Rashid, *The Taliban*, 25; Anthony Davis, "How the Taliban Became a Military Force," in Maley, ed., *Fundamentalism Reborn?* 44; multiple interviews.
3. Interview with Mullah Roketi, Kabul, January 2006.
4. Marquand, "The Reclusive Leader Who Runs the Taliban."
5. Multiple interviews with former Afghan, Pakistani, and U.S. officials.
6. Griffin, *Reaping the Whirlwind*, 153.
7. See documents 1–8, *The Taliban File, 9/11 Sourcebook*, national security archive electronic briefing book no. 97, Sajit Ghandi, ed., NSA/GWU, especially document 1, "New Fighting and New Forces in Kandahar," U.S. Consulate (Peshawar) cable; document 3, "The Taliban—Who Knows What the Movement Means?" U.S. embassy (Islamabad) cable; document 5, "[excised] Believe Pakistan Is Backing Taliban," U.S. embassy (Islamabad) cable; document 6, "The Taliban: What We've Heard," U.S. embassy (Islamabad) cable. The collection is available online at http://www.gwu.edu/~nsarchiv/NSAEBB/NSAEBB97/index.htm.
8. These quotes come from Ghandi, ed., *Sourcebook*, documents 3 and 6.
9. Ibid., document 6.
10. Ibid., "Meeting with the Taliban in Kandahar: More Questions Than Answers." U.S. embassy (Islamabad) cable.
11. The U.S. embassy cable documenting this meeting has excised the name of the Afghan official, but describes him as a native of Maroof district, where Ghaus is from, and someone tipped to be a senior foreign ministry official in the new Taliban government.
12. He died in 2000.
13. That Issa Noorzai was a major smuggler and a member of the Quetta Alliance comes from multiple interviews with Afghan and Pakistani officials, as well as Noorzai tribesmen. Another alleged member of the Quetta Alliance, "Sakhi Jan" Dost Notezai, was briefly arrested in October 1990 in connection with the multiton seizure of heroin, hashish, and opium referenced in

Operation Jihad. Notezai, through a combination of legal maneuvering and wielding his significant political influence, largely avoided incarceration. Today his son, Amanullah Notezai, is a provincial minister in the Baluchistan government and a member of the Pakistan Muslim League faction, which supported former president Pervez Musharraf.

14. "TKO Proposal," [name exised] Islamabad Country Office, Drug Enforcement Administration.
15. Bob Clark, a former DEA agent posted to Islamabad in the 1990s, says most TKO designations were given to Latin American drug smugglers, since Southwest Asian drugs "weren't seen as something that made its way into the U.S. market."
16. This is according to an Afghan who accompanied Noorzai to one of the meetings and who was able to accurately identify DEA agents serving in the Islamabad embassy at the time.
17. Ghandi, ed., *Sourcebook*, document 8, "Finally, a Talkative Talib: Origins and Membership of the Religious Students' Movement," U.S. Embassy (Islamabad) cable.
18. "First Heroin Kingpin Ever Extradited from Afghanistan Pleads Guilty to Smuggling Heroin into the United States," news release from U.S. Attorney's Office, Department of Justice, Southern District of New York, July 11, 2006.
19. Interview with an Afghan official, Peshawar, January 2008.
20. Davis, "How the Taliban Became a Military Force," 44; Ghandi, ed., *Sourcebook*, document 3. Abdur Ghaffar was the younger brother of Nasim, the Helmand strongman who was assassinated and succeeded by his brother Rasul (see Chapter 2). When Rasul died of cancer in the early 1990s, Abdur Ghaffar took over the business.
21. Davis, "How the Taliban Became a Military Force," 50–51.
22. The DEA document is cited in Griffin, *Reaping the Whirlwind*, 154.
23. Interview with a U.S. official, Kabul, March 2005.
24. Ahmed Rashid, "Pakistan and the Taliban," in Maley, ed., *Fundamentalism Reborn*, 77.
25. Ghandi, ed., *Sourcebook*, document 5.
26. Davis, "How the Taliban Became a Military Force," 45–46; Coll, *The Ghost Wars*, 291.
27. Rashid, *The Taliban*, 28–29.
28. Ibid., 29.
29. Information for this paragraph comes from Rashid, *The Taliban*, 27–29, and multiple interviews.

30. For more detail, see Barbara Elias, ed., *Pakistan: "The Taliban's Godfather"? Documents Detail Years of Pakistani Support for Taliban, Extremists,* national security archive electronic briefing book no. 227, NSA/GWU, at http://www.gwu.edu/~nsarchiv/NSAEBB/NSAEBB227/index.htm.
31. Coll, *The Ghost Wars*, 293.
32. Rashid, "Pakistan and the Taliban," 88.
33. Elias, ed., *Pakistan*, "Afghanistan: Russian Embassy Official Claims Iran Interfering More Than Pakistan," U.S. Embassy (Islamabad) cable.
34. Coll, *The Ghost Wars*, 293.
35. Ghandi, ed., *Sourcebook*, document 15, "A/S Raphel Discusses Afghanistan," U.S. Embassy (Islamabad) cable.
36. Coll, *The Ghost Wars*, 332.
37. Transnational Institute, "Afghanistan, Drugs and Terrorism: Merging Wars," TNI briefing series no. 2001/2, December 2001, http://www.tni.org/reports/drugs/debate3.pdf.
38. Both the U.S. government and UNODC perform annual surveys of Afghanistan's poppy crop. The U.S. government uses satellite technology, while the UN conducts ground surveys, which is why there are discrepancies in their total estimates. The drop-off in opium production in 2001 is due to the Taliban's decision to ban poppy cultivation, a subject to be discussed later in this chapter.
39. Rubin, "The Political Economy of War and Peace in Afghanistan," 1795.
40. Telephone interview with Bernard Frahi, UNODC official, August 2007. This is also cited in Rubin, "Political Economy," 1796.
41. Rashid, *The Taliban*, 118.
42. Interview with a former Pakistani counternarcotics official, Islamabad, April 2007.
43. Jeffrey Bartholet and Steve Levine, "The Holy Men of Heroin," *Newsweek*, December 6, 1999.
44. Director of Central Intelligence, "National Intelligence Daily," Central Intelligence Agency, May 1, 1998, 7, NSA/GWU. In this document, yet to be assigned to a collection at the NSA, Haji Bashir Noorzai's name has been redacted. It reads: "Under one such agreement [name excised]—the son of key Quetta Alliance member [name excised] pays the Taliban about $230 for each kilogram of either heroin or morphine base being exported through the Jalalabad and Qandahar Airports." Other public reference documents on Noorzai specifically refer to his export deal with the Taliban.
45. Telephone interview with Julie Sirrs, former U.S. official, June 5, 2007.
46. Interview with a retired ISI agent, Islamabad, June 2006.
47. Macdonald, *Drugs in Afghanistan*, 102.

48. Interview with David Macdonald, Kabul, September 26, 2007.
49. Macdonald, *Drugs in Afghanistan*, 51. Various Afghan officials believe the Taliban today gives drugs to young soldiers—and specifically suicide bombers—to make them fearless. Several have raised the issue with U.S. officials, asking for kits to perform blood tests on attackers captured before they self-detonate. "When we have captured suicide bombers before they could set off their charge, they often seem to be high on drugs—really out of it and wild," a former governor told me in 2007.
50. "National Intelligence Daily," 7.
51. Ibid.
52. Interview with Bob Clark, former DEA agent, Islamabad, February 2, 2008.
53. Interview with a former UN official, Islamabad, November 18, 2007.
54. Telephone interview with a former CIA official, September 5, 2008.
55. Jonathan Oliver, "West Will Hit the Taliban's Opium Trade," *Mail on Sunday*, September 30, 2001.
56. Perl, "The Taliban and the Drug Trade."
57. Benjamin and Simon, *The Age of Sacred Terror*, 155.
58. Barry Meier, "Super Heroin Was Planned by Bin Laden, Report Says," *New York Times*, October 4, 2001. Bin Laden's only two known public statements on opium can be found in Lawrence, ed., *Messages to the World*, 98, 167. In one statement, bin Laden praises Mullah Omar for "the prohibition of growing opium," calling it a "great Islamic decision." In a separate diatribe against Americans he says, "You are a nation that permits the production, trading and usage of intoxicants. You also permit drugs, and only forbid the trade of them, even though your nation is the largest consumer of them."
59. Perl, "The Taliban and the Drug Trade," 4.
60. Multiple interviews. This subject also gets a mention in Rubin, "Political Economy," 1796, and in Coll, *The Ghost Wars*, 613, footnote citing a Human Rights Watch report.
61. A copy of Bashir's deposition was given to the author by his American lawyer, Ivan Fisher. In it, Noorzai went on to claim the Emirati sheik sought to continue the lease arrangement after the Taliban government collapsed, and, curiously, invited HBN to help smooth the process. Other public documents from the trial report on meetings between HBN and two American investigators on August 9, 2004, in Dubai, in which HBN described in detail a trip he had made to Dubai in 2001 with Gul Agha Sherzai, the man who took over Kandahar following the U.S. invasion. HBN said Sheikh Mohammed had sent a plane for them in Kandahar, and they had met with the sheik's Afghan representative, Rahim Balouch. In the written testimony he said Balouch had

given Sherzai a suitcase with 1 million dhirams ($270,000) and said, "This is your gift."

62. Multiple interviews.
63. Farah and Braun, *Merchant of Death*, 141.
64. Braun and Pasternak, "Long Before Sept. 11, Bin Laden Flew Aircraft Under the Radar."
65. Interview with Mohammad Fedawi, former president of Ariana Airlines, Kabul, March 2007.
66. Interview by research assistant 1 with Hayat Zalmay, Jalalabad, June 2007.
67. Farah and Braun, *Merchant of Death*, 117, 139.
68. Ibid., 121. Fedawi also described Ahmed in an interview with the author.
69. Ibid., 117–118.
70. Braun and Pasternak. "Long Before Sept. 11."
71. Benjamin and Simon, *Sacred Terror*, 289.
72. This information is compiled from Farah and Braun, *Merchant of Death*, 63–64; Brunwasser, "The Embargo Buster"; and Phillip Van Niekerk and André Verlöy, "Africa's Merchant of Death Sold Arms to the Taliban," Washington, D.C.: Center for Public Integrity, January 31, 2002, http://www.publicintegrity.org/assets/pdf/pi_2002_02.pdf.
73. Interview, July 2007.
74. Farah and Braun, *Merchant of Death*, 64.
75. Van Niekerk and Verlöy, "Africa's Merchant of Death."
76. Farah and Braun, *Merchant of Death*, 128.
77. Ibid., 140.
78. Interview with a U.S. official, Washington, D.C., May 8, 2007.
79. Van Niekerk and Verlöy, "Africa's Merchant of Death."
80. Farah and Braun, *Merchant of Death*, 146; Brunwasser, "The Embargo Buster."
81. Telephone interview with Julie Sirrs, former DIA analyst, June 5, 2007.
82. Telephone interview with Karl Indurfurth, May 10, 2007.
83. "Taliban File Update: U.S. Pressed Taliban to Expel Usama bin Laden Over 30 Times," news release, State Department, January 30, 2004, NSA/GWU, http://www.gwu.edu/~nsarchiv/NSAEBB/NSAEBB97/index3.htm.
84. Transnational Institute, "Afghanistan, Drugs, and Terrorism: Merging Wars."
85. Ibid.
86. Martin Jelsma, "Learning Lessons from the Taliban Opium Ban," *International Journal on Drug Policy* 16, no. 2 (March 2005), http://www.tni.org/detail_page.phtml?page=archives_jelsma_taliban.
87. Jelsma, "Learning Lessons from the Taliban Opium Ban"; House Government Reform Committee Subcommittee on Criminal Justice, Drug Policy, and

Human Resources, statement of Asa Hutchinson, 107th Cong., 1st sess., October 3, 2001, http://www.usdoj.gov/dea/pubs/cngrtest/ct100301.html.

88. The estate is described in Coll, *The Ghost Wars*, 549. The author has also reviewed photos of the compound.
89. William Sami and Charles Recknagel, "Iran's War on Drugs," *Transnational Organized Crime* 5, no. 2 (Summer 2002).
90. Transnational Institute, "Afghanistan, Drugs and Terrorism: Merging Wars."
91. Ibid.
92. Rashid, *The Taliban*, 122.
93. "Worldwide Drug Threat Assessment: A Joint Intelligence Report," Committee on Narcotics Intelligence Issues.
94. Pakistan had 3 million addicts by 1996, 5 million by 1999, according to Rashid, *The Taliban*, 122.
95. Interview with a former Pakistani official, Islamabad, October 2006.
96. Interview with a Pakistani counternarcotics official, Rawalpindi, September 13, 2007.
97. Hannah Bloch, "A Skirmish Over Drugs," *Time*, June 2, 1997, 25.
98. Ibid.
99. See document collection at Elias, ed., *Pakistan*.
100. Ibid., document 15, "[excised]/Pakistan Interservice Intelligence/Pakistan (PK) Directorate Supplying the Taliban Forces," from [excised] to DIA, [excised] cable; document 17, "IIR [excised] Pakistan Involvement in Afghanistan," from [excised] to DIA.
101. Interview with a western official, Kabul, September 26, 2007.
102. Telephone interview with William Milam, former U.S. diplomat, August 2007.
103. In a subsequent interview, Chamberlain retreated from the testimony she made under oath, saying aggressive questioning backed her into an assessment based on "unclassified reporting—what you know." She added, "I regretted it the moment I said it." The full transcript of her testimony is available at http://commdocs.house.gov/committees/intlrel/hfa85841.000/hfa85841_0f.htm.
104. Interview with a western official, Kabul, September 26, 2007.
105. Elias, ed., *Pakistan*, document 34, "Pakistan Support for Taliban," U.S. Embassy (Islamabad) cable.
106. Musharraf, *In the Line of Fire*, 209.
107. Interview with a U.S. official, Washington, D.C., May 2007.
108. Coll, *The Ghost Wars*, 560.
109. National Commission on Terrorist Attacks upon the United States, Kean and Hamilton, *The 9/11 Commission Report*, 259.
110. Coll, *The Ghost Wars*, 552.

111. House Government Reform Subcommittee on Criminal Justice, Drug Policy, and Human Resources, statement of Asa Hutchinson.
112. "Another Powder Trail," *Economist*, October 18, 2001.
113. Woodward, *Bush at War*, 212.
114. Risen, *State of War*, 154.
115. Interview with Robert Charles, former INL chief, Washington, D.C., May 23, 2007.
116. Telephone interview with Dana Rohrabacher, U.S. congressman, October 2006.
117. Woodward, *Bush at War*, 228.
118. Risen, *State of War*, 154.

4. The New Taliban

1. Colonel Tom Collins, a U.S. military spokesman, confirmed Osmani was killed with two associates and identified one of them as Mullah Zahir: e-mail to author, January 9, 2007. Separately, three Afghan officials in Helmand identified the third man as Haji Masooq, a major heroin dealer, to two research assistants.
2. Michael Smith, "Taliban Leader 'Killed' After RAF Tracks Phone," *London Sunday Times*, December 24, 2006.
3. Telephone interview with an Afghan official, October 15, 2007.
4. Mujahid and Peters, "Buddhist Relics Latest Casualties of Pakistan's Talibanization."
5. For a useful discussion on ungoverned territories, see Rabasa, Boraz, Chalk, Cragin, Karasik, Moroney, O'Brien, and Peters, *Ungoverned Territories: Understanding and Reducing Terrorist Risks* (monograph).
6. E-mail to author, October 18, 2007.
7. The insurgents who operate along the Pakistan-Afghanistan frontier don't recognize the border, and for the sake of fighting smugglers and insurgents it would be easier if the international community did not have to, either. I define the region as a swath of territory, narrow at parts, widening at others, extending from Nuristan Province in northeast Afghanistan and the Chitral district of Pakistan across the border, all the way down to the Rabat triangle where Baluchistan (Pakistan), Sistan al Baluchistan (Iran), and Nimroz (Afghanistan) come together.
8. Interview with a UN official, Kabul, March 1, 2007.
9. Here I am including operations, however sporadic and ineffectual they may have been, by the Pakistan military in the federally administered tribal areas (FATA).

10. For more on CENTCOM's refusal to dispatch U.S. Marines who were also in theater to Tora Bora, see Mary Ann Weaver, "Lost at Tora Bora," *New York Times Magazine*, September 11, 2005. Weaver accurately blames the U.S. Special Forces' reliance on two corrupt warlords, Hazrat Ali and Haji Zaman—both of whom are suspected of ties to opium trafficking—for bin Laden's escape. U.S. and Afghan officials believe a multimillion-dollar bribe was paid to secure bin Laden's great escape. "It was more of a great release," a senior Afghan security official complained to me.
11. Telephone interview with journalist Rahimullah Yusufzai, October 10, 2007.
12. Schroen, *First In*, 92.
13. Maass, "Gul Agha Gets His Province Back."
14. International Crisis Group, "Countering Afghanistan's Insurgency: No Quick Fixes" (report), 3.
15. *International Narcotics Control Strategy Report 2002*, U.S. State Department, vii–3, http://www.state.gov/p/inl/rls/nrcrpt/2002/.
16. Interview with Bob Woodruff, New York City, August 11, 2007.
17. McDowell, "As Disruption from War on Taliban Ends, Traffickers Moving Big Heroin Shipments."
18. Bearak, "Unreconstructed."
19. Interview with a DEA agent, Islamabad, March 2003.
20. Matt Pennington, "Afghanistan Stops Paying Farmers to Give Up Growing Opium," Associated Press, August 25, 2003.
21. Rubin, "In the Land of the Taliban."
22. Drug dealers in at least one instance may have aided a senior Taliban commander in securing his escape from the U.S.-led invasion. A March 2004 intelligence report seen by the author says Mullah Dadullah paid northern smuggler Shamuk Haq $1 million to escape Mazar e Sharif when the Taliban fell from power there. Haq was a dealer based in northern Balkh Province who allegedly smuggled heroin and weapons between the north and Helmand.
23. Interview with a U.S. official, Washington, D.C., July 25, 2007.
24. Peters, "Hostilities Flare in America's Other War."
25. Rahimullah Yusufzai, "Taliban Aims to Regain Power," BBC News, March 28, 2003, http://news.bbc.co.uk/2/hi/south_asia/2897137.stm.
26. Rahimullah Yusufzai, quoted in ICG's "No Quick Fixes." He names the original 2003 members as Jalaluddin Haqqani, Saifur Rahman Mansoor, Mullah Dadullah, former Taliban army chief Akhtar Mohammad Osmani, Akhtar Mohammad Mansoor, former Taliban defense minister Mullah Obaidullah, Kandahar's ex–security chief Hafiz Abdul Majeed, former Nimroz provincial governor Mullah Mohammad Rasul, Mullah Barodar, and

former Taliban corps commander in northern Afghanistan Mullah Abdur Razzaq Akhundzada.

27. E-mail interview with Mirwais Yasini, October 16, 2007.
28. Sly, "Opium Cash Fuels Terror, Experts Say." Prices calculated from UNODC's world drug report, available at http://www.unodc.org/pdf/WDR_2006/wdr2006_chap5_opium.pdf, 4.
29. From a U.S. Department of Homeland Security report cited in Rabasa et al., *Ungoverned Territories*, 66.
30. A kilo of refined heroin might sell for $1,000 along the border. On the streets of Europe and the United States, it will fetch as much as $130,000, according to the UNODC.
31. "Coalition Forces Make Second Major Drug Seizure in Five Days," story no. NNS031220-01, U.S. Naval Forces Central Command/Commander, U.S. 5th Fleet Public Affairs, December 20, 2003; "USS Decatur Captures Possible Al-Qaida Associated Drug-Smuggling Dhow in Arabian Gulf," story no. NNS031219-09, U.S. Naval Forces Central Command/Commander, U.S. 5th Fleet Public Affairs, December 19, 2003.
32. Interview with a U.S. official, Kabul, March 2004.
33. Mintz, "15 Freighters Believed to Be Linked to Al Qaeda."
34. Interview with an Afghan commander, Islamabad, October 25, 2007.
35. Tohid, "Bumper Year for Afghan Poppies."
36. Macdonald, *Drugs in Afghanistan*, 103.
37. Interviews with Major General Khalid Jaffery, director general of Pakistan's Anti Narcotics Force, Rawalpindi, September 13, 2007; General Kamal Sadat, former chief of Afghanistan's Counter Narcotics Police, Kabul, February 28, 2007; and Hashem Zayyem, drugs liaison officer at the Iranian embassy, Kabul, March 1, 2007.
38. Interview with Major General Khalid Jaffery, Rawalpindi, September 13, 2007.
39. The author was shown dozens of still classified State Department, DoD, and CIA documents; many of them, like this one, were raw intelligence reports outlining links between the drugs trade and terrorist groups, which were cabled back to Washington from the U.S. embassies in Kabul and Islamabad.
40. Interview with a western diplomat, Islamabad, August 2, 2006.
41. Telephone interview with a U.S. official, May 12, 2007.
42. Telephone interview with a former CIA official, September 5, 2008.
43. In Afghanistan, Iran, and Pakistan, many users smoke or consume unrefined opium gum. The most common product on the regional market is partially refined opium base, known locally as "brown sugar." Crystal heroin, the more

potent white powder produced from boiling opium base with acetic anhydride, is what gets smuggled to the West.

44. Burnett and Huband, "UK Trains Afghans in Anti-Drugs Drive."
45. Telephone interview with a western official, June 12, 2007.
46. Interview by research assistant 1 with a former Force 333 commander, Ghazni, August 2007.
47. A copy of the letter was shown to the author.
48. Multiple interviews with farmers and Afghan citizens by research assistant 3, Helmand, July 2007.
49. Interview with a western diplomat, Kabul, March 4, 2008.
50. Interview by research assistant 2 with Haji Bado Khan, Lashkar Gah, July 2007. Research assistant 1 also heard similar accounts.
51. Interview by research assistant 3 with Haji Khan, Sangin, July 2007.
52. Haytullah Gaheez, "Daughters Sold to Settle Debts," Institute for War and Peace Reporting, ARR no. 155, December 30, 2004, http://www.iwpr.net/?s=f&o=152229&p=arr&l=EN&apc_state=henarcaDaughters%20Sold%20to%20Settle%20Debts_2______publish_date_1_10_compact.
53. Tom Coghlan, "Even the School Playground Has Been Turned into a Poppy Field," *Telegraph*, February 8, 2007; multiple interviews with local farmers in Helmand.
54. Smith, "Talking to the Taliban: Globe Special Report." The figure of 8 percent comes from the UNODC's "Afghanistan Opium Survey 2007," 6, http://www.unodc.org/pdf/research/Afghanistan_Opium_Survey_2007.pdf.
55. See, for example, David Mansfield and Adam Pain, "Opium Poppy Eradication: How to Raise Risk When There Is Nothing to Lose?" Afghanistan Research and Evaluation Unit, Briefing Paper Series, August 2006, http://www.areu.org.af/index.php?option=com_docman&task=doc_view&gid=426.
56. Abubakar Siddique and Muhammad Salih Salih, "Afghanistan: Poor Helmand Farmers Find Themselves in Eye of Drug Storm," Radio Free Europe/Radio Liberty, October 10, 2007, http://www.globalsecurity.org/military/library/news/2007/10/mil-071010-rferl07.htm.
57. Interviews by research assistants with local farmers, Helmand, June and July 2007.
58. Interview by research assistant 2 with Dastagir Khan, Sangin, July 2007.
59. Their full reports are available at http://iwpr.net/?p=arr&s=f&o=340973&apc_state=henfarr340968.
60. Aziz Ahmad Tassal, "Winning Hearts and Minds," Institute for War and Peace Reporting, ARR no. 275, November 27, 2007, http://www.indybay.org/newsitems/2005/01/04/17127681.php.

61. Shafe, "Taleban Ghost Town."
62. Tassal, "Winning Hearts and Minds."
63. Information in this paragraph is from Khan, "Taliban Collected Taxes, Ran Heroin Labs, Had Own Judge in Afghan Town" and Khan, "Taliban Hang Three Alleged Afghan Informers."
64. Stephen Grey and Anna Schecter, "Exclusive: 11 Tons of Opium Discovered in Taliban Town," ABC News, December 20, 2007, http://blogs.abcnews.com/theblotter/2007/12/exclusive-11-to.html.
65. Jean MacKenzie, Aziz Ahmad Tassal, and Mohammad Ilyas Dayee, "What Next for Musa Qala?" Institute for War and Peace Reporting, ARR no. 277, December 12, 2007, http://www.iwpr.net/?p=arr&s=f&o=341358&apc_state=henparr.
66. Callinan, "Taliban Back in Drugs, Terror Business."
67. Siddique and Salih, "Poor Helmand Farmers"; multiple interviews.
68. Telephone interview by research assistant 1 with an Afghan official, August 2007.
69. Interview by research assistant 3 with Mohammed Gulab Achakzai, Kandahar, August 2007.
70. Grey and Schecter, "Exclusive: 11 Tons of Opium."
71. Interviews by research assistant 4, Quetta, October 8 and 9, 2007.
72. Interviews by research assistant 1 with an Afghan official, Afghanistan, July 2007.
73. Ahto Lobjakas, "Afghanistan: NATO Downplays 'Conventional' Threat in South," Radio Free Europe, January 23, 2007, http://www.rferl.org/content/article/1074237.html.
74. Interviews by research assistant 1 with Afghan officials, Kabul, August 2007.
75. Interviews by research assistant 1 with Afghan and UN officials, March 1, 2008.
76. Ibid.
77. Hekmatyar's party was known as Hizb-i-Islami until 1979, when it split into two factions. The faction Hekmatyar controls is what is now referred to as Hizb-i-Islami Gulbuddin, or HIG.
78. Interview with a U.S. official, Washington, D.C., July 13, 2008.
79. This group remains nominally commanded by Jalaluddin Haqqani, but serious illness and old age took him out of day-to-day operations in 2006. Many say his son Sirajuddin Haqqani now runs the network.
80. Interviews by research assistant 3 with police, district officials, and intelligence agents, Pakistan, August 2007.
81. Interview with a U.S. official, Washington, D.C., July 25, 2007.

82. Rashid, *Jihad*, 165; Catseel, "Narco-Terrorism: International Drug Trafficking and Terrorism—a Dangerous Mix"; Makarenko, "Central Asia's Opium Terrorists."
83. Telephone interview with Ahmed Rashid, July 16, 2007.
84. According to Rashid and a U.S. intelligence document seen by the author.
85. Rashid, *Jihad*, 165.
86. Mark Burgess, "Profile of the IMU," The Terrorism Project, Washington, D.C.: Center for Defense Information, March 25, 2002, http://www.cdi.org/terrorism/imu.cfm; Rashid, *Jihad*; Makarenko, "Central Asia's Opium Terrorists."
87. Multiple interviews with western and Pakistani officials; Tohid, "Al Qaeda's Uzbek Bodyguards."
88. Habibullah Khan, "Pakistan Claims Control of Al Qaeda Haven," ABC News, April 11, 2007, http://blogs.abcnews.com/theblotter/2007/04/pakistan_claims.html; Declan Walsh, "Toll Hits 250 as Pakistani Tribesmen Fight to Expel Foreign Militants," *Guardian*, April 5, 2007.
89. Information on these individuals was compiled by the author and research assistants.
90. John Ward Anderson, "Emboldened Taliban Reflected in More Attacks, Greater Reach," *Washington Post*, September 25, 2007.
91. Interview with Karen Tandy, Islamabad, September 28, 2007.
92. Interview with an Afghan official, Kabul, October 2005.
93. Interview with a UN official, Kabul, February 25, 2007.
94. James Risen, "Reports Link Karzai's Brother to Afghanistan Heroin Trade," *New York Times*, October 4, 2008.
95. Interview with Ahmed Wali, Islamabad, April 2007.
96. Interview by research assistant 3 with Sadoo Agha, Gereshk, July 2007.
97. Interview by research assistant 2 with a senior interior ministry official, Lashkar Gah, July 2007.
98. Interview with Kamal Sadat, Kabul, February 26, 2007.
99. Ibid.
100. Interview with a western diplomat, Islamabad, March 2007.
101. Interview with a European official, Islamabad, April 2007.
102. Interview with a western military official, Islamabad, December 2007.
103. Interview with a Pakistani officer, Quetta, July 10, 2008.
104. David Rohde, "Afghan Police Are Set Back as Taliban Adapt," *New York Times*, September 2, 2007.
105. Karen DeYoung, "U.S. Notes Limited Progress in Afghan War," *Washington Post*, November 25, 2006.

106. Christie Blatchford, "Canadian Troops Forced to Start from Scratch," *Globe and Mail*, September 1, 2007.
107. Interview by research assistant 2 with Shaystah Gul Khan, Gereshk, July 2007.
108. United Nations Assistance Mission in Afghanistan, *Suicide Attacks in Afghanistan 2001–2007*.; Ansar Abbasi, "Should FBI Be Invited for Karachi Blasts Probe?" *News*, Islamabad, October 29, 2007.
109. Abdul Sattar, "Jihadist Video Shows Boy Beheading Man," Associated Press, April 20, 2007. AP reported that Ghulam Nabi, the man killed in the video, was accused of providing the evidence to the Americans that led to Mullah Osmani's death in December 2006. After receiving the video, the AP confirmed with Nabi's father, Ghulam Sakhi, that Nabi had routinely hosted Osmani and Mullah Dadullah at the madrassa he ran in western Baluchistan Province. Sakhi told AP that his son had traveled to Peshawar and Wana, in southern Waziristan, to "collect money" for guns and food, and that he had personally spoken with Dadullah immediately before his son was killed. "They are the enemies of Islam," he said of the Taliban. "They are behaving like savages."
110. Peters, "They're Back: A New, Vicious Taliban Take Shape in Afghanistan; Opium Funds a New Type of Taliban Army"; Pam Constable, "Afghan Corps Faces a Resurgent Taliban," *Washington Post*, June 10, 2006; Institute for War and Peace Reporting, "Living Under the Taliban," ARR no. 249, April 4, 2007, http://www.reliefweb.int/rw/rwb.nsf/db900sid/KHII-7253JT?OpenDocument.
111. "Taliban Chop Drivers' Noses, Ears in Eastern Afghanistan," Reuters, March 18, 2007.
112. Interview by research assistant 2 with Haji Batoor Khan, Sangin, July 2007.
113. International Crisis Group, "Pakistan's Tribal Areas: Appeasing the Militants," 6.
114. "Opium Trade Is Halal in Islam: Bara Scholar," *Pakistan Daily News*, January 21, 2005.
115. Interview with a western counternarcotics official, Kabul, February 2007.

5. The Kingpin

1. Interview with General Ali Shah Paktiawal, Kabul, May 2005.
2. Interview with an Afghan police official, Kabul, July 2007
3. Interview with an Afghan official, Peshawar, February 2007.
4. Interviews by research assistant 1 with Afghan officials and tribal sources, Kabul, July and August 2007.
5. The short-lived Saffarid dynasty was led by a coppersmith, Ya'qub bin Laith as-Saffar, who like HJK rose from humble origins to became a powerful

warlord. With his base in modern-day Zaranj, the capital of Nimroz Province, he eventually conquered all of Afghanistan and what are today parts of eastern Iran and western Pakistan. At its height, the Saffarid dynasty nearly conquered Baghdad but was defeated.

6. Interview by research assistant 5 with a tribal elder, Dalbandin, October 3, 2007.
7. Interview with an Afghan police official, Kabul, September 26, 2007.
8. Interview with Hashem Zayyem, Kabul, March 1, 2007.
9. Interview with a former British official, Kabul, November 2007.
10. Interview with a U.S. official, Kabul, June 30, 2005.
11. Tim McGirk, "Terorism's Harvest," *Time*, August 9, 2004.
12. Interview with a Pakistani official, Islamabad, March 12, 2008.
13. Baramcha is spelled Baramshah in some intelligence reports shown to the author.
14. Interview by research assistant 1 with an Afghan interior ministry official, Kabul, July 2007.
15. Interview with an Afghan security official, Kabul, September 2006.
16. McGirk, "Terorism's Harvest"; multiple interviews.
17. Ibid.
18. Multiple interviews by research assistant 1 with Afghan officials.
19. Interview by research assistant 1 with an Afghan official, Kabul, July 2007.
20. Ibid.
21. Interview with General Ali Shah Paktiawal, Kabul, May 2004.
22. Interviews by research assistant 1 with an Afghan interior ministry official, Kabul, July and August 2007; http://www.usdoj.gov/usao/nys/pressreleases/October08/usvkhansignedindictment.pdf.
23. Gretchen Peters and Brian Ross, "U.S. Military Links Karzai Brother to Drugs," ABC News, June 22, 2006, http://blogs.abcnews.com/theblotter/2006/06/us_military_lin.html.
24. Interview with a Pakistani officer, Islamabad, March 12, 2008.
25. Interview by research assistant 5 with a smuggler, Quetta, October 2, 2007.
26. Interview with a western official, Kabul, September 2006.
27. Robert Burns, "Gates: Taliban Fighters Use Iranian Weapons," Associated Press, June 4, 2007.
28. Interview with an Afghan official, Peshawar, December 2007.
29. Interviews by research assistants 1 and 2 with Afghan officials, Kabul and Helmand, July 2007.
30. Interview by research assistant 2 with an Afghan security official, Helmand, July 2007.
31. Interview with a smuggler, Quetta, April 2006.

32. Interviews by research assistants 1 and 2 with tribal sources, Kabul and Helmand, July 2007.
33. Interview with a former U.S. official, Washington, D.C., June 16, 2007.
34. Larry Neumeister, "Afghan Man Arrested in New York Narco-Terrorism Case," Associated Press, October 24, 2008; "Afghan Charged in N.Y. Drug-Terrorism Case," Associated Press, October 24, 2008.
35. "Afghan Drug Kingpin Charged with Financing Taliban Terrorist Insurgency," U.S. Drug Enforcement Administration press release, http://www.usdoj.gov/dea/pubs/pressrel/pr102408.html.
36. Telephone interview by research assistant 6 with border resident, December 2008.
37. Interview by research assistant 6 with a Pakistani intelligence official, Quetta, December 2008.
38. Telephone interview by research assistant 6 with an Intelligence Bureau official, December 2008.
39. Interview by research assistant 6 with a border source, Quetta, December 2008.
40. Telephone interview by research assistant 6 with a border resident, December 2008.

6. Follow the Money

1. Interview with Riaz, Dubai, December 10, 2007.
2. See http://newdelhi.usembassy.gov/pr060206.html and http://www.ustreas.gov/press/releases/js909.htm. Groups like the FARC and the United Self-Defense Forces of Colombia also have double designations.
3. Mehta, *Maximum City Bombay Lost and Found*, 134–140; Kaplan, "Paying for Terror."
4. See http://www.ustreas.gov/press/releases/reports/fact_sheet.pdf.
5. Telephone interview with a former CIA official, September 5, 2008.
6. Carolyn Lochhead, "Bush Goes After Terrorists' Funds," *San Francisco Chronicle*, September 25, 2001.
7. See http://www.ustreas.gov/press/releases/po727.htm.
8. For a transcript of the speech, go to http://edition.cnn.com/TRANSCRIPTS/0112/20/se.05.html.
9. See http://www.treas.gov/offices/enforcement/ofac/reports/tar2006.pdf, 15.
10. Interview with John Cassara, Washington, D.C., June 29, 2007.
11. Interview with Robert Charles, Washington, D.C., May 23, 2007.
12. It's also known as "Hundi" in Pakistan, where it specifically refers to a balancing of trade accounts.

13. Maimbo, "Money Exchange Dealers of Kabul: A Study of the Hawala System in Afghanistan," 9.
14. Edwina Thompson, "The Nexus of Drug Trafficking and *Hawala* in Afghanistan," in Byrd and Buddenberg, eds., *Afghanistan's Drug Industry* (report), 177–179.
15. Behar, "Kidnapped Nation."
16. Interview with Raymond Baker, Washington, D.C., July 17, 2007.
17. "U.S. Designates Suspects in Pakistani Drug Lord's Ring."
18. Interview with Gulbaz Khan, Peshawar, January 2008.
19. "Dubai Has 30,000 Construction Cranes," *Gulf News*, June 18, 2006.
20. Interviews with bankers and former Pakistani officials, Karachi, March 2008.
21. Telephone interview with Tariq Hassan, February 18, 2008.
22. Sherbaz Khan, "Big Fish Allowed to Escape the Net: Tariq, Ex-SECP Issues White Paper," *Dawn*, July 8, 2006.
23. See http://www.akdsecurities.net.
24. "Investors Lost $13bn in 2005 Stock Crisis," *Dawn*, July 8, 2006.
25. Nadeem, curiously, is the son of Swaleh Naqvi, the former chief executive of BCCI, according to other brokers and bankers in Karachi.
26. Mark Smith, "With Vast Sums in Transit, Even Entire Nations Put at Risk," *Houston Chronicle*, December 3, 1995.
27. Jon Henly, "City 'Haven' for Terrorist Money Laundering," *Guardian*, October 10, 2001.
28. Patrick Radden Keefe, "Quartermasters of Terror," *New York Review of Books*, February 10, 2005, 2.
29. Office of the Director of National Intelligence, "The Terrorist Threat to the U.S. Homeland," news release, July 17, 2007, 6, http://www.dni.gov/press_releases/20070717_release.pdf.
30. As well, there is evidence that bin Laden banned his supporters and trainees in his camps, not just from using alcohol and hashish, but even from smoking tobacco. For example, see Sifaoui, *Inside al Qaeda*, and http://cns.miis.edu/pubs/reports/.pdfs/binladen/060201.pdf.
31. "Monograph on Terrorist Financing," 9/11 Commission.
32. Lee Wolosky, "Statement to the National Commission on Terrorist Attacks upon the United States," April 1, 2003, http://govinfo.library.unt.edu/911/hearings/hearing1/witness_wolosky.htm.
33. Interview with a U.S. official, Islamabad, February 5, 2008.
34. Rashid, *Jihad*, 165; Catseel, "Narco-Terrorism: International Drug Trafficking and Terrorism—a Dangerous Mix"; Makarenko, "Central Asia's Opium Terrorists."

35. See http://cns.miis.edu/pubs/reports/pdfs/binladen/060201.pdf.
36. Radden Keefe, "Quartermasters of Terror," 5.
37. Farah, "Al Qaeda's Road Paved with Gold."
38. Cassara, *Hide and Seek*, 178.
39. Benjamin and Simon, *The Age of Sacred Terror*, 112.
40. Farah, "Al Qaeda's Road."

7. Mission Creep

1. The author was given copies of the correspondence by staff at the Foreign Relations Committee.
2. Multiple interviews; Meyer, "Pentagon Resists Pleas for Help in Afghan Opium Fight."
3. A copy of the letter was given to the author by staff at the Foreign Relations Committee.
4. Meyer, "Pentagon Resists Pleas."
5. Risen, *State of War*, 157.
6. Ibid.
7. Interview with a U.S. official, Washington, D.C., May 14, 2007. GPS stands for "global positioning system."
8. Meyer, "Pentagon Resists Pleas"; Blanchard, "Afghanistan, Narcotics and U.S. Policy"; see also UNODC's *Annual Drug Survey 2004*, 206, http://www.unodc.org/afg/reports_surveys.html.
9. Declan Walsh, "How Anti-Corruption Chief Once Sold Heroin in Las Vegas," *Guardian*, August 28, 2007.
10. David Kaplan and Aamir Latif, "A Stash to Beat All," *U.S. News & World Report.*, August 10, 2005. Sher Mohammed was the nephew of Nasim Akhundzada (cited in Chapter 2). As with his uncle, Sher Mohammed appears to have set poppy quotas for Helmand. Antonio Maria Costa, the executive director of the UNODC, blamed Sher Mohammed specifically for Helmand's soaring poppy crop. President Karzai, meanwhile, has repeatedly pressed for him to be restored to power.
11. Quoted in John Risen, "Poppy Fields Are Now a Front Line in the Afghan War," *New York Times*, May 16, 2007.
12. David Rohde, "The Afghanistan Triangle," *New York Times*, October 1, 2006; Gretchen Peters, "Law Lessons for Afghan Police," *Christian Science Monitor*, January 7, 2003.
13. David Rohde, "Afghan Symbol for Change Becomes a Symbol of Failure," *New York Times*, September 5, 2006.
14. Telephone interview with Beverly Eighmy, May 15, 2007.

15. Karen Tandy, "Statement Before the Committee on Armed Services." U.S. House of Representatives, 66–73; Michael Braun, "U.S. Counternarcotics Policy in Afghanistan," testimony, Committee on International Relations.
16. Telephone interview with Rand Beers, August 5, 2007.
17. "Rumsfeld: Major Combat Over in Afghanistan," CNN, May 1, 2003, http://www.cnn.com/2003/WORLD/asiapcf/central/05/01/afghan.combat/.
18. Risen, *State of War*, 158.
19. Victoria Burnett, "Crackdown on Afghanistan's Cash Crop Looms," *Boston Globe*, September 18, 2004.
20. A copy of the cable was shown to the author.
21. Interview with a U.S. official, Washington, D.C., July 25, 2007.
22. Risen, *State of War*, 153.
23. Interview with Robert Charles, Washington, D.C., May 23, 2007.
24. A copy of the cable was shown to the author.
25. A copy of his testimony was given to the author by Bashir's American lawyer, Ivan Fisher.
26. The details on this can be found in Chapter 3, "Narco-Terror State."
27. See: http://www.usdoj.gov/dea/pubs/states/newsrel/2008/nyc092408.html.
28. Ibid.
29. The indictment can be found at http://www.house.gov/kirk/pdf/Norzai Indictment.pdf.
30. Powell, "Warlord or Druglord?"
31. Mark Corcoran, "America's Blind Eye," *Foreign Correspondent*, Australian Broadcasting Corporation, April 10, 2002.
32. According to HBN's testimony, author's interviews, and local news reports from the time.
33. Risen, *State of War*, 164.
34. Gregg Zoroyya and Donna Leinwand, "Rise of Drug Trade Threat to Afghanistan's Security," *U.S.A. Today*, October 26, 2004.
35. The author obtained transcripts of the meetings from Bashir's lawyer, Ivan Fisher. The documents identify Mike's surname variably as Kistimos or Acimos. Brian's surname is given as Allen on one document and Malone on another. The spellings appear to be phonetic, so first names only are used.
36. Gul Agha and Khalid Pashtun, along with the Karzai family, are all members of the Zirak Durrani federation. The Noorzai clan is part of the rival Panjpai branch, which prevailed during the Taliban regime. It's not a clean divide: some Noorzai clansmen are members of the Karzai regime; some of Karzai's Popalzai tribe are Taliban.
37. Maass, "Gul Agha Gets His Province Back."

38. Brian Ross and Gretchen Peters, "U.S. Military Links Karzai's Brother to Drugs," ABC News, June 22, 2006, http://blogs.abcnews.com/theblotter/2006/06/us_military_lin.html; Sifton and Coursen-Neff, *Killing You Is a Very Easy Thing for Us*, Human Rights Watch report.
39. Ahmed Wali Karzai's wife is Arif Noorzai's sister.
40. Interview with a Noorzai relative, Kabul, March 15, 2007.
41. Interestingly, in "Warlord or Druglord?" Babar is identified as Saitullah Khan Babar, a friend of Noorzai's and a former officer in the ISI, Pakistan's military intelligence service.
42. According to the motion filed on his behalf.
43. Powell, "Warlord or Druglord?"
44. Risen, *State of War*, 165.
45. This is according to his lawyer.
46. Perhaps not surprisingly, Fisher was unwilling to share those documents with the author.
47. Telephone interview with Ivan Fisher, October 20, 2008.
48. Interview with Ivan Fisher, New York City, April 24, 2007.
49. Benjamin Weiser, "Manhattan Jury Convicts Man Linked to Taliban Leader in Drug Smuggling Case," *New York Times*, September 23, 2008.
50. And its parliament is highly unlikely to pass one, given that a fair number of its members themselves are accused of ties to the drugs trade.
51. See http://www.usembassy.gov/pakistan/h05102402.html.
52. See http://www.usdoj.gov/usao/nys/pressreleases/May 07/essaarrivalpr.pdf.
53. See http://www.usdoj.gov/dea/pubs/states/newsrel/nyc051107a.html.
54. Interview with a western official, Kabul, March 4, 2008.
55. Interview with a U.S. official, Washington, D.C., July 13, 2008.
56. Karen Tandy, "Remarks in Islamabad, Pakistan," U.S. Embassy (Islamabad), press release, September 28, 2007.
57. Tandy, "Remarks in Islamabad."
58. Committee on Armed Services, statement of Karen P. Tandy, http://www.globalsecurity.org/military/library/congress/2006_hr/060628-tandy.pdf.
59. Blanchard, "Afghanistan, Narcotics and U.S. Policy."
60. See, for example, Tandy, "Statement Before the Committee on Armed Services."
61. Meyer, "Pentagon Resists Pleas."
62. Tandy, "Statement Before the Committee on Armed Services."
63. Risen, "Poppy Fields."
64. James Glantz and David Rohde, "Report Faults Training of Afghan Police," *New York Times*, December 4, 2006.
65. Ibid.

66. Rohde, "Afghan Symbol for Change."
67. Interview with an Afghan official, Kabul, September 2005.
68. Rohde, "Overhaul of Afghan Police Is New Priority."
69. Multiple interviews with UN and Afghan officials, March 2007.
70. Constable, "Poor Yield for Afghans' War on Drugs."
71. Jeremy Page, "Wanted for Empty Prison: Some Convicted Afghan Drug Barons," *Times* (London), February 23, 2008.
72. Moore, "Struggling for Solutions as Opium Trade Blossoms."
73. Gall and Cloud, "U.S. Memo Faults Afghan Leader on Heroin Fight."
74. Interview with Doug Wankal, Helmand, May 2006.
75. David Rohde, "Taliban Raise Poppy Production to a Record Again," *New York Times*, August 26, 2007.
76. Joseph Coleman, "World Bank Urges Counter Opium Measures," Associated Press, February 5, 2008.
77. Coghlan, "School Playground."
78. Burch, "Afghan Airport to Help Switch from Drugs to Fruit."
79. Hafvenstein, *Opium Season*, 64–65.
80. Ed Johnson, "Gates Wants NATO to Reorganize Afghanistan Mission," *Bloomberg*, December 13, 2007; Thomas Harding, "Canadians to Quit Afghanistan," *Telegraph*, February 22, 2008.
81. Interview with Thomas Schweich, Washington, D.C., June 1, 2007.
82. Read the full report at http://www.state.gov/documents/organization/90671.pdf.
83. Hollbrooke, "Still Wrong in Afghanistan"; multiple interviews.
84. "UN Urges NATO to Stop Afghan Opium Trade," CNN, November 17, 2007, http://www.cnn.com/2007/WORLD/asiapcf/11/17/afghan.opium/index.html.
85. Interview with a western official, Islamabad, February 5, 2008.

8. Zero-Sum Game

1. "Helmand Heads for Record Poppy Harvest," Institute for War and Peace Reporting, ARR no. 241, February 9, 2007, http://www.iwpr.net/?p=arr&s=f&o=329222&apc_state=henparr.
2. See http://www.state.gov/p/inl/rls/nrcrpt/2007/vol1/html/80858.htm.
3. I am not suggesting the *entire* Afghan drug trade is being managed in Pakistan. Some smugglers who traffic Afghan drugs live in Iran, Central Asian states, or Afghanistan itself. Research for this project found that the majority of businessmen running the southern Afghan poppy trade, which intersects the insurgency, live and operate their businesses in Pakistan.

4. Tomsen, "Statement on Afghanistan: In Pursuit of Security and Democracy" (speech).
5. Docherty, *Desert of Death*, 185.
6. Smith, "Doing It the Dutch Way in Afghanistan."
7. Moore, "NATO Confronts Surprisingly Fierce Taliban."
8. See http://abcnews.go.com/images/PollingUnit/1049a1Afghanistan-WhereThingsStand.pdf.
9. Seth Jones, "America Is Making a Difference in Eastern Afghanistan," *Globe and Mail*, April 1, 2008.
10. Bronwen Roberts, "Afghans Learning a Better Way to Match Taliban Pay," Agence-France Presse, March 24, 2008.
11. This isn't only a U.S. affliction: British, Pakistani, European, and Afghan officials interviewed for this project complained their law enforcement agents and spies don't cooperate well, either.
12. Interview with a U.S. military officer, Islamabad, September 10, 2007.
13. Karen Tandy, "Remarks in Islamabad, Pakistan," U.S. Embassy (Islamabad), press release, September 28, 2007.
14. Interview with a western official, Kabul, October 30, 2006.
15. Rubin and Sherman, *Counter-Narcotics to Stabilize Afghanistan*, 8.
16. Paul Taylor Sun, "Afghan Urges 'Name and Shame' War on Graft, Drugs," Reuters, March 16, 2008.
17. See http://www.incb.org/incb/en/press_release_2007-11-12_01.html.
18. See http://www.state.gov/p/inl/rls/nrcrpt/2007/vol1/html/80858.htm and Chouvy, "Licensing Afghanistan's Opium: Solution or Fallacy?"
19. Rubin et al., *Too Early to Declare Success*, Afghanistan policy brief.
20. Interview with William Byrd, Washington, D.C., June 11, 2007.
21. Rubin, *Road to Ruin*, 3.
22. Interview with a U.S. official, Islamabad, February 21, 2007.
23. Moore, "Struggling for Solutions as Opium Trade Blossoms."
24. Interview with Noorullah Delawari, Kabul, March 27, 2007.

Afterword

1. Del Quentin Wilber, "Afghan Farmer Helps Convict Taliban Member in U.S. Court," *Washington Post*, December 23, 2008.
2. "Afghanistan Opium Survey 2008," UNODC, August 2008, vii, www.unodc.org/documents/publications/Afghanistan_Opium_Survey_2008.pdf.
3. Although these gains seemed less impressive when reports emerged that many northern farmers simply switched to growing marijuana.
4. "Afghanistan Opium Survey 2008," 5, 24–25.

5. Pir Zubair Shah and Jane Perlez, "Pakistan Marble Helps Taliban Stay in Business," *New York Times*, July 14, 2008.
6. Jason Straziuso, "Record 151 U.S. Troops Die in Afghanistan in 2008," Associated Press, December 31, 2008.
7. Thom Shanker, "Obstacle in Bid to Curb Afghan Trade in Narcoticsa," *New York Times*, December 23, 2008.
8. Vivienne Walt, "Is the Taliban Stockpiling Opium? And If So, Why?" *Time* magazine, October 29, 2008.
9. "Afghanistan Opium Survey 2008," viii.
10. Seth Jones et al., "How Terrorist Groups End," Rand Corporation, July 2008, http://www.rand.org/pubs/monographs/MG741/.
11. "Taliban Leader Omar Denies Talks," *BBC News*, December 23, 2008, http://news.bbc.co.uk/2/hi/south_asia/7797274.stm.

BIBLIOGRAPHY

Books

Baker, Raymond. *Capitalism's Achilles Heel.* Hoboken: Wiley, 2005.

Benjamin, Daniel, and Steven Simon. *The Age of Sacred Terror.* New York: Random House, 2003.

Bergen, Peter. *Holy War, Inc.* New York: Touchstone Press, 2002.

Booth, Martin. *Opium.* New York: St. Martin's Griffin, 1996.

Cassara, John. *Hide and Seek.* Washington, D.C.: Potomac Books, 2006.

Charles, Robert B. *Narcotics and Terrorism.* Philadelphia: Chelsea House, 2004.

Coll, Stephen. *The Ghost Wars.* New York: Penguin Press, 2004.

Cooley, John K. *Unholy Wars.* London: Pluto Press, 1999.

Courtwright, David. *Forces of Habit.* Cambridge, MA: Harvard University Press, 2001.

Crile, George. *Charlie Wilson's War.* New York: Atlantic Monthly Press, 2003.

Davenport-Hines, Richard. *The Pursuit of Oblivion.* New York: W. W. Norton, 2002.

Docherty, Leo. *Desert of Death.* London: Faber and Faber, 2007.

Escohotado, Antonio. *A Brief History of Drugs.* Rochester, NY: Park Street Press, 1996.

Farah, Douglas, and Stephen Braun. *Merchant of Death.* Hoboken, NJ: Wiley, 2007.

Griffin, Michael. *Reaping the Whirlwind.* London: Pluto Press, 2001.

Hafvestein, Joel. *Opium Season.* Guilford, UK: Lyons Press, 2007.

Hanes, W. Travis, and Frank Sanello. *The Opium Wars.* Naperville, IL: Sourcebooks, 2002.

Haq, Ikramul. *Pakistan.* Lahore: Annoor Printers and Publishers, 1991.

Haq, M. Emdad-ul. *Drugs in South Asia.* New York: St. Martin's Press, 2000.

Haqqani, Hussain. *Pakistan Between Mosque and Military.* Lahore: Vanguard Books, 2005.

Hussein, Zahid. *Frontline Pakistan.* London: I. B. Taurus, 2007.

Hoffman, Bruce. *Inside Terrorism.* New York: Columbia University Press, 2006.

Lawrence, Bruce, ed. *Messages to the World.* London: Verso Press, 2005.

Lesser, Ian, Bruce Hoffman, John Arquilla, David Ronfeldt, and Michele Zanini. *Countering the New Terrorism.* Santa Monica: Rand Corporation, 1999.

Macdonald, David. *Drugs in Afghanistan.* London: Pluto Press, 2007.
Maley, William, ed. *Fundamentalism Reborn?* London: Hurst, 1998.
Marks, Howard. *Mr. Nice.* London: Vintage Books, 1996.
McCoy, Alfred. *The Politics of Heroin,* rev. ed. Chicago: Lawrence Hill, 2003.
——— and Alan Block, eds. *War on Drugs.* Boulder: Westview Press, 1992.
Mehta, Suketu. *Maximum City Bombay Lost and Found.* New York: Vintage Books, 2004.
Musharraf, Pervez. *In the Line of Fire.* London: Simon & Schuster, 2006.
Naím, Moisés. *Illicit.* New York: Doubleday, 2005.
Napoleoni, Loretta. *Terror Incorporated.* London: Penguin Books, 2003.
Nasiri, Omar. *Inside the Jihad.* New York: Basic Books, 2006.
National Commission on Terrorist Attacks upon the United States, Thomas H. Kean, and Lee Hamilton. *The 9/11 Commission Report.* New York: W. W. Norton, 2003.
Rashid, Ahmed. *Descent into Chaos.* New York: Penguin Books, 2008.
———. *Jihad: The Rise of Militant Islam in Central Asia.* New Haven, CT: Yale University Press, 2002.
———. *The Taliban.* New Haven, CT: Yale University Press, 2000.
Risen, James. *State of War.* New York: Simon & Schuster, 2006.
Rubin, Barnett R. *The Fragmentation of Afghanistan,* second ed. New Haven, CT: Yale University Press, 2002.
Schroen, Gary. *First In.* New York: Presidio Press, 2005.
Sifaoui, Mohamed. *Inside al Qaeda.* London: Granta Books, 2003.
Tenet, George. *At the Center of the Storm.* New York: HarperCollins, 2007.
Woodward, Bob. *Bush at War.* New York: Pocket Books, 2003.
Yousaf, Mohammed, and Mark Adkin. *The Bear Trap.* Lahore: Jang Publishers, 1992.

U.S. Government Documents

"Afghanistan: Foreign Secretary Mulls Over Afghanistan." U.S. Embassy (Islamabad) cable, October 1996. Barbara Elias, ed., *Pakistan: "The Taliban's Godfather"? Documents Detail Years of Pakistani Support for Taliban, Extremists,* National Security Archive electronic briefing book no. 227, National Security Archive/George Washington University (NSA/GWU hereafter), http://www.gwu.edu/~nsarchiv/NSAEBB/NSAEBB227/index.htm.
"Afghanistan, Iran, Pakistan Country Profiles." Office of Intelligence Drug Enforcement Administration, January 1992. Narcotics Collection, box 11, folder: Drug Trafficking/Pakistan. NSA/GWU.
"Afghanistan: Russian Embassy Official Claims Iran Interfering More Than Pakistan." U.S. Embassy (Islamabad) cable, November 30, 1995. *Pakistan,* Elias, ed., NSA/GWU.

"Afghanistan: Taliban Rep Won't Seek UN Seat for Now." U.S. Embassy (Islamabad) cable, December 1996. *The Taliban File, 9/11 Sourcebook*, National Security Archive electronic briefing book no. 97, Sajit Ghandi, ed., NSA/GWU, http://www.gwu.edu/~nsarchiv/NSAEBB/NSAEBB97/index.htm.

"Afghanistan: Taliban Victory's Impact [excised]." National Intelligence Daily, CIA, September 30, 1996. *Pakistan*, Elias, ed., NSA/GWU.

"Afghanistan: U.S. Interests and U.S. Aid." Letter to U.S. State Department, 1992. Document collection of Peter Tomsen, former U.S. Special Envoy (Tomsen collection, hereafter).

"A/S Raphel Discusses Afghanistan." U.S. Embassy (Islamabad) cable, April 22, 1996. *Taliban File*, Ghandi, ed., NSA/GWU.

"Daily Muslim Article on Balochistan Heroin Seizure." U.S. Embassy (Islamabad) cable, December 1990. Narcotics Collection, box 30, folder: Pakistan/Afghanistan FOIA Documents. NSA/GWU.

"[excised] Believe Pakistan Is Backing Taliban." U.S. Embassy (Islamabad) cable, December 6, 1994. *Taliban File*, Ghandi, ed., NSA/GWU.

"[excised]/Pakistan Interservice Intelligence/Pakistan (PK) Directorate Supplying the Taliban Forces." From [excised] to DIA, Washington, D.C., [excised] cable, October 22, 1996. *Pakistan*, Elias, ed., NSA/GWU.

"Finally, a Talkative Talib: Origins and Membership of the Religious Students' Movement." U.S. Embassy (Islamabad) cable, February 20, 1995. *Taliban File*, Ghandi, ed., NSA/GWU.

"GOP Begins Cleanup of Smugglers Den at Sohrab Goth." U.S. State Department cable from Karachi consul, December 1986. Narcotics Collection, box 30, folder: Pakistan/Afghanistan FOIA Documents. NSA/GWU.

"Heroin, Guns and the War in Pakistan." Robert Oakley, U.S. Embassy (Islamabad) cable to Secretary of State, December 1988. Narcotics Collection, box 30, folder: Pakistan/Afghanistan FOIA Documents. NSA/GWU.

"Heroin in Pakistan: Sowing the Wind." CIA. Published in *The Friday Times* (Lahore), September 3, 1993.

"HFAC International Narcotics Control Task Force Hearings, May 22." U.S. State Department document, June 1986. Narcotics Collection, box 29, folder: Pakistan. NSA/GWU.

"IIR [excised] Pakistan Involvement in Afghanistan." From [excised] to DIA, Washington, D.C., November 7, 1996. *Pakistan*, Elias, ed., NSA/GWU.

International Narcotics Control Strategy Reports 2001–2007, U.S. State Department Bureau for International Narcotics and Law Enforcement Affairs, Washington, D.C.

"Meeting with the Taliban in Kandahar: More Questions Than Answers." U.S. Embassy (Islamabad) cable, February 15, 1995. *Taliban File*, Ghandi, ed., NSA/GWU.

"Monograph on Terrorist Financing." 9/11 Commission, August 21, 2004, http://www.9-11commission.go/staff_ statements/911_TerrFin_Monograph.pdf.

"Narcotics and the New Government." U.S. Embassy (Islamabad) cable, December 1988. Narcotics Collection, box 30, folder: Pakistan/Afghanistan FOIA Documents. NSA/GWU.

"Narcotics—FY 90 Budget." Robert Oakley, U.S. Embassy (Islamabad) cable to INM Assistant Secretary Ann Wrobleski, March 1989. Narcotics Collection, box 30, folder: Pakistan/Afghanistan FOIA Documents. NSA/GWU.

"The Narcotics Issue and Contacts with Politicians." U.S. State Department letter to U.S. Embassy (Islamabad), September 1988. Narcotics Collection, box 30, folder: Pakistan/Afghanistan FOIA Documents. NSA/GWU.

"Narcotics Production/Trafficking in Northern Helmand." U.S. Embassy (Islamabad) cable, June 1989. Narcotics Collection, box 30, folder: Pakistan/Afghanistan FOIA Documents. NSA/GWU.

"Narcotics Trafficking and the Military." Near East and South Asia briefs, CIA, January 30, 1987. Narcotics Collection, box 30, folder: Pakistan: Narcotics Control Preparedness. NSA/GWU.

"Narcotics Trafficking from Afghanistan." U.S. Embassy (Islamabad) cable, March 1989. Narcotics Collection, box 11, folder: Drug Trafficking/Pakistan. NSA/GWU.

"National Intelligence Daily." Director of Central Intelligence, CIA, May 1, 1998. This document has not yet been assigned to a collection. NSA/GWU.

"National Narcotics Intelligence Consumers Committee Report for 1985–1986." Afghanistan Collection, box 12. NSA/GWU.

"New Fighting and New Forces in Kandahar." U.S. Consulate (Peshawar) cable, November 3, 1994. *Taliban File*, Ghandi, ed., NSA/GWU.

"Pakistan: Countering an Expanding Drug Industry." Intelligence assessment, CIA, September 1988. Narcotics Collection, box 11, folder: Drug Trafficking/Pakistan. NSA/GWU.

"Pakistan." DEA country analysis, undated. Narcotics Collection, box 30, folder: Pakistan. NSA/GWU.

"Pakistan's Narcotics Control Program." Letter from Edward Fox, Asst. Secretary of Legislative and Intergovernmental Affairs, to the Chairman of the Foreign Affairs Committee, U.S. House of Representatives. Narcotics Collection, box 30, folder: Pakistan Narcotics Preparedness. NSA/GWU.

"Pakistan Support for Taliban." U.S. Embassy (Islamabad) cable, September 26, 2000. *Pakistan*, Elias, ed., NSA/GWU.

"Request for Afghan Opium Crop Figures." U.S. State Department cable to U.S. Embassy (Islamabad), October 1992. Tomsen collection.

"The Taliban: What We've Heard," U.S. Embassy (Islamabad) cable, January 26, 1995. *Taliban File*, Ghandi, ed., NSA/GWU.

"The Taliban—Who Knows What the Movement Means?" U.S. Embassy (Islamabad) cable, November 28, 1994. *Taliban File*, Ghandi, ed., NSA/GWU.

"TKO Proposal." [name exised] Islamabad Country Office, Drug Enforcement Administration, March 25, 1993. Narcotics Collection, box 30, folder: Pakistan. NSA/GWU.

U.S. Counternarcotics Strategy Afghanistan 2007. Thomas A. Schweich, UNODC, http://www.state.gov/documents/organization/90671.pdf.

"U.S. Engagement with the Taliban on Usama bin Laden." U.S. State Department summary, circa July 16, 2001. *Taliban File*, Ghandi, ed., NSA/GWU.

"Veteran Afghanistan Traveler's Analysis of al Qaeda and Taliban Exploitable Weaknesses." Defense Intelligence Agency cable, October 2001. *Taliban File*, Ghandi, ed., NSA/GWU.

"Visit of INM Assistant Secretary Wrobleski: Meeting with President Zia." U.S. Embassy (Islamabad) cable, September 1987. Narcotics Collection, box 29, folder: Pakistan. NSA/GWU.

"Worldwide Drug Threat Assessment: A Joint Intelligence Report." Committee on Narcotics Intelligence Issues. Document prepared by representatives from the DEA, DIA, U.S. Customs, U.S. Coast Guard, and the National Drug Intelligence Center. April 2000, http://jeremybigwood.net/FOIAs/FOIA.htm.

Reports and Studies

Alexiev, Alexander. "Inside the Soviet Army in Afghanistan." Santa Monica: Rand Corporation, May 1988. Afghan Collection, NSA/GWU.

Byrd, William, and Christopher Ward. *Drugs and Development in Afghanistan*. Social Development Papers: Conflict Prevention and Reconstruction. Washington, D.C.: World Bank, December 2004.

———, and Doris Buddenberg, eds. *Afghanistan's Drug Industry*. Vienna: UNODC/World Bank, 2007.

Curtis, Glenn E., and Tara Karacan. *The Nexus Among Terrorists, Narcotics Traffickers, Weapons Proliferators and Organized Crime Networks in Western Europe*. Washington, D.C.: Library of Congress Federal Research Division, December 2002.

International Crisis Group. "Afghanistan's Endangered Compact." Asia briefing no. 59, January 29, 2007, http://www.crisisgroup.org/home/index.cfm?l=1&id=4631.

———. "Central Asia: Drugs and Conflict." November 26, 2001, http://www.crisisgroup.org/home/index.cfm?l=1&id=1430.

———. "Countering Afghanistan's Insurgency: No Quick Fixes." Asia report no. 123, November 2, 2006, http://www.crisisgroup.org/home/index.cfm?id=4485.

———. "Pakistan's Tribal Areas: Appeasing the Militants." Asia report no. 125, December 11, 2006, http://www.crisisgroup.org/home/index.cfm?id=4568.

Katzman, Kenneth. "Terrorism: Near Eastern Groups and State Sponsors, 2001." Washington, D.C.: Congressional Research Service, September 10, 2001.

Maimbo, Samuel Munzele. "Money Exchange Dealers of Kabul: A Study of the Hawala System in Afghanistan." Finance and Private Sector Unit South Asia Region. Washington, D.C.: World Bank, June 2003.

Perl, Raphael. "The Taliban and the Drug Trade." Washington, D.C.: Congressional Research Service, October 5, 2001.

Porteous, Samuel D. *The Threat from Transnational Crime.* Canadian Security Intelligence Service, commentary no. 70, 1996.

Rabasa, Angel, Steven Boraz, Peter Chalk, Kim Cragin, Theodore W. Karasik, Jennifer D. P. Moroney, Kevin A. O'Brien, and John E. Peters. *Ungoverned Territories: Understanding and Reducing Terrorist Risks.* Santa Monica: Rand Corporation, 2007.

Rubin, Barnett R. "The Political Economy of War and Peace in Afghanistan." *World Development* 28, no. 10 (2000): 1789–1803.

———. *The Road to Ruin.* Center on International Cooperation, New York University, October 7, 2004.

——— and Abubakar Siddique. *Resolving the Pakistan-Afghanistan Stalemate.* U.S. Institute of Peace, special report 176, October 2006.

——— and Jake Sherman. *Counter-Narcotics to Stabilize Afghanistan.* Center on International Cooperation, New York University, February 2008.

——— et al. *Too Early to Declare Success.* Afghanistan policy brief. Center on International Cooperation, New York University, March 2005.

Sifton, John, and Zama Coursen-Neff. *Killing You Is a Very Easy Thing for Us.* New York: Human Rights Watch, July 2003.

Torabi, Yama, and Lorenzo Delesgues. "Afghan Perceptions of Corruption: A Survey Across Thirteen Provinces." Integrity Watch Afghanistan, February 2007.

United Nations Assistance Mission in Afghanistan. *Suicide Attacks in Afghanistan 2001–2007.* UNAMA, September 2007, http://www.unama-afg.org/docs/_UN-Docs/UNAMA%20-%20SUICIDE%20ATTACKS%20STUDY%20-%20SEPT%209th%202007.pdf.

United Nations Office on Drugs and Crime. "Afghanistan: Opium Survey, 2001–2007." http:www.unodc.org.

———. *The Opium Economy in Afghanistan.* New York: UNODC, 2003.

Weiss, Martin, et al. *Terrorist Financing.* Washington, D.C.: Congressional Research Service, August 3, 2005.

Wilder, Andrew. *Cops or Robbers?* Kabul: Afghanistan Research and Evaluation Unit, July 2007.

Speeches and Testimony

Beers, Rand. "Narco-Terror: The Worldwide Connection Between Drugs and Terrorism." Testimony, Committee on the Judiciary, U.S. Senate, 107th Cong., 2nd sess., March 13, 2002.

Blair, Tony. "Prime Minister's Statement to Parliament on the September 11 Attacks." October 4, 2001, www.number10.gov.uk.

Braun, Michael. "U.S. Counternarcotics Policy in Afghanistan: Time for Leadership." Testimony, Committee on International Relations, U.S. House, 109th Cong., 1st sess., March 17, 2005.

Casteel, Steven. "Narco-Terrorism: International Drug Trafficking and Terrorism—a Dangerous Mix." Statement, Committee on the Judiciary, U.S. Senate, 108th Cong., 1st sess., May 20, 2003.

Cilluffo, Frank J. "Threat Posed by the Convergence of Organized Crime, Drug Trafficking, and Terrorism." Statement, Committee on the Judiciary, Subcommittee on Crime, U.S. House, 106th Cong., 2nd sess., December 13, 2000.

Costa, Antonio Maria. "Briefing to the Committee on International Relations." Washington, D.C., September 20, 2006.

Tandy, Karen. "Statement Before the Committee on Armed Services." U.S. House of Representatives, Washington, D.C., June 28, 2006.

Tenet, George. "Challenges in a Changing Global Context." Testimony, Select Committee on Intelligence, U.S. Senate, 108th Cong., 2nd sess., February 24, 2004.

———. "Converging Dangers in a Post 9/11 World." Testimony, Select Committee on Intelligence, U.S. Senate, 107th Cong., 2nd sess., February 6, 2002.

———. "Worldwide Threat in 2000: Global Realities of Our National Security." Statement, Select Committee on Intelligence, U.S. Senate, 107th Cong., 2nd sess., February 2, 2000.

Tomsen, Peter. "Statement on Afghanistan: In Pursuit of Security and Democracy." Speech before the U.S. Senate Committee on Foreign Relations, Washington, D.C., October 16, 2003.

Scholarly and Magazine Articles

Abbas, Hassan. "Pakistan Through the Lens of the 'Triple A' Theory." *Fletcher Forum of World Affairs* 30, no. 1 (Winter 2006).

BIBLIOGRAPHY

"Afghanistan's Tribal Complexity." *Economist*, January 31, 2008.

Anderson, Jon Lee. "The Taliban's Opium War." *New Yorker*, July 9, 2007.

Bearak, Barry. "Unreconstructed." *New York Times Magazine*, June 1, 2003.

Beehner, Lionel. "Musharraf's Taliban Problem." Council on Foreign Relations, September 10, 2006, http://www.cfr.org/publication/11401/musharrafs_taliban_problem.html.

———. "NATO and the Afghan-Pakistani Border." Council on Foreign Relations, August 3, 2006, http://www.cfr.org/publication/11237/nato_and_the_afghanpakistani_border.html.

Behar, Richard. "Kidnapped Nation." *Forbes*, April 29, 2002.

Blanchard, Christopher M. "Afghanistan, Narcotics and U.S. Policy." Congressional Research Service, Washington, D.C., December 7, 2004, and May 26, 2005.

Burgess, Mark. "In the Spotlight: Islamic Movement of Uzbekistan (IMU)." Center for Defense Information, the Terrorism Project, Washington, D.C., http://www.cdi.org/terrorism/imu.cfm.

Carpenter, Ted Galen. "How the Drug War in Afghanistan Undermines America's War on Terror."CATO Institute, Washington, D.C., November 10, 2004.

Chouvy, Pierre-Arnaud. "Drugs and the Financing of Terrorism." *Terrorism Monitor* 2, no. 20 (October 21, 2004), http://www.jamestown.org/publications_details.php?volume_id=400&issue_id=3116&article_id=2368732.

———. "Narco-Terrorism in Afghanistan." *Terrorism Monitor* 2, no. 6 (March 25, 2004), http://www.jamestown.org/publications_details.php?volume_id=400&issue_id=2929&article_id=23648.

Dalrymple, William. "On the Long Road to Freedom Finally." *Tehelka Magazine* 5, no. 9 (March 8, 2008), http://www.tehelka.com/story_main38.asp?filename=Ne080308on_the.asp.

Felbab-Brown, Vanda. "A Better Strategy Against Narco-Terrorism." Audit of the Conventional Wisdom series, MIT Center for International Studies, Cambridge, Mass. January 2006, http://web.mit.edu/cis/pdf/Audit_01_06_Vanda.pdf.

Galen Carpenter, Ted. "How the Drug War Undermines America's War on Terror." Foreign policy briefing, CATO Institute, Washington, D.C., November 10, 2004.

Glassner, Susan, and Walter Pincus, "Seized Letter Outlines al Qaeda Goals in Iraq," *Washington Post*, October 12, 2005.

"A Godfather's Lethal Mix of Business and Politics." *U.S. News & World Report*, December 5, 2005.

Goodhand, Jonathan. "From Holy War to Opium War?" *Central Asian Survey* 19, no. 2 (June 1, 2000): 265–280.

Grare, Frederic. "Pakistan: The Myth of an Islamist Peril." Policy brief, Carnegie Endowment for International Peace, Washington, D.C., February 2006.

Hasnain, Ghulam. "Karachi's Gang Wars: Portrait of a Don." *Newsline*, September 2001.

Hersh, Seymour M. "The Other War: Why Bush's Afghanistan Problem Won't Go Away." *New Yorker*, April 12, 2004.

Hitz, Frederick. "Obscuring Propriety: The CIA and Drugs." *International Journal on Intelligence and Counterintelligence* 12, no. 4 (Winter 1999): 448–462.

Hussein, Zahid. "Narco Power." *Newsline*, December 1989.

Kaplan, Eben. "Terror's Twisted Money Trail." Council on Foreign Relations, New York, April 4, 2006.

Lifschultz, Lawrence. "The Death Toll of Educated Afghans in Peshawar Is Now More Than One Thousand." *Newsline*, October 1989.

———. "Heroin Empire." *Newsline*, July 1989.

Maass, Peter. "Gul Agha Gets His Province Back." *New York Times Magazine*, January 6, 2002.

McGirk, Tim. "Terrorism's Harvest." *Time*, August 9, 2004.

Powell, Bill. "Warlord or Druglord?" *Time*, February 8, 2007.

Rashid, Ahmed. "Afghanistan on the Brink." *New York Review of Books*, June 22, 2006.

Rubin, Barnett R. "Saving Afghanistan." *Foreign Affairs*, January-February 2007.

Rubin, Elizabeth. "In the Land of the Taliban." *New York Times Magazine*, October 22, 2006.

Sancton, Thomas. "Dispatches." *Time*, April 4, 1994.

Schweich, Thomas. "Is Afghanistan a Narco-State?" *New York Times Magazine*, July 27, 2008.

News Stories

Ahmed, Shafiq. "Taliban Accounts Frozen." *Dawn*, January 24, 2006.

Baldauf, Scott, and Owais Tohid. "Taliban Appears to Be Regrouped and Well-Funded." *Christian Science Monitor*, May 8, 2003.

Bergen, Peter. "The Taliban: Regrouped and Rearmed." *Washington Post*, September 10, 2006.

Bonner, Arthur. "Afghanistan's Other Front: A World of Drugs." *New York Times*, November 2, 1985.

———. "Afghan Rebel's Victory Garden: Opium." *New York Times*, June 18, 1986.

Braun, Stephen, and Judy Pasternak. "Long Before Sept. 11, Bin Laden Flew Aircraft Under the Radar." *Los Angeles Times*, November 18, 2001.

Brunwasser, Matthew. "The Embargo Buster." *Frontline*, PBS, May 2002, http://www.pbs.org/frontlineworld/stories/sierraleone/bout.html.

Burch, Jonathon. "Afghan Airport to Help Switch from Drugs to Fruit." Reuters, August 4, 2008.

Burnett, Victoria, and Mark Huband. "UK Trains Afghans in Anti-Drugs Drive." *Financial Times*, January 10, 2004.

Callinan, Rory. "Taliban Back in Drugs, Terror Business." *Australian*, May 31, 2004.

Chivers, C. J. "Dutch Soldiers Stress Restraint in Afghanistan." *New York Times*, April 6, 2007.

Chouvy, Pierre-Arnaud. "Licensing Afghanistan's Opium: Solution or Fallacy?" *Asia Times*, February 1, 2006.

Cole, Matthew. "Killing Ourselves in Afghanistan." *Salon.com*, March 10, 2008, http://www.salon.com/news/feature/2008/03/10/taliban/.

Coll, Stephen. "Anatomy of a Victory: The CIA's Covert Afghan War." *Washington Post*, July 19, 1992.

Constable, Pamela. "A Poor Yield for Afghan's War on Drugs." *Washington Post*, September 19, 2006.

Cooper, Helene. "NATO Chief Says More Troops Needed in Afghanistan." *New York Times*, September 22, 2006.

DeYoung, Karen, and Douglas Farah. "Infighting Slows Hunt for Hidden al Qaeda Assets." *Washington Post*, June 18, 2002.

Farah, Douglas. "Al Qaeda's Gold: Following the Trail to Dubai." *Washington Post*, February 18, 2002.

———. "Al Qaeda's Road Paved with Gold." *Washington Post*, February 17, 2002.

Gall, Carlotta. "Afghans Accuse U.S. of Secret Spraying to Kill Poppies." *New York Times*, February 27, 2005.

———. "Taliban Battle Afghan Forces in Drug Region." *New York Times*, February 3, 2006.

——— and David Cloud. "U.S. Memo Faults Afghan Leader on Heroin Fight." *New York Times*, May 22, 2005.

Ghani, Ashraf. "Where Democracy's Greatest Enemy Is a Flower." *New York Times*, December 11, 2004.

Guggenheim, Ken. "U.S. Official Says Taliban Behind Opium Surge." Associated Press, October 3, 2001.

Higgins, Holy Barnes. "The Road to Helmand." *Washington Post*, February 4, 2007.

Hollbrooke, Richard. "Still Wrong in Afghanistan." *Washington Post*, January 23, 2008.

Hsu, Spencer, and Walter Pincus. "U.S. Warns of Stronger al Qaeda." *Washington Post*, July 12, 2007.

Kaplan, David. "Paying for Terror." *U.S. News & World Report*, December 5, 2005.

———. "The Saudi Connection." *U.S. News & World Report*, December 15, 2003.

——— and Joshua Kurlantzick. "How a Terror Network Funds Attacks." *U.S. News & World Report*, October 1, 2001.

Khan, Noor. "Taliban Collected Taxes, Ran Heroin Labs, Had Own Judge in Afghan Town." Associated Press, December 12, 2007.

———. "Taliban Hang Three Alleged Afghan Informers." Associated Press, April 1, 2007.

Kroft, Steve. "Afghanistan: Addicted to Heroin." *60 Minutes*, CBS, October 16, 2005.

Lifschultz, Lawrence. "Inside the Kingdom of Heroin." *Nation*, November 14, 1988.

Lowinson, Joyce H., and David F. Musto. "Drug Crisis and Strategy." *New York Times*, May 22, 1980.

Makarenko, Tamara. "Central Asia's Opium Terrorists." *Wide Angle Productions*, PBS, http://www.pbs.org/wnet/wideangle/printable/centralasia_briefing_print.html.

Marquand, Robert. "The Reclusive Leader Who Runs the Taliban." *Christian Science Monitor*, October 10, 2001.

Mazzetti, Mark, and David Rohde. "Al Qaeda Chiefs Are Seen to Regain Power." *New York Times*, February 18, 2007.

McDowell, Patrick. "As Disruption from War on Taliban Ends, Traffickers Moving Big Heroin Shipments." Associated Press, March 3, 2002.

Meyer, Josh. "Al Qaeda 'Co-Opts' New Affiliates." *Los Angeles Times*, September 16, 2007.

———. "Pentagon Resists Pleas for Help in Afghan Opium Fight." *Los Angeles Times*, December 5, 2006.

———. "U.S. Anti-Drug Efforts in Afghanistan to Be Bolstered." *Los Angeles Times*, December 8, 2006.

Mintz, John. "15 Freighters Believed to Be Linked to Al Qaeda." *Washington Post*, December 31, 2002.

Moore, Molly. "NATO Confronts Surprisingly Fierce Taliban." *Washington Post*, February 26, 2008.

———. "Struggling for Solutions as Opium Trade Blossoms." *Washington Post*, March 21, 2008.

Mujahid, Islam, and Gretchen Peters. "Buddhist Relics Latest Casualties of Pakistan's Talibanization." ABC News, October 15, 2007, http://blogs.abcnews.com/theblotter/2007/10/buddhist-relics.html.

Peters, Gretchen. "Afghan War Flares Anew." *Christian Science Monitor*, April 6, 2003.

———. "American Voice on New Terror Video." *Christian Science Monitor*, October 29, 2004.

———. "Hostilities Flare Again in America's Other War." *Christian Science Monitor*, March 31, 2003.

———. "Opium Bumper Crop Seen to Benefit Taliban." ABC News and ABC News Radio, September 3, 2006, http://abcnews.go.com/International/Story?id=2390033&page=1.

———. "Taliban Drug Trade: Echoes of Colombia." *Christian Science Monitor*, November 21, 2006.

———. "Taliban Stamping Out Hashish but Opium Production Continues to Flourish." Associated Press, April 14, 1997.

———. "They're Back: A New, Vicious Taliban Take Shape in Afghanistan; Opium Funds a New Type of Taliban Army." ABC News and ABC News Radio, June 27, 2006, http://abcnews.go.com/International/story?id=2124643&page=1.

———. "Violence Grows in Pakistan's Tribal Zone, Despite Army Presence." *Christian Science Monitor*, December 12, 2005.

———. "Weary Taliban Come In from the Cold." *Christian Science Monitor*, December 14, 2004.

Rashid, Ahmed. "Wages of War." *Far Eastern Economic Review*, August 5, 1999.

Rohde, David. "Overhaul of Afghan Police Is New Priority." *New York Times*, October 18, 2007.

Risen, James. "An Afghan's Path from U.S. Ally to Drug Suspect." *New York Times*, February 2, 2007.

Rupert, James, "A Pakistani Officer Wages Jihad Against U.S." *Newsday*, October 7, 2007.

——— and Steve Coll. "U.S. Declines to Probe Afghan Drug Trade; Rebels, Pakistani Officers Implicated." *Washington Post*, May 13, 1990.

Sciolino, Elaine. "U.S. Urging Afghan Rebels to Limit Opium." *New York Times*, March 26, 1989.

Scott Tyson, Ann. "Taliban Gains Forestall U.S. Troop Reductions in Afghanistan." *Washington Post*, September 22, 2006.

Sly, Liz. "Opium Cash Fuels Terror, Experts Say." *Chicago Tribune*, February 9, 2004.

Smith, Graeme. "Doing It the Dutch Way in Afghanistan." *Globe and Mail*, December 2, 2006.

———. "Talking to the Taliban: Globe Special Report." *Globe and Mail*, March 24, 2008, http://www.theglobeandmail.com/talkingtothetaliban.

Tohid, Owais. "Al Qaeda's Uzbek Bodyguards." *Christian Science Monitor*, September 28, 2004.

———. "Bumper Year for Afghan Poppies." *Christian Science Monitor*, July 24, 2003.

Tolchin, Martin. "CIA Admits It Failed to Tell Fed About BCCI." *New York Times,* October 26, 1991.

"U.S. Designates Suspects in Pakistani Drug Lord's Ring." Associated Press, November 27, 2007.

Vaknin, Sam. "Hawala, or the Bank That Never Was." United Press International, February 2, 2002.

Witte, Griff. "Emerging Epicenter in the Afghan War." *Washington Post,* March 15, 2007.

Graphs here and on following page are from the author's 2007 survey of 350 people who work in or alongside the opium trade in southern Afghanistan and along the Pakistan border.

Please circle which activities the Taliban engage in:

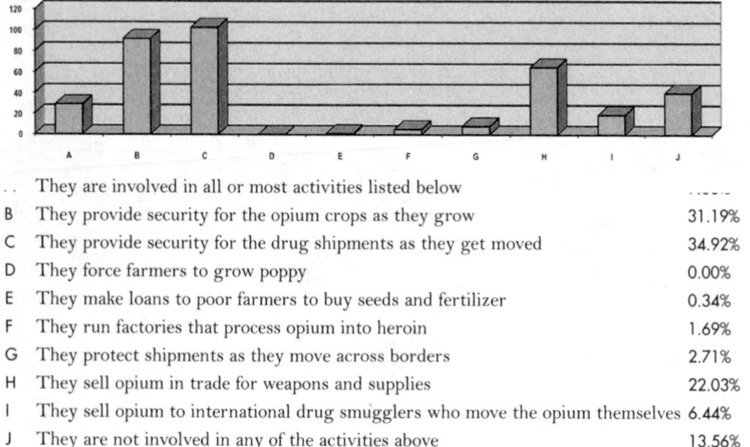

[illegible]	They are involved in all or most activities listed below	[illegible]
B	They provide security for the opium crops as they grow	31.19%
C	They provide security for the drug shipments as they get moved	34.92%
D	They force farmers to grow poppy	0.00%
E	They make loans to poor farmers to buy seeds and fertilizer	0.34%
F	They run factories that process opium into heroin	1.69%
G	They protect shipments as they move across borders	2.71%
H	They sell opium in trade for weapons and supplies	22.03%
I	They sell opium to international drug smugglers who move the opium themselves	6.44%
J	They are not involved in any of the activities above	13.56%

Which of the following is the most true and fair statement:

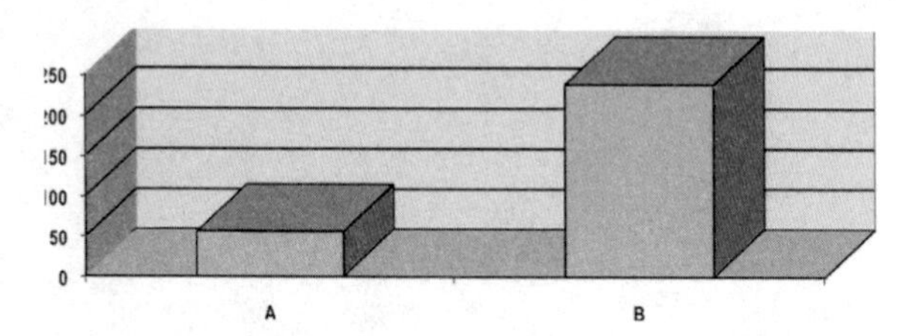

A	Taliban commanders are fighting for their religion and freedom of Afghanistan	18.98%
B	Taliban leaders are mainly trying to make money	81.02%

Activities that foreign *jihadis*, including al Qaeda, engage in:

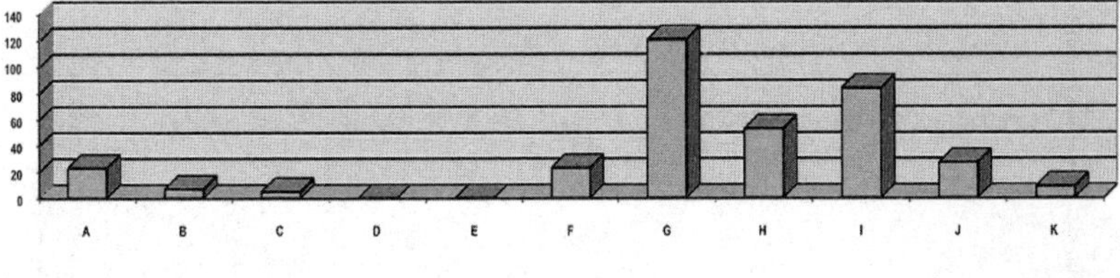

A They are involved in all or most activities listed below 7.80%
B They provide security for the opium crops as they grow 2.37%
C They provide security for the drug shipments as they get moved 1.69%
D They force farmers to grow poppy 0.00%
E They make loans to poor farmers to buy seeds and fertilizer 0.00%
F They run factories that process opium into heroin 7.80%
G They protect shipments as they move across borders 41.02%
H They sell opium in trade for weapons and supplies 17.97%
I They sell opium to international drug smugglers who move the opium themselves 28.47%
J They are not involved in any of the activities above 9.15%
K Don't know 3.05%

Opium poppy cultivation in Afghanistan 1994–2008

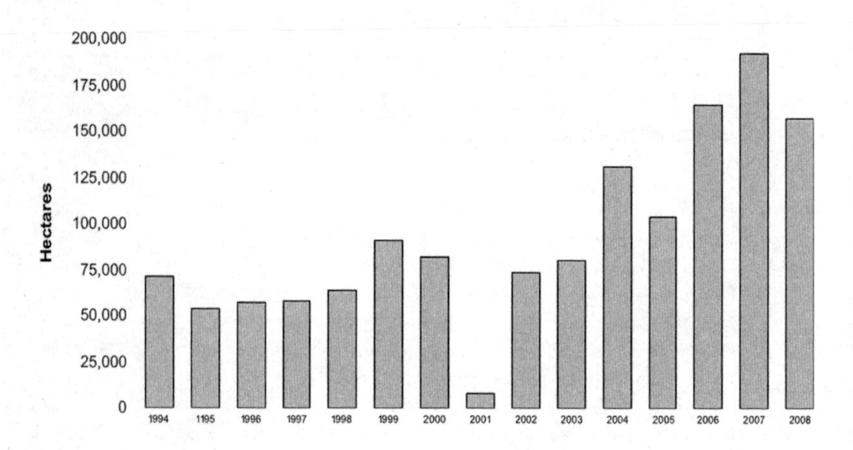

UNODC CHART

INDEX

INDEX

INDEX

INDEX

INDEX